I0054700

Strategies for the Online Day Trader

Strategies for the Online Day Trader

Advanced Trading Techniques for Online Profits

Fernando Gonzalez

William Rhee

McGraw-Hill

New York   San Francisco   Washington, D.C.   Auckland   Bogotá
Caracas   Lisbon   London   Madrid   Mexico City   Milan
Montreal   New Delhi   San Juan   Singapore
Sydney   Tokyo   Toronto

Library of Congress Cataloging-in-Publication Data

Gonzalez, Fernando
    Strategies for the online day trader : trading techniques for
online profits / by Fernando Gonzalez and William Rhee.
      p. cm.
    ISBN 0-07-135153-1
    1. Electronic trading of securities.   2. Stocks—Data processing.
    I. Rhee, William.   II. Title.
HG4515.95.G66   1999
332.63′2′0285—dc21   99-15644
                                                           CIP

McGraw-Hill

A Division of The **McGraw·Hill** Companies

Copyright © 1999 by The McGraw-Hill Companies, Inc. All rights reserved.
Printed in the United States of America. Except as permitted under the United
States Copyright Act of 1976, no part of this publication may be reproduced or
distributed in any form or by any means, or stored in a database or retrieval
system, without the prior written permission of the publisher.

1 2 3 4 5 6 7 8 9 0 DOC / DOC 9 0 3 2 1 0 9 8
ISBN-13: 978-0-07-158997-0
ISBN-10: 0-07-158997-X

*The sponsoring editor for this book was Stephen Isaacs, the editing supervisor was
John M. Morriss, and the production supervisor was Modestine Cameron. It was set
in Palatino by Inkwell Publishing Services.*

Printed and bound by R.R. Donnelley & Sons Company.

McGraw-Hill books are available at special quantity discounts to use as premiums and sales promotions, or for use in corporate training programs. For more information, please write to the Director of Special Sales, McGraw-Hill, 11 West 19th Street, New York, NY 10011. Or contact your local bookstore.

This book is printed on recycled, acid-free paper containing a minimum of 50% recycled de-inked fiber.

Disclaimer

This book is designed for educational purposes only. It is not designed to provide all the information required to be successful in day trading. Day trading may involve a significantly higher level of risk in comparison to other common forms of capital management such as long-term investments in stocks, bonds, or mutual funds. Proficiency at day trading may take a very long period of time to develop, depending on an individual's capacity to understand the high degree of risk involved, the aptitude to manage these high risks in order to preserve capital, and the potential to develop any and all necessary skills to create profitable results. Day trading may result in the loss of all of a trader's capital and, in cases that involve the use of extended buying power or margin, you may lose all your capital and assume liability for owing additional funds that are substantially more than your capital invested.

The authors and publisher will not assume any responsibility due, but not limited to, losses incurred as a result of applying what is discussed in this book. The authors and publisher do not claim or guarantee your success at day trading or suggest that any past performance mentioned in this publication indicates the same results will occur in the future.

Contents

PART III: Appendices

Acknowledgments

We would like to thank our wives, Mara and Kelly, as well as our parents and families for their unending support and confidence.

Our thanks to Jorge Jimenez of Momentum Securities, Irvine, CA for his assistance and for persuading us to write this book.

Our thanks to the following firms for having provided us with data and software for research and reference purposes:

The Executioner
www.executioner.com

CyberCorp Inc.
www.cybercorp.com

Window on Wall Street
www.windowonwallstreet.com

Equis for MetaStock
www.equis.com

Momentum Securities, Inc.
www.soes.com

Management of Momentum Securities, Irvine, CA
www.tradingacademy.com

Our thanks to Stephen Isaacs, our editor at McGraw-Hill, for his patience and valuable assistance.

Introduction

Since the beginning of time, people have been fascinated with the concepts of speculation, competition, and the accumulation of wealth. Although the stock market was not established with these intentions, it nevertheless provides a forum for individuals to test their skills and act out their fascination with those concepts. Of course there is an alternative way to speculate, compete, and profit from such games. It is called gambling, and casinos are the forums for individuals to test their luck. Those whose career path leads to the stock market are called traders, while those who are bitten by the casino bug are called gamblers. If you have read enough, it would be a good idea to put this book down and return to the workforce. If you cannot resist the urge to go on and attempt to act out your fascination with speculating, competing, and hopefully profiting from taking such risks, then you should read this book before you start day trading. While it is true that trading, especially day trading, borders on gambling, it is also true that trading involves hard work in preparing for the market; a determination to succeed; and the capacity to absorb, decipher, and react to the constant flow of information that affects the market on a daily basis.

Until recently, market makers, specialists, and institutional traders had advantages over the public in determining the course of the stock market and in the availability of valuable and timely information and the ability to profit from the ignorant public. Today however, with the speed of information, high-speed access to real-time quotes, and instant execution of computerized trading, the public has every opportunity that the professionals have to profit from trading in the dynamic arena of the stock market. The difference is education and experience.

By now you probably understand and are familiar with the impact of day trading on stocks. You have heard of the risks and horror stories of others attempting to day trade who lose everything. You may also have heard of a select few who are making more money in one month than most people make in a year. The truth is that while there is unlimited potential to profit from the stock market, the failures greatly outnumber the sucesses.

Most individuals who attempt to day trade are quite intelligent and have the mental capacity, determination, and intent to succeed. However, the nature of trading involves not only competing with other participants in the market, but struggling with the internal conflicts of pride, fear, despair, greed, and of course, distaste for losing money. These mental obstacles are not easily overcome, even for the most experienced trader.

The purpose of this book is to familiarize you with the obstacles of day trading, the psychology and philosophy behind it, and the pitfalls that plague most novice day traders. It will help you to prepare for day trading in a step-by- step process so that you too can take advantage of the cutting-edge technology that has helped thousands of other individuals to profit from the stock market.

This book is divided into two parts. Part I, containing Chapters 1 through 4, lays the foundation for understanding market basics; understanding yourself in relation to the market; gaining an overall perspective on the market; and understanding the forces that affect the market.

Part II includes Chapters 5 through 12. Chapters 5 and 6 help you to understand price action; learn how to anticipate and develop your timing; and understand momentum, trends, and the technical analysis behind charts, which attempts to systematize the movement of prices. Chapter 7 focuses on order execution, because it is your extremities in cyberspace. Being able to execute orders at the command of your thoughts will help you to buy and sell with split-second precision so that you will not miss key price levels. We then lay out the basics of fundamental and technical analysis. While day trading involves a micro-version of price volatility, understanding the overall perspective of fundamental and technical analysis will give a better indication of the intrinsic value of stocks and where the course of momentum may encounter support and resistance from the opposite forces. Next, we provide an overview of trading strategies and styles in Chapter 8—different techniques for trading that vary according to scales of price and time, personal inclinations, and risk tolerance levels. In Chapters 9 through 11, we present examples taken from our own trades. We provide the details of various trades and document the split-second as well as longer-term decisions that trigger an entry point, and the management of risk that leads to different exit points. Finally, Chapter 12 includes a variety of important trading notes.

Most individuals fail in their attempt to day trade not from any lack of mental capacity, but from a stubborn refusal to avoid a head-on collision with the market's forces. Rather than facing the full impact, using the market's forces as leverage to ride the waves of buying and selling pressures will help you to surface from the turmoil of a volatile day in the market not just unscathed, but victorious and profitable. The strategies outlined in this book will help you to apply that leverage as you participate in the growth of on-line trading. With competition growing from major exchanges around the world and technological breakthroughs occurring in order handling, on-line day traders are part of a major revolution in the stock market as we enter the next millennium. Good luck!

PART I
Trading Foundations

1
Market Basics

At the top of the list of advancements that technology has brought forth to better our everyday lives are the refinements implemented to improve the efficiency of our financial markets. The powerful PC with its new ability to communicate information through networks has paved the way for a highly efficient method of data and order processing. Now that we are entering the new millennium, what many consider to be the greatest winds of change are blowing upon the stock market, affecting nearly all facets of its domain. In fact, as we write this book, it seems that we can never keep up with the additions and improvements, both planned and achieved. Nevertheless, we are confident of the timelessness of stock trading. Given the advent of the new technologies, we would like to present the same speculation and street-smarts that have been written in hundreds of volumes before, but now in a setting that has finally brought forth what our trading ancestors have clamored over in the last hundred years: a level playing field, high speed, and lower trading costs. The ability to extract information and send orders at lightning-fast speed and at lower cost has always been a crucial factor in efficient stock trading. Now that we have that ability, many have discovered, with great dismay, that access to high-tech trading tools has not softened the competition for profits in the stock market.

Historically, the investing public has stayed away from stock trading, despite its glamour, because of the apparent advantage of the experienced professional over the newcomer. Even before the explosion of online trading in the latter part of the 1990s, the mere mention of stock trading would immediately elicit the question that many of us have heard countless times: "Isn't that *risky*?" The refusal to confront the reality of that question launches a journey that often ends in the destruction of trading capital. Many newcomers have been lulled into believing that the new speed and lower costs of stock trading present a greater advantage to the general population and a level playing field with the professionals. While this is true in a technical sense, it is certainly not the case for rookie traders. First, the small window of opportunity to get ahead of the rest of the investing public has already been closed. Next, the professional's experience, the heart of success, is only acquired by the intangible: *time.* Thus, now that we all have access to the best tools imaginable—and there are more to come— what is an inexperienced trader to do? As with all other challenges, you must prepare to compete using your best wits, your discipline, your patience, your diligence in educating yourself, and most of all, your passion for trading

Day Trader Markets

In an effort to gain an understanding of the game, let us first study the basic rules and the different playing grounds.

In stock trading, there are two major trading arenas, which represent our two largest stock markets: the National Association of Securities Dealers Automated Quotation System (NASDAQ) and the New York Stock Exchange (NYSE). There are many differences between the two markets, but for day traders there are two basic distinctions: *order execution* and *volatility.* Stocks are traded differently on each market. With enough technology and practical application, perhaps one day the best characteristics of each market will be combined to create a singular and highly efficient market. Separately, however, each market presents a multitude of opportunities for the day trader.

NYSE (Listed Issues)

The NYSE is our traditional stock market and is also the largest stock exchange in the world. The majority of the country's best and most established companies have their stocks listed for trading on this exchange. The many great companies whose stock are traded here, such as GE, IBM, and J.P. Morgan (JPM), represent the foundation of our country's economy.

The NYSE is an auction-oriented market, where a single person or entity, known as a *Specialist,* organizes and matches buyers and sellers, and acts in favor of providing liquidity. The Specialist is responsible for maintaining a high degree of order and fairness between buyers and sellers in the trading of the stock. There is much power in being a Specialist. With the assistance of clerks, Specialists have the power to shift the price of the stock in order to provide liquidity. The manner in which they provide liquidity to the stocks is carefully measured by the management of the stock exchanges, who have a great interest in providing a fair market to the investing public.

While it was not possible before, anybody with the correct trading account can now have orders sent directly to a Specialist through a system known as SuperDOT, the electronic order routing system for listed stocks. On SuperDOT, you are quoted the buying and selling prices of the different member exchanges on which the listed stocks are traded (New York, Boston, Philadelphia, Chicago, Pacific, and Cincinnati). By far the most liquid and significant of the exchanges is the NYSE.

Stocks listed on the exchanges are generally less volatile in nature than those traded on the NASDAQ. Listed stocks are generally larger and more established companies, and as a result, they are less of a haven for very active day traders who seek (and almost require) enough volatility and price extension to find profit opportunities in the trading day. Despite the less volatile nature of listed stocks, there are nevertheless numerous opportunities for profit.

The method of execution for your orders on listed exchanges has advantages and disadvantages. Because the Specialist on the NYSE may have larger orders to process, your order may occasionally be filled at a price better than expected, a virtually impossible feat on the NASDAQ. Order executions, however, are not as instantaneous on the NYSE in comparison to the NASDAQ. Scalping on listed stocks is generally more difficult to time because the Specialist has full control and discretion over your orders. However, swing and core trades (which hold through larger time periods than scalps) on both markets follow the same set of rules, because of the longer-term nature of the price moves.

NASDAQ (Over-the Counter, OTC)

The NASDAQ is the second largest stock market in the U.S. In contrast to the exchanges, it is the home of most technology stocks and stock of other emerging companies. Speculation is normally higher than for stocks traded on the NYSE, which houses more established companies. As a result of the higher level of speculation, NASDAQ stock prices often reflect the most extreme levels of human optimism, uncertainty, and fear. The fact that there is considerably more volatility and greater control over your orders in this market makes the NASDAQ a day trader's favorite playground.

In this market, the ownership of stock is exchanged in a much different way than the NYSE. The NASDAQ is a negotiated market, where many *Dealers* or Market Makers (member firms who represent the stock) and day traders alike compete fiercely for the best prices. There is no single entity to maintain order in the way a Specialist does in the exchanges. Buy and sell orders are not routed to a single entity (with some exceptions), but rather are posted as Bids and Offers (Ask) for the market to see and take advantage of. While price fluctuations are more prevalent in this environment, it is nevertheless a highly efficient market.

Trading directly on the NASDAQ is far more complicated than trading on the exchanges. While sending orders to the SuperDOT system for listed exchanges is as easy as choosing between market or limit types of orders, the NASDAQ is comprised of several different methods or order routing systems, such as SOES, SelectNet, and ECNs (discussed in greater detail in Chapter 7). Because of this complexity, we place greater emphasis on NASDAQ-based trading when we discuss order execution and

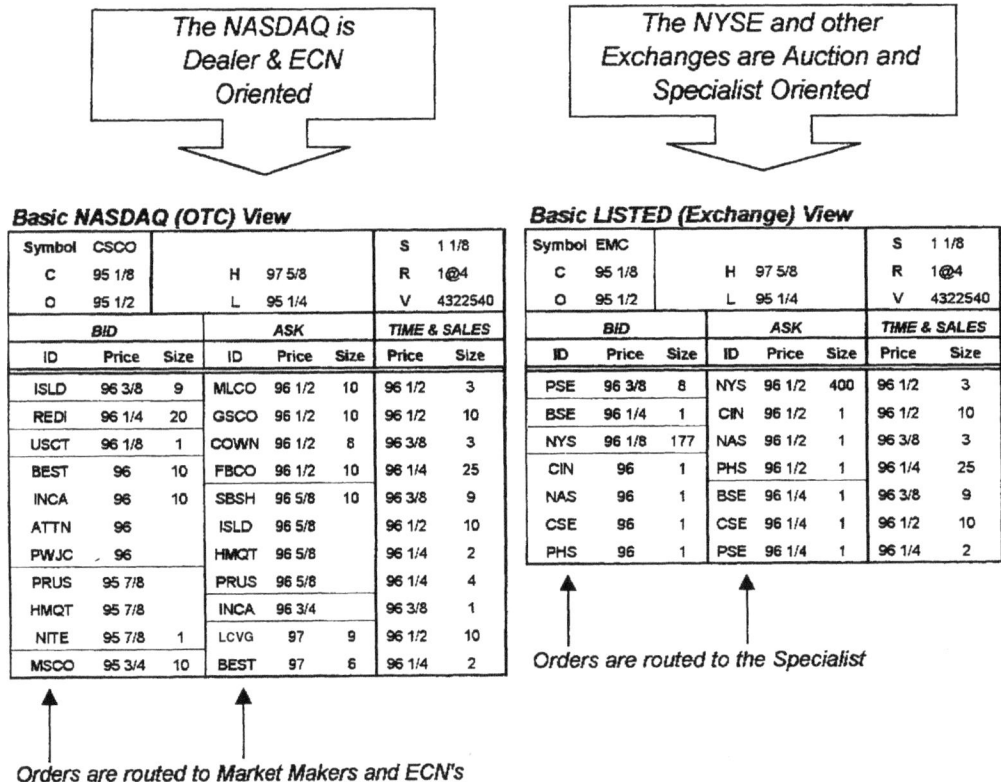

The NASDAQ is Dealer & ECN Oriented	The NYSE and other Exchanges are Auction and Specialist Oriented

Basic NASDAQ (OTC) View

Symbol CSCO						S	1 1/8
C	95 1/8		H	97 5/8		R	1@4
O	95 1/2		L	95 1/4		V	4322540

BID			ASK			TIME & SALES	
ID	Price	Size	ID	Price	Size	Price	Size
ISLD	96 3/8	9	MLCO	96 1/2	10	96 1/2	3
REDI	96 1/4	20	GSCO	96 1/2	10	96 1/2	10
USCT	96 1/8	1	COWN	96 1/2	8	96 3/8	3
BEST	96	10	FBCO	96 1/2	10	96 1/4	25
INCA	96	10	SBSH	96 5/8	10	96 3/8	9
ATTN	96		ISLD	96 5/8		96 1/2	10
PWJC	96		HMQT	96 5/8		96 1/4	2
PRUS	95 7/8		PRUS	96 5/8		96 1/4	4
HMQT	95 7/8		INCA	96 3/4		96 3/8	1
NITE	95 7/8	1	LCVG	97	9	96 1/2	10
MSCO	95 3/4	10	BEST	97	6	96 1/4	2

Orders are routed to Market Makers and ECN's

Basic LISTED (Exchange) View

Symbol EMC						S	1 1/8
C	95 1/8		H	97 5/8		R	1@4
O	95 1/2		L	95 1/4		V	4322540

BID			ASK			TIME & SALES	
ID	Price	Size	ID	Price	Size	Price	Size
PSE	96 3/8	8	NYS	96 1/2	400	96 1/2	3
BSE	96 1/4	1	CIN	96 1/2	1	96 1/2	10
NYS	96 1/8	177	NAS	96 1/2	1	96 3/8	3
CIN	96	1	PHS	96 1/2	1	96 1/4	25
NAS	96	1	BSE	96 1/4	1	96 3/8	9
CSE	96	1	CSE	96 1/4	1	96 1/2	10
PHS	96	1	PSE	96 1/4	1	96 1/4	2

Orders are routed to the Specialist

Figure 1-1. NASDAQ Level 2 and SuperDOT.

momentary data interpretation. Efficient order routing on the NASDAQ has become complicated because of the constant additions and improvements to this market. In fact, the NASDAQ today is completely different and considerably more efficient than it was in its orginal inception.

The NASDAQ makes two levels available for public access, quite simply distinguished as *Level One* and *Level Two*. Level One reflects the basic inside market—the best current buying and selling price. This is generally used by stockbrokers and regular online investors who give little priority to efficient order execution because of the longer-term nature of their involvement with the stock. Level Two is for more active participants who would like to see a clearer picture of the actual stock price. If you are going to actively day trade, it is imperative that you have a Level 2 account. On this type of system, not only is the inside market quoted, but also what is beneath the inside market, as well as the Time and Sales Report. Level 2 is as far as an investor can go in a NASDAQ quotation system and is the professional NASDAQ trader's choice.

NASDAQ Level 2 Basics

For active day trading, familiarity with NASDAQ Level 2 is crucial to get the most efficient price, as well as for using high-velocity scalping techniques. Figure 1-2 is an example of a Level 2 screen with definitions. From a day trader's point of view, correctly understanding how Level 2 works is extremely important. While there have been many attempts to simplify the direct buying and selling methods of the NASDAQ through the creation of special one-key formulas to help you decide, the best execution is "worked" manually by a trader who understands exactly what to do, what type of order to send, and when to send it. Let us begin by examining the distinction between a Market Maker and an Electronic Communication Network (ECN).

Market Makers

Market Makers are NASDAQ member firms that subscribe to represent a stock to the public. They are also known as dealers. There are many Market Makers that represent our most actively traded stocks, and in the interest of providing the best prices to the public, they compete with one another. While the fairness of this practice has always been questioned, the NASD has gone and continues to go to great lengths to prevent collusion or price fixing, and it imposes heavy fines for violations. They have three primary functions:

Symbol	CSCO					S	1 1/8
C	95 1/8	↑	H	97 5/8		R	1@4
O	95 1/2		L	95 1/4		V	4322540

| BID | | | ASK | | | TIME & SALES | |
MM/ECN ID	Price	Size	MM/ECN ID	Price	Size	Price	Size
ISLD	96 3/8	9	MLCO	96 1/2	10	96 1/2	3
REDI	96 1/4	20	GSCO	96 1/2	10	96 1/2	10
USCT	96 1/8	1	COWN	96 1/2	8	96 3/8	3
BEST	96	10	FBCO	96 1/2	10	96 1/4	25
INCA	96	10	SBSH	96 1/4	10	96 3/8	9
NITE	96	1	INCA	96 1/4	9	96 1/2	10
MSCO	96	10	ISLD	96 1/4	6	96 1/4	2

ECN's

Market Makers

List of Posted Buyers   List of Posted Sellers   Trade Reports

NASDAQ Level 2 Basic Definitions:

Symbol: Stock Symbol (NASDAQ stocks consist of 4 or 5 symbols, listed stocks have 1 to 3 symbols)
C Yesterday's Closing Price
O Today's Opening Price
H Today's Highest Price Traded
L Today's Lowest Price Traded
S Status (+ or -) based on the last trade compared to yesterday's close.
Some proprietary software may be adjusted based on last trade vs opening price
R Number of Market Makers or ECN's at the Inside Bid vs Inside Ask
Some proprietary software may be adjusted based on total size on Inside Bid vs Ask
V Number of Shares traded since the Open
BID List of Buyers with ID, price posted, and size
ASK List of Sellers with ID, price posted, and size (also known as "Offer")
Inside BID Best Current Buying Price
Inside ASK Best Current Selling Price
TIME & SALES Report of actual transactions. While all trades must be reported immediately, this column
may occasionally reflect delayed or erroneous reports.
Time & Sales are also known as "prints" or "trades"
MM/ECN ID Four Character symbol indentifying the Market Maker or ECN
Price Price posting. Prices are usually rounded to 1/16 increments, but some proprietary
software may reflect non-rounded smaller fractions such as 1/32, 1/64, 1/128 etc.
Size Size of the the Order, usually quoted in 100 share multiples
MM Market Makers (Dealers): NASDAQ member firms who make a market in the stock.
Holds inventory, executes orders for customers and trades for its own accounts.
Must always post a buying and selling price. Consist of brokerage houses and
wholesale brokerages. Market Makers are also responsible to fill SOES orders.
ECN Private Electronic Communication Networks operating as vehicles for non-market making
participants to post Bids and Offers directly into the NASDAQ. This is the most common
order execution vehicle for professional Day Traders. Currently, there are nine ECN's:
INCA, ISLD, TNTO, BTRD, REDI, ATTN, BRUT, STRK & NTRD. ECN's are not required to
make a market by always post buying and selling prices. They are also not SOESable.

Figure 1-2. Basic NASDAQ Level 2 Screen with Definitions.

- **To provide liquidity or "make a market."** Market Makers must constantly have a buying (Bid) and selling (Ask) price. They profit from the difference between the buying and selling prices—the spread.

- **To execute customer orders.** Market Makers execute both large institutional orders and orders from their own small investor customers. They profit by charging a mark-up (if they represent the stock on the NASDAQ) or commission.

- **To trade for their own accounts.** Because they are experienced in the trading and price activity of the stock and have access to the flow of orders, Market Makers can profit by taking positions for their own accounts if they feel strongly about the direction of a stock price.

Historically, Market Makers are known enemies of day traders. They are, however, a big part of what allows the NASDAQ to function and a crucial part of our trading. Sometimes their presence will help our trade, other times not. Regardless, they are part of what makes the machine work. We observe their activity on NASDAQ Level 2 and use them as a resource to get in and out of trades and to gauge temporary strength or weakness.

Electronic Communication Networks (ECNs)

The introduction of ECNs to the NASDAQ market has been no less than revolutionary. Their presence has greatly augmented market efficiency in many ways. The ability of small investors and institutions alike to manually post Bids and Offers directly into the market has allowed for better liquidity, higher competition, and thus better prices. You will find quite frequently that prices posted to the market through ECNs are more competitive than those posted by Market Makers.

In number, there are far fewer ECNs than Market Makers on the NASDAQ. While each ECN has its own distinct characteristics, they share a common function that is very different from that of a Market Maker. ECNs provide electronic networks that allow traders to communicate their intentions to buy or sell to one another. Unlike their Market Maker and Specialist counterparts, ECNs are not responsible for providing liquidity. This is because an ECN is a network of traders, like yourself, who do not bear the duty (or burden) of representing the stock to anybody. In these networks, if nobody wants to buy or sell, nobody is obligated to do either. You will often observe that when a stock is tanking, there are few or no realistic Bids on any of the ECNs. As active NASDAQ traders, we use this advantage to communicate our Bids and

Offers electronically to other traders. In fact, a large percentage of our orders involve some sort of ECN activity.

While there are numerous Market Makers, there are only nine ECNs in the NASDAQ to date: ISLD, BTRD, TNTO, REDI, ATTN, BRUT, STRK, NTRD, and INCA. For the newcomer, it may appear difficult to distinguish one from the other. However, remembering these ECNs is second nature to a seasoned Level 2 trader, and newcomers will gain greater familiarity with them the longer they use Level 2. In addition there are popular Level 2 software packages that allow a trader to color-code the ECNs on the quotation window in order to distinguish them from Market Makers, who are also identified by a unique four-letter symbol on NASDAQ Level 2.

We discuss Level 2 in greater detail in Part II, as well as specific techniques, strategies, and thought processes that we employ when trading on this system. There is an enormous economy that exists within the confines of the Bid and Ask. Great price moves begin and end in this territory that is occupied by the best professionals, institutional and day trader alike, who employ all methods to gain a greater advantage over other traders. Your discipline and skills will assist you in navigating through this territory. The key to a safe entry into this economy is your education and its practical application. It is important that you take your time and control the excitement to trade and the need for immediate gratification. This is your first test of self-discipline. Your patience and discipline will pay off greatly, first by saving you from massive losses and next by revealing a realistic opportunity to profit.

2

Risk Management, Psychology, and Discipline

In the spring of 1997, William had a humbling experience that we think is important to share with you:

I was on top of the world. Two years before that, I was broke. Well, I was actually worse than broke—I was $100,000 in debt from getting my butt handed to me by trading the T-Bond futures. Now I was trading again, but this time on the NAS-DAQ Level II SOES system. I was scalping the NASDAQ stocks, and I was making more money than I had ever thought possible. This day was memorable though. Why am I taking this stupid short position in Novellus? Because the market is tanking, I thought, but Novellus hadn't sold off yet. Besides, I had already profited $8,000 from other stocks that I had shorted that day, and Novellus was soon to follow—I just knew it. . . so I thought. There went the Dow selling off again. I addressed Winston, my order inputter. "Winston, sell short another Novellus at the market." A new short was opened: 1,000 at 71. Now averaging that with my first 1,000 short at 70, my breakeven is 2,000 at 70½. I knew I should not have been doubling down on this loser, but I was positive that NVLS would go down. "Goldman keeps holding the Bid, what an idiot." Uh-oh, the Dow's bouncing. It should be a dead cat bounce. It'll come back off. Now why is Novellus running up again? Is this market stupid? Don't they know the market's gonna sell off again? See, there it is. "Winston, where's Novellus?" 72¾ Bid, 73 Ask. Look at that size to sell on that Ask. "Winston, sell short another Novellus at the market! I know I'm already short! Just short it again and shut up!" Doesn't he realize I know what I'm doing? Shit, the Dow's bouncing again. "Grace, call Brad. I need an Instinet quote on Novellus." NVLS started rallying. How could I possibly have gotten into this mess? I'm never this stupid. The 74's are showing. It should stop here. This price is too high. Now the 74's are clearing, Shit!!! "Winston, get ready to cover these shorts if it breaks 75." I felt sick but I couldn't *decide if I should cover here. I thought it was already too much money to lose—it had to come back down now. NVLS broke through the 75's. They're just taking out stop orders. It will come tanking back. . .I hope. The Dow was starting to look strong. Oh, shit, NVLS is ripping through the 76's! "Winston, buy it. Buy all my Novellus. Grace, give me Instinet! Winston, what did I get?" 77, 77$^{1}/_{4}$, 77$^{1}/_{2}$. I just lost $18,000. I just lost all my profits and another ten thousand. I gotta go throw up.*

This scenario illustrates some of the pitfalls of novice traders. Although William had been trading for seven years before this event, he still violated every rule of trading. His story highlights the importance of discipline in trading. All it takes is a moment of emotional frenzy, and your entire risk management strategy falls apart. A day, week, or month of hard work can be wiped out in a single moment of frivolity. It turns out that if William had kept all his short positions, he would have made a killing the next day. NVLS reported better than expected earnings, but a lawsuit was filed against it by a competitor for violation of copyright laws. NVLS opened down 15 points. William was right, but at that moment, the price of the stock moved against him, beyond his risk tolerance. He lost money, so no matter what happened later, he was wrong. Most novice traders realize the effort and discipline needed to analyze the market, but the single most common cause of failure is the inability to cope with internal conflicts. Whether because of emotions or lack of discipline, many are unable to accept small losses. Procrastination sets in, followed by panic. By this time, novices either blow up their accounts, or lose confidence and give up. The purpose of this chapter is to help you understand the philosophy and psychology of trading. Some may think we are overstating the point, but we can't stress it enough. And any trader, no matter how good, can't hear it enough.

Risk

Many traders fail because of their inability to deal with the emotions of trading. Despite thorough analysis and sound methodology for trading, many fail to recognize the limits and tolerance for risk, resulting in loss of equity. These traders rarely progress beyond the level of vast textbook knowledge and mediocrity as traders. Success in trading requires more than just a comprehensive study of technical and fundamental analysis; it requires the careful orchestration of risk management, discipline, and patience, and keeping tight control of the emotions of greed and fear.

What is risk? For most of us, our knowledge and experience of the relationship between risk and reward is limited to gambling and events of chance. However, progress throughout history—whether political, social, or economic—has been achieved through various channels of problem solving, which often meant taking risks. People realized that by identifying past events, they could anticipate predictable results for the future. The desire to see the future and to choose based on that knowledge is inherent in all of us. The search for this knowledge led Pascal and Fermat to the discovery of the Theory of Probability, and thus began the study of statistics and the science of quantifying risk. By understanding the nature of risk, its consequences and possibilities, we have been able to transform our fears of the unknown into a catalyst that drives the advancement of science and technology, business, and the quality of life we experience.

Risk taking is manifested in a wide range of our decision-making processes, from having children to buying insurance and doing estate planning, from choosing a career to purchasing an automobile. It is present in our willingness to accept mistakes and failure, with the intent of moving forward toward the possibility of success. The advancement of technology—the overwhelming presence of computers to aid our everyday tasks, and the evolution of the Internet—would not be feasible without embracing the nature of risk and managing it to guide our vision of the future.

Many individuals equate trading with gambling for the obvious reason of wagering one's capital in the hopes of winning or profiting from that risk. The qualities that make up a good gambler are also evident in a good trader. They are always in control of their emotions. But how do you stay calm when you are losing money? Successful traders will admit to being wrong and accept a small loss. They understand what risk is. Rather than avoiding it, they learn the value of risk management as a tool for assessing the profit potential in the marketplace.

Like gambling, trading is a fascinating method of obtaining money, not from labor, but from a game of chance. It inspires our passion for risk taking, but without the social stigma of gambling. Trading offers the opportunity to realize one's dreams of freedom, accumulation of wealth, and now, with the growth of online trading through the Internet, the sophistication of partaking in technological advances. However, trading should never be an alternative to gambling. While gambling requires some skill and money management, a large part of a gambler's success relies on dumb luck. Somebody once said, "I would rather be lucky than smart any day." We would too, and so would most of you. It is easy to convince yourself that this is your lucky day, or even to be so bold as to think that you have an instinct for recognizing good fortune. But luck is only one outcome of probability, and it plays an inconsequential role in the consistent success of a trader.

In a game of seven-card stud, the best hand before any betting begins is two aces in the hole and an ace showing. But if you make any attempt to build the pot, everyone will fold, and you will win only the ante. Obviously, your reward is directly proportional to your risk in playing this hand. However, if you hold a hand that has a high probability of becoming the best hand, you have a number of choices:

1. Call all the bets, but not raise.
2. Call the bets to see a few more cards, then fold if the probability of winning decreases.
3. Raise the bets and build the pot.

While you still have the risk of losing, how much money you wager is determined by your course of action in playing out this hand. However, you also have the opportunity to collect a colossal reward if your calculated probability is realized. Whichever scenario you choose, your chance of winning, even with a statistical advantage, depends largely on luck. Depending on the amount of your wager, your winnings will vary. This is the relationship between risk and reward. The discipline in controlling risk is not to wager more than you can afford to lose.

Most individuals trade for the same reasons—the freedom to make your own hours, the freedom to become your own boss and not have to answer to anyone, and the freedom of someday being financially independent. But if it were that easy, we would all be wealthy, and we certainly would not be here to share our thoughts. Trading is a difficult business. It is a business in which knowledgeable and skillful traders compete to profit from dynamic price action determined by the market participants' interpretation of the stock price equilibrium at any given moment. Simply put, prices move constantly and randomly. At any instant, the price of a stock perfectly reflects the market's consensus on the value of that stock. It is dynamic because the movement in price (the instantaneous point at which buyer and seller agree to transact) is always in motion. As in operating a business, the approach to trading must be structured in order to ensure longevity and growth. This can only be accomplished by:

1. assessing and managing risk;
2. maintaining discipline;
3. controlling the emotions of pride, greed, and fear; and
4. developing a style or method of trading that's comfortable and consistent with your risk tolerance and ultimate goals.

Risk Management

The efficiency of an engine is measured by the maximum displacement of energy per incremental intake of the potential energy of fuel. Similarly, risk management maximizes the output of profits per incremental risk exposed and energy utilized to analyze the market. Just as maintaining an efficient engine requires fine-tuning the intricate parts, risk management must be maintained by fine-tuning the intricacies of all your emotions, discipline, and confidence. Furthermore, the energy expended to analyze the market and establish a strategy must be efficiently transferred into your decision-making process by assessing and managing your risk exposure. Without risk management, one moment of excitement or panic can cause you to lose your head and that can be an expensive lesson.

When a market is running against you, like in the Novellus example, one must always consider where to place the stop loss for that particular trade before the entry. No trader should get into any trade that presents a poor risk-to-reward ratio, such as risking one point to make a quarter of a point. It should be the other way around. In the Novellus example, had William cut his losses early and walked away, he would have protected most of the profits he had already made for the day rather than giving them right back to the market and then some. Dollar cost averaging works well if used correctly in trading or investing for the long haul. But if you are a day trader, using intraday dollar cost averaging in a market that is running against you is like piling on more pillows in front of a locomotive. You will still get run over and you will lose more money.

The diversification of one's portfolio reduces unnecessary risk exposure for the risk-averse investor. While the same concept applies to trading, risk can never be completely avoided. Opportunities abound in the marketplace because volatility allows the astute trader to convert short-term price swings into profits. However, getting caught on the wrong side of that movement can be painful and costly. The potential for profit cannot exist without the risk of a loss. Taking a long position when the market appears strong seems to be a safe trade. But is it? A look at market sentiment shows that the higher the bullish sentiment, the higher the potential for the market to fall. Why? Because a high sentiment means more people are long the market already. They are confident and wish the market to go higher. In order for the prices to climb any higher, more new buyers need to come into the market. But if everyone is already on the long side, who is left to buy? A lack of buyers means more sellers, and the slightest hesitation can trigger a sell-off. But to sell or go short at this point appears risky, because you are violating the trend and prices can still go higher. If you hesitate, it may be too late. There is no right or wrong answer. However, successful traders enter a trade to take advantage of price fluctuations, knowing that if they are wrong, they will take a small loss and exit the trade quickly.

Risk management is not a definite series of procedures that will eliminate risk altogether. Rather, it encompasses controlling all aspects of your emotions, confidence, and discipline; and using the resources available to you in order to develop certain guidelines for mitigating risks. The guidelines are as follows:

1. Factor in all pertinent information regarding the market, including any uncertainties facing the market. The market is the ultimate arbiter, digesting all relevant information and factoring in any uncertainties about the future.

2. Set the risk limits by calculating the options available to you so that your decisions will be structured. For example, set stop losses and higher stops as the position goes in your favor.

3. Mitigate your risk whenever possible by developing a style of trading and share size consistent with your personality and tolerance for risk. Once the position is in your favor, reduce the risk by locking in part of the profit early and letting the rest of your winning position run.

Longevity, Preservation of Capital, and Equity Building

Contrary to popular belief, trading is a game of longevity. The myth in trading is that you will easily strike it rich over a short period of time or find the golden trade that will allow you to retire and live happily ever after. The reality is that trading is a game or business that is played out over a period of time and that involves hard work, analysis, and soul-searching. It is a profession based on consistency, preservation of capital, and equity building.

The willingness to accept small losses increases the trader's odds of preserving capital and ensuring longevity. The idea is to keep losses to a minimum while allowing the winners to run. If you have difficulty taking small losses, the inevitable end would be the pain of large losses. We all fantasize about accumulating vast amounts of wealth with almost every trade. However, when in any trade, rather than listening for the cash register ringing in your head, you must first consider the potential downside, and how and when you are going to eliminate this trade if the market turns against you and tears to the opposite direction. Good poker players fold as soon as they realize the odds of winning are against them. The same goes for good traders. It is a consistent, habit-like practice of capital preservation. Because every trade has the potential for turning into a loss, a good trader must always be prepared to exit the trade at the first indication of being wrong. Many novice traders make the mistake of holding on to losers in the hope of a retracement back to the original entry point. While many stocks do come back and recover, it takes only one or a few bad trades to wipe out all previous recoveries and even more. A string of losses can cause serious damage not only to a trader's account, but perhaps more importantly to a trader's confidence—your ability to believe in yourself. You will become a prisoner of your own trades.

Every trader experiences periods of gains and periods of losses. However, only those who can endure the series of losses will survive. Dr. Alexander Elder writes, in *Trading for a Living,* "The hallmark of a successful trader is his ability to accumulate equity." This can only be achieved by letting the profits grow while cutting losses quickly, before they wipe out the profits altogether. Trading seems easy when the trader is making money. It is the losing streak that hinders progress, and even eliminates us from the game. When sustaining a string of losses, the trader must stop, take a break, and take as much time as needed to regain composure.

Too often, a biased trader in a losing position becomes angry at the market and, to show who's boss, exercises the power of doubling down. Do you really think the market will be intimidated? All this will do is increase the risk in a losing trade and perpetuate the destruction. Take the losses, swallow your pride, and come back to trade another day. The endeavors of most novice traders to succeed are cut short by their inability to sustain longevity and preserve their capital. A good trader once said, "My best trades are yet to come. . ." This helps to remind him that he must preserve his capital to trade again tomorrow.

Discipline and Objectivity

Discipline is the ability to control one's behavior, despite the temptation to deviate from what is right. Objectivity is a function of discipline. The former is not possible without the latter. In trading, discipline goes beyond the basic interpretation of rules of conduct. It is the ability to maintain self-control and to exercise the management of risk. Discipline requires commitment, motivation, and the willingness to struggle in the pursuit of your goals. But discipline is not an innate quality. It can be cultivated. It is the conditioning of the mind, much like an athlete's training of the body. Objectivity is the ability to remain impartial, to distance yourself from your emotions. To become a successful trader, both qualities are needed.

Developing your skills as a trader means improving both the capability to observe the market as objectively as possible and the discipline to execute your plans. When trading, you can easily become emotionally involved because your money is on the line. If the market goes your way, it is exhilarating. A few winning trades and you can easily think you are infallible. However, if the market moves in the opposite direction you may become stubborn, then angry, then scared. The forces that move the market are not easily detected. But we do know that the market is dynamic and moves randomly. The aggregate activity of all the participants makes up the market. Remember, for every buyer, there is a seller. The market is not your foe—*you* are. If you are biased, you are unable to see what the market is thinking or doing. You may have the discipline, but without allowing the market to tell you which way it is going, you cannot exercise the discipline to become part of the move or get out of the way if you are caught on the wrong side. Inversely, you may be objective and see the market's intentions, but without discipline, you will be unable to execute the proper trades and become part of that move.

Here are some points to remember:

1. Make the effort to analyze the market, collect the information, and study the charts. Be prepared. Without preparation, you will miss the major moves, or worse, you may get caught on the wrong side. Preparation will guide your instincts and teach you to anticipate the market.

2. After assessing the risk versus profit potential, execute the trade. Don't be afraid to lose. If you let fear take over, you will never be able to enter a trade because the thought of losing will be overwhelming. Distance yourself from your emotions—especially fear.

3. Learn to take profits when you have exhausted the profit potential. Conversely, learn to exit a losing trade when you realize that you are wrong.

4. Let the market tell you which way it is going. Do not make the mistake of thinking that you are correct and the market is wrong, especially when managing an open position. You may eventually be right, at a later time. But if the market is moving in the opposite direction right now, that means you are losing money and therefore *you* are wrong.

5. If you are a novice, keep your bets small, trade lightly, and do a lot of observing. Get educated before you trade.

Because trading intensifies human emotions, staying objective allows traders to distance themselves from those emotions. It is also easier to accept being wrong when you make an effort to be objective. The market moves in only two directions, so a trader is wrong quite often. That is the nature of trading. Admitting to being wrong hurts our egos, and taking a loss hurts the pocketbook. If discipline does not make you take losses, then the depletion of your capital will. Being wrong is not a measure of failure. Refusing to admit to yourself when you are wrong and eventually being forced out of the game is what constitutes failure. Lack of discipline clouds your judgment and keeps you from staying objective. Losing that objectivity prevents you from seeing your mistakes. Therefore, a lack of discipline results in failure.

Greed and Fear

"I have imbibed such a love for money that I keep some sequins in a drawer to count, and cry over them once a week." —LORD BYRON

Greed, in connection to money, is the insatiable appetite to acquire more. Money in its singular form is meaningless, yet it is the center of our existence. We are all greedy about money, and the more we have, the greedier we get. Greed is what keeps us in the market. It is the never-ending fuel that propels us to continue to trade in search of more profits. But it is also the flaw that keeps us in a losing trade. Greed can be constructive or destructive, with no distinctive boundaries. It is the seed of our own destruction.

Like greed, fear is constructive, to a certain degree. It makes us cautious. It makes us take protective measures and sharpens our perception. But too much fear evokes anxiety and panic. We respond by avoiding the cause of our fears. In trading, fear is the antithesis to greed. It keeps our greed in check. We protect our profits and refrain from a risky trade out of fear. But too much fear leads to panic and hinders progress. The reluctance to trade is a symptom caused by fear. If you cannot overcome your fears, you will thwart your own efforts. Strike a balance between fear and greed.

Confidence

During the course of our trading careers, we have seen too many people attempt to day trade and eventually get wiped out. Of the few who did become successful, we have tried to identify what characteristics or events transformed these select few from losers into winners. The distinctions vary, but the one key ingredient common to all the profitable traders was confidence in their ability to trade. This is not to say that they were confident in their picks of the direction of the market, but in their ability to see the direction of price moves and utilize their resources to take advantage of that price fluctuation. Even the most successful traders are sometimes wrong about a market call. But their confidence gives them the freedom to change their minds and to exercise discipline. How do you become confident when you are losing money and are unsure of what you are doing? Don't you need to be making money to become confident? These are valid questions. If you have diligently done your homework in examining the market and studying the fundamentals, and if you have set aside a certain amount of risk capital to test your skills at the elusive art of trading, then at some point you must take that plunge with confidence. Even the smallest animal, once it has decided to take a stand, will confront its opponent with confidence. If you are unable to confront the market with confidence, then we advise you to walk away. You do not have to walk away and never trade again. Once you have regained your composure you can face the market again. The market will always be there, brimming with opportunities. If you attempt to trade in a state of uncertainty, your hesitation will definitely translate into losses due to bad timing or freezing up when you should be acting.

When we have a series of losing days, we walk away from the market for a few days to collect our thoughts and confidence. In the fourth quarter of 1998, one of us had a bad slump in trading and decided to take a vacation. However, the market was very active, and he hurried back to trade. Because his mind was still focused on not losing money, he was unable to trade objectively and his confidence was further eroded. So he took a longer vacation. Eventually, he stopped thinking about losing money and became more relaxed. When he returned this time, he started out with smaller share sizes so that money would not be the primary concern, and he became increasingly more confident. His confidence was restored because he focused on his trading ability and reduced his concerns about losing money. He saved not only his career, but also his sanity.

The reason that one sets aside a predetermined amount of risk capital is that trading is a risky venture. This risk capital should be money that can be lost without destroying your life. Then your dependency on the income from trading or even the equity itself will not affect your judgement and hinder your trading decisions. If these parameters for risk are set and you are willing to take the risk with that capital, then trade with confidence. Of course, you have to put in the time and effort to prepare and study the market. But when you consider yourself ready, do not hesitate.

A trader once asked us how we enter trades so easily when the market looks so scary. We told him that we are able to execute trades because of our confidence in our ability to get out if we are wrong. Although we are never one hundred percent sure of the trade when we enter, we know that if we do not take the risk when we see an opportunity, we would never be able to enter trades, and we would never make any money. After this conversation, we decided to observe his trading. When he saw the opportunity for the right trade, he would mutter to himself that this was it! But he kept rubbing his clammy palms on his legs, and he could never enter the trade at the right time. His lack of confidence forced him to wait for more confirmation, and when it came, he jumped in too late. He ended up losing on a trade that he would have made a profit on if he had entered when he first realized the opportunity. His fear of losing money destroyed his confidence and potential.

Without confidence, your fear will be magnified and you will be unable to trade. Timing, discipline, and risk management can only be practiced if you have confidence. Without confidence, you will act only when the market convinces you that a trade is a sure thing. We all know that there are no sure things in the stock market.

When traders tell us that they have been losing money and that they need to make money soon or stop trading, we advise them to stop trading immediately. Remaining in the market under those conditions is the perfect setup for getting wiped out. If you feel that you have to make money soon, then get a job. Trading is not for you. Take the rest of your money and use it for something else. Needing to make money soon is equivalent to hoping for it. In the stock market, there is no room to *hope,* only room to act.

Confronting the market is like facing a mural of your inner self. All your emotions and thoughts are combined into one mosaic. Focus on what will help you become confident and do not lose sight of it. If you find your thoughts wandering, take a break until you can focus again on what is important to help you regain that confidence.

Patience

Patience may be a virtue, but in trading it can mean the difference between timing the market to become profitable and chasing the market, or overtrading. Patience is not waiting for the perfect trade to land in your lap. It is allowing the market to tell you what direction it is headed in, so that you can time a good entry. It is waiting for the market to move to your target level or stop you out if you are wrong. Too often traders chase the market and enter the end of a run, or get a good price level but take profits prematurely because they are anxious to lock in the profits. This is fine if you are a good scalper and are willing to get back in if the market continues to move. However, too much movement in and out of trades can lead to over-trading. Your commissions will add up quickly and your marginal rate of profits per trade will diminish to a level at which you are giving away more in commissions than you are earning in profits. Patient traders learn to let the market tell them when the profit potential has been exhausted, or if you are wrong for the market to prove you wrong and stop your losses. Patient traders use the time factor to maximize their profitability while taking losses only if the market proves them wrong.

Patience also plays a critical role for newcomers to the market. Newcomers must allow themselves the time to mature as traders and time to apply logic to the abstracts of the market. Like good wine, a trader gets better with time. Some traders take years to mature, while others learn more rapidly. Those who are new must allow themselves as much time as it takes to develop. While most will probably experience some losses, consistent study and observation of the market *and* the inner self while practicing strict risk management and capital preservation are critical during this time. Some newcomers are profitable very early in trading. Regardless, patience and consistency in applying sound risk management will be critical to your long-term success.

Whether you are an experienced trader or a newcomer, patience will help you succeed. Practice it.

Reality Check

New traders must be realistic about their progress. Most, if not all, new traders will lose money in the beginning. Consider these early losses your "tuition" paid to the market. However, keep in mind that the first step toward becoming profitable is to minimize these early losses while acquiring the skills necessary to continue, so that you too will be able to take advantage of the numerous opportunities that abound in the marketplace.

Nobody likes to lose money. But whenever there is the possibility of success, there exists the risk of failure. Many attempt to master the speculative art of trading but fail, not from a lack of knowledge or capital as most people conclude, but from their inability to control their anxieties and to accept losses. Don't associate losses with failure. Making mistakes and losing money is a natural progression in trading. Once you understand this concept, you can understand the concept of risk management. A trader can never avoid risk, because complete risk avoidance leads to an inability to face the challenges of the market. Ultimately, the desire to avoid risk instills fear and hinders progress. But by confronting it, risk management becomes a valuable tool for assessing the potential for profit in the market.

Remember, sometimes the scariest or riskiest trade turns out to be the most profitable trade. Unfortunately, knowing what to do and actually doing it are two different things. Trading successfully requires discipline—the discipline to execute the trade, the discipline to remain objective, and the discipline to take profits and losses. Most of the qualities that make up a good trader are not innate; they are qualities that can be developed. Condition your mind and your emotions. It can be done!

3
Market Preparation

In every field, the biggest difference between the professional and the amateur is experience. This is perhaps more so in trading than in any other area. The amateur trader carries a significantly higher risk than the seasoned trader, even on the very same trade. If we are in the business of minimizing risk, and if experience plays such a crucial factor that it can directly and significantly affect levels of risk, then how does the novice compensate? While it is obvious that there is no substitute for time, it is possible to accelerate the learning process through proper education and making a conscious effort to mimic the mind of a professional. You must understand the playing field, its rules (written or unwritten), the forces that affect it, and the basic laws of supply and demand. Along with psychology and risk management, mastering these aspects of trading provides a trader with a solid foundation of skills.

In studying hundreds of novice traders, it is very clear to us that many stumble because they lack a"big picture" awareness. Realize that the individual is merely a tiny bolt in a complex machine. Do not nurture the false belief that your trading is the center of the market's attention. Many day traders take months or years and large losses to learn this—that is, if it is ever learned. Individuals must acknowledge that their trading must find synchronicity with the market's progression. The market, through its natural course, can and will quickly punish, and eventually eliminate, traders who are out of sync, whether they are aware of it or not.

Professionals do not fear the market, but rather respect and accept its inherent risks, because of a deep understanding of its currents and inner workings. They are aware of its activity at all times and acknowledge that its various tides can and will directly affect their profitability. To the professional, the entire stock market, despite its millions of components, is a massive entity that behaves like an individual. It is human, and therefore we can anticipate its behavior, given certain input, to a reasonable degree of accuracy.

Professionals may often have difficulty in explaining the reasons for their trades, or why they stopped out early or reversed position. Perhaps it was because of an event that occurred weeks ago or the unusual progression of the stock's price action since the open that they were instinctively reacting to. Regardless, they are drawing upon *a total awareness of the market's evolution through time.* This is one of the most crucial factors affecting trading that novices fail to explore. Novices must look into the market, break it down, follow its progression, and react to that progression, not fight it. They must understand that one can anticipate the market's next move, but also understand that it is dynamic and not predictable to any single person one hundred percent of the time. The ability to correctly anticipate the market's next wave, and the discipline to acknowledge that one can just as easily miscalculate, is best developed by the amateur trader through making a conscious effort to magnify a total awareness of the market, the response of its components (sectors and stocks), and the trader's own reactions. Novices are too often engrossed in their trades (which may seem the world to them at the moment) and fail to properly pay attention to the massive market that surrounds them and to the tides that will determine whether the traders will be profitable or not.

Picture the stock market as a complicated maze that is best examined from an overall perspective—a bird's eye view. It is a common misconception that the professional day trader ignores the big picture. While this may hold true for some profitable day traders, the majority of the best, most profitable, and most consistent traders pay attention to and correctly understand the big picture. Total awareness of the market is akin to having a mental compass. While not often perfect, it serves as a guide to traders toward the best-odds direction of the market—be it an individual stock, a specific sector, or the entire stock market—and helps them to avoid dead ends and traps.

The Importance of Educating Yourself

The development of information technology has made an abundance of resources available for any trader, from more direct and faster access to the markets to affordable commissions and a variety of sources of information. Favorable SEC and NASD regulations, the individual's desire for independence, and the opportunity to reap large profits have caused a tremendous surge in the popularity of trading. The fact that trading is incredibly popular does not mean that trading has become safe. It is still a business for those who are prepared and still quite a cruel one for the unprepared. Whether there are ten participants or ten million does not change the fact that only a small group with the best skills will reap the majority of trading profits. To the dismay of many, the market is designed to operate that way. Just like any other competitive environment, in sports or in business, the dominance of the few outshines the rest. It is the same in the stock market. You must educate and train yourself before taking up the challenge of trading, or you will constantly fall behind those who have more experience than you.

We believe in the "no shortcuts" approach to learning how to trade. Take as much time as you need to learn how. While the lure of making a lot of money is very strong, and especially so if you see other traders do it with apparent ease, strive to be an educated trader from the very beginning: Make sure you know that where there is opportunity for profits, there is the danger of losses. This applies to all traders, regardless of experience. Before you learn how to run, you must first learn how crawl, then how to walk, then how to fall with grace and how to pick yourself up. Only then can you learn how to run.

The Two Opposing Forces of the Market

It is a fairly common and simple notion that the market is a daily, minute-by-minute battle between buyers and sellers. However, as simple as it sounds, many day traders fail to take note of how significantly the simple laws of supply and demand affect any given trading day. It is a surprising phenomenon that many newcomers and intermediates alike are unaware of the importance of these basic economic principles. What makes a market? What makes a stock price move? Buyers and sellers? Supply and demand? Call it what you will, but in this business, the market comes down to order flow—the volume of buy versus sell orders. Order flow is at the heart of the market. Anyone with a clue to the direction of order flow (majority buying or selling) has a goldmine of information. While it is impossible for us to be certain about the direction of today's order flow, it is best estimated by day traders through constantly monitoring price activity.

Upon beginning the trading day, ask yourself whether the buyers or the sellers are going to be visiting the market today. Who has the upper hand? A trader behaves like a storeowner, constantly watching the door to see who is coming in. The trading day begins with gauging market sentiment, paying close attention to the headlines, activity, and direction at the open. As the day progresses, traders monitor price activity and interpret fundamentals for clues and patterns as to whether the market or stock will likely continue its trend, reverse, or just fluctuate. Observe the strength of a rally or sell-off, and its relative pullbacks. Were they strong or weak? Did the market pull back at all? Maybe there is more coming. Regardless, traders must constantly think ahead of the crowd, eliminate the obvious, factor in the hype and uncertainty, and react accordingly. Then they must confront the tough possibility that they and their peers, who believe that they are thinking ahead of the crowd, are actually wrong. These are the psychological twists and turns that make trading no easy task, whether for the professional or the novice. One thing is certain: Trading skills are accompanied by the habit of thinking ahead and being prepared to react correctly when the next turn in the market presents itself.

Buyers and Sellers

The birth of any market begins with a need or demand. Similarly, the beginning of a trading day is always a search for solid Bids (buyers). It is the market's assurance of survival and good health. Market makers, specialists, and professional traders need to move inventory and quite obviously, without the Bids, the market will eventually die a natural death. Quite a gloomy thought, but true. Understanding that the market or a single stock is constantly in search of good Bids is key to understanding the market's intrinsic nature. When the Bids are strong and the market is advancing, the path is paved for overexuberance; conversely the lack of Bids opens the door to panic—a frenzy to grab the last of the remaining good Bids. While these make for ripe trading territory, it is important to understand two things. First, stocks fall quicker than they rise; fear is a stronger emotion than optimism (most people will send order flow on emotion). Second, stock prices tend to advance in stages (testing for good Bids) but they tend to sell off sharply (see Chapter 6). As far as technique is concerned, for example, profits on the short side are booked in a shorter time span than they are through the long side. An awareness of who (buyers or sellers) is launching an attack on the market at any given moment, and familiarity with the simple laws of supply, demand, panic, and exuberance are basic but crucial tools in a trader's arsenal.

Sources of Information for the Day Trader

"What should I do for homework?" is a question often asked by a novice or intermediate trader. As much as we do not like to simply say, "Read and watch anything and everything," it is nevertheless true. It is always beneficial for traders to read or watch whatever they can about the business, especially in the quest to improve their trading skills. Remember, though, to keep an objective point of view.

Exercise caution. With the number of new resources for traders growing so rapidly, the overabundance of available information can cause confusion for anyone seeking to enter the trading world or enhance trading skills. Also, a novice or intermediate trader is always vulnerable to others' opinions, largely because of the novice's desire for guidance. Make an effort to remain objective. Avoid opening a position based on the opinions of others or an incredible news article without doing the proper research. What if the analyst was talking in terms of years, while you want to trade and profit from a stock tomorrow? What if the stock has just moved up by 38 points? Be diligent and filter the information that you receive. Always cross-reference it with other information. Adjust the time value, confront the downside, and weigh out the pros and cons before you risk your valuable trading capital based on the opinion of somebody else. Be a professional! Derive your own trades. If you don't do this, you might as well place your money with an investment advisor, where it will probably be better off.

A common misconception in the day trading world is that day traders don't need to watch what the public is watching. Nothing could be further from the truth. Keep in mind that the best traders possess a higher level of knowledge and expertise in the business than the investing public. It is a shame to find a day trader with less market knowledge than a casual investor. Long-term investors put all their faith in either a broker or the management teams of the companies they own stock in. Professional traders primarily place their faith in only three things: their decisions, their systems, and their brokerage houses (whose only job is to keep their money and clear their trades correctly). Keep in mind that we are in the business of gathering and processing information with the goal of profiting by reacting correctly to that information. We want to hear and watch what the majority is hearing and watching, so as to anticipate potential direction. We are not watching the news or listening to opinions to seek advice, but rather to gain the information needed to anticipate the market's reaction, observe the market's progression, eliminate the obvious, develop a plan, and speculate on best-odds scenarios.

Television

CNBC and Bloomberg TV are perhaps the best television resources for our business. Real-time market monitoring and healthy discussion of the trading day's headlines and general market issues are beneficial to the trader in many aspects. However, the notion of "buy on rumor, sell on news" is no different today than it ever was. This is not to say that you should take a short position on a hot stock with great news today. It is to say that stocks in the headlines are often too extended for a day trade play by the time you are ready to execute in your exuberance. It's a large market and you must adhere to your trading rules. There are few better experiences in trading than finding out that a stock you are already profiting nicely on is just now being heralded on the news. Perhaps this may even be the hint to exit a position.

CNBC and Bloomberg TV are excellent real-time market monitors with very intelligent viewpoints. We have one of them on almost constantly. Learn from them and use them as resources to monitor the market. In most cases, they are not good resources for day trader techniques, or worse yet, buy, sell, or hold recommendations for application in day trading. A great majority of the information reported and opinions expressed by guests on the program are more applicable to the long-term investor and can be very dangerous for the day trader. The day trader must learn to decipher and interpret the news *in day trading terms.*

CNBC After Hours, CNN, MoneyLine, and other nightly or weekly financial news resources on TV are also terrific sources of general information. Keep in mind that most of the investing public only has time to watch financial news in the evenings or on the weekends. While many of these reports may be old news to the day trader by the time the evening or weekend news comes along, it is fascinating to view the market from the general public's viewpoint. Also, the macro-view of the market as discussed from a variety of angles (different charts, oscillators, commentary, etc.) helps to keep a trader abreast of the general market and, often, in good perspective.

The Internet

The development of trading resources (or any information resource, for that matter) on the Internet has been no less than amazing. What used to cost hundreds of dollars in data subscriptions is now readily available at extremely affordable prices or even for free. The Internet makes available to the day trader an abundance of resources: headlines; technical and fundamental data about the market, sectors, and individual stocks; and other resources that are essential to the day trader.

Here are some of the various types of information available online.

- **Headlines and Commentary.** This is an excellent alternative to television because the information is summarized through lists and is interactive. Thus, you can read exactly what you prefer. A multitude of Web sites offer a list of headlines you can scroll through. You will reach a point when, most of the time, simply reading the headlines will be sufficient. That saves precious time, especially at pre-market open, and allows the trader to ingest more information.

- **Technical and Fundamental Information.** If you have a Level 2 account, you will most likely be provided with sufficient technical (especially intraday) data from that service. Fundamental data, such as P/E ratios, market capitalization, EPS, and so on can be retrieved from a variety of free resources.

- **Public Message Boards and Public (Unmoderated) Chat Rooms.** These are more amusing than informative. This is where the Longs and Shorts battle it out verbally, and where rumors often proliferate. Some comments on the message boards are impressively intuitive; however, the majority of the information here is rubbish and good only for a few laughs. As a student of mass psychology, it is beneficial for you to visit the public chat rooms and message boards. Too much involvement here, however, could be counterproductive.

- **Private Real-Time Trading Rooms.** Some of these are excellent sources of information, while others are not. The key is to find reputable trading rooms that are operated by real and experienced traders. The best trading rooms are moderated by professional traders who are intent on educating its subscribers. Many of them also act as excellent guides to navigating the ins and outs of the trading day. The users in these types of chat rooms are often required to conform to a higher code of conduct than is found in the public chat rooms. These sites are also excellent forums for traders who are trading alone; you can benefit greatly from interaction with others in a managed environment.

- **Training Classes and Seminars.** As with the private trading rooms, what is important here is reputation. Because these can be very expensive, do not hesitate to ask questions before signing up. Make sure that the training program is designed and conducted by an experienced trader and educator whose primary objective is to educate you on managing your risks in the market, rather than teach you how to use a specific piece of software or the rules of the NASDAQ. It is also very important that the training course does not impose a specific trading style that may be detrimental or unsuitable to your level of risk tolerance and your ability. Make an effort to speak to previous attendees who share similar goals to yours, and get a variety of opinions on the worthiness of the course. Do not hesitate to ask questions, and be wary of claims and lures that concentrate too much on how much money you can make in the business.

- **Computerized (Automatic) Trading Systems.** There is not much need for comment here. Think about it: If you had developed an automatic trading system that worked, would you need to be selling it? Probably only when it doesn't work anymore. Systems that work are not for sale.

- **Scanning Software.** A number of software packages are available to traders to help identify specific patterns they are looking for and to assist in daily market scanning. While we believe that scanning through hundreds of charts manually helps a trader develop a good eye for chart patterns, these software packages can be very helpful to those who do not have the time to scan manually.

Publications

Like television, publications are extremely beneficial sources of information for the day trader. We have noticed that popular publications such as the *Investor's Business Daily (IBD)* and the *Wall Street Journal* have increased the amount of information published for the active stock trader during the last few years. *IBD,* in particular, takes a contemporary approach and may serve as an excellent source for potential day trade targets. It also helps the trader keep abreast of earnings announcements, economic reports, and a variety of fundamental issues that may affect a specific trading day.

Barron's and *Businessweek* are among many weekly publications that are worthy of reading because of their "week in recap" approach. Just like the nightly news, the investing public finds more time to read these publications in the evening hours or on weekends, when they have time to track their investments. It is not uncommon to find specific articles that affect the next few trading days on a stock. As momentum traders, we not only use these popular periodicals (and all other resources) to educate ourselves and keep abreast of developments in the financial market, but also to anticipate shifts in order flow by anticipating the investing public's reaction to the media.

Real-Time Financial News Wires

Bloomberg, Reuters, Dow Jones, and Telerate are among the popular financial news wires used by analysts, fund managers, market makers, and professional traders to stay at the cutting edge of the market's headlines. The amount of research data on these services is extensive, and it is presented for professional use. A fully dedicated news and research terminal with a data feed is set up in the trading area. While they are expensive, many professional traders consider these tools to be indispensable in trading because of the speed of news reports and trading alerts (many of which directly and instantaneously affect order flow). In addition these services provide a vast amount of accurate data that is immediately searchable and available from one source. Many day traders trade primarily on the scrolling news of these services alone. Despite the many advantages of these machines, the cost an individual trader may incur by having one at home may outweigh the benefits.

Technical Analysis: A Synopsis

The random-walk theory suggests that stock prices move at random and that analyzing past price movements is of no use in anticipating future prices. While there are many market participants (including profitable day traders) who believe that the theory holds true and who trade primarily on the basis of order flow, we believe that the study of technical analysis, price action, and trends (at least, of the most basic concepts) is extremely beneficial to the day trader. Technicians of the market believe that there is a systematic approach to trading stocks, despite the random theory, through the analysis of pricing patterns, price relationships, and volume. The absolute popularity of technical analysis, especially its basics, makes it a formidable force in the market. Because we are in the business of studying mass psychology, it also makes perfect sense to monitor what is popular.

A Guide for the New or Intermediate Trader

The practice of technical analysis serves as a legitimate guide to the novice or intermediate trader who is often lost in the large world of stocks. The attention to these factors, especially to common patterns and price relationships, serves as a solid point of reference in the quest to familiarize oneself with the stock market. As a new trader, you must make a serious attempt to gain familiarity with such basic factors as: how trading in a larger, more influential stock has a tendency to affect the smaller stocks in the same sector; how price action at S&P500 futures trading affects a large majority of stocks, some with incredible accuracy and others not so; the power of the trend; how a stock or index all too often rebounds off a support level or perhaps a 200-day moving average; and how a trading gap often seems to act as a magnet for price action. The study of price movement, relationships, trends, and volume is a valuable learning experience for any trader. Making a conscious effort to observe, study, and monitor basic factors such as support, resistance, opening and closing prices, and basic technical patterns while exercising strict risk management and discipline paves the way for any novice or intermediate trader to achieve a professional viewpoint of the equities market. We discuss these topics in more detail in Chapter 6.

Fundamental Analysis: A Synopsis

Fundamental analysis is the knowledge and study of:

- Economic, social, and political factors that affect the stock market, and
- Accounting-related factors and the potential to generate earnings of a particular company or group of companies so as to determine whether stock prices are valued correctly, undervalued, or overvalued.

Contrary to popular understanding, knowledge of the fundamentals is a very beneficial component to day trading for several reasons. It plays a key role in the day trader's ability to interpret news announcements and headlines for potential price direction, and it comes very much into play when there is technical uncertainty. The key here is correct interpretation with respect to time value. Interpreting the fundamentals in professional trading terms gives one a great advantage in day trading. As a rule of thumb, the longer the time period, the more fundamentals come into play. Also, the hotter the news, the more immediate the effect on the stock price. There are factors that cause an immediate effect on stock price, while others take more time. Some headlines, which may be news to you, may already have had an effect on price because of the proliferation of a rumor. A trader must keep a keen eye on how certain fundamental factors affect price activity, by how much, and how long. The market factors in uncertainty and the fundamentals justify the price because of their effect on intrinsic value. But a surprise fundamental announcement may set a trend for the day, or perhaps longer, and can be very beneficial to trading.

Trading on News

Many profitable traders rely heavily on the immediate delivery of news, so as to quickly take, dispose, or reverse positions before the news spreads to the trading and investing majority. Some news that is reported intraday, such as the announcement of a stock split, lawsuit, merger deal or cancellation, or stock buyback, affects order flow so greatly that it is a tremendous source of profits for the day trader. However, one must have the ability to interpret the news accurately and swiftly so as to take maximum advantage of the opportunity.

In a popular case, for example, when news about the U.S. Justice Department's legal action against Microsoft was first announced intraday during the latter part of 1997, it was a sure reason to take a short position immediately on Microsoft. In fact, MSFT was already beginning to sell off as Janet Reno was beginning her announcement. It had also set a foreboding tone in the entire market. However, because of the commotion at MSFT, many traders that day were too late to recognize that this caused a strong positive reaction to Netscape's price action (the company perceived by many to benefit the most from the negative headline). While it was extremely difficult to catch a short position on Microsoft (MSFT), opening a long position on Netscape (NSCP) was easier. The rally on NSCP was exhilarating.

Moreover, many traders who were trying to open a short position on MSFT gave up after the stock had pulled back 3 or 4 points. Of those who had been lucky enough to open as position, many took profits too quickly. To a trader who is in tune with fundamentals, the gravity of that kind of news would have translated to a shaving of 6 or 7 points off the pre-announcement stock price (MSFT was in the 130's at the time). It turned out to be a 10-point intraday haircut for MSFT. There were more than a few opportunities to open the short position here or to open long on NSCP, and the proper interpretation of the facts opened a larger window of opportunity for the perceptive day trader.

Intermediate-Term Trades

We believe that while day traders profit from taking advantage of intraday price fluctuations (where fundamentals are often not in play as much as technicals), knowledge of fundamental factors is key to setting up the day trader for intermediate-term trades such as swing and core positions (where fundamentals become more of an issue). In the Microsoft example, the opportunity would open up to a swing trade to hold a short position (with lower share size) in order to allow the news to be digested by the general public. This made for a profitable short-side swing trade based on fundamentals. The upside was limited by the gravity of the news.

Technical and Fundamental Knowledge Combined

We are ardent believers in taking a combination approach to trading, be it to trade by different time spans or to trade by different schools of study.

Cross-referencing technical and fundamental studies makes you a powerful and complete trader with less restriction for time, price, or direction. The combined approach builds a good foundation of knowledge that will be used in preparation, in precaution, and in the search for the numerous opportunities available for profit every day in the stock market.

While you must avoid playing against a technical price progression (bucking the trend!), you must understand that fundamental factors often supplement technical price activity and vice versa. The market is so dynamic that there are times when fundamentals are in charge of the trading day while the technicals lag. Keep in mind that the market also factors in the immeasurable: uncertainty. A combined knowledge of fundamentals and technicals increases a trader's odds of correctly interpreting the market: when to enter, when to exit, or whether to trade at all.

The Trading Day

Wake up early. Be an early bird. We don't mean just your physical presence, but your mental presence as well. The key here is preparation, speed, and scenario building. Take in the news and keep it in. Watch how the market plays out the headlines through order flow and price action, from the open all the way to the close, not just during the first couple of hours. Watch the market change as news comes in. See how stocks have a tendency to move together. See how a gap affects price activity (Chapter 6). See how big news on larger stocks affects the little stocks in the same sector. Did you know that a strong earnings announcement by Intel can rally the entire technology sector? Keep an eye on that Dow, the NASDAQ 100, and the S&P 500 futures! If you are inexperienced, you don't even have to trade—just watch. The market is fascinating! Create a scenario, and see if you were right or wrong. Don't worry if you were right and you didn't make money because you didn't trade. There will be hundreds of opportunities again later. Now take notes and do it all over again tomorrow; this time you will be wiser. Build yesterday's facts into today's activities. There will come a day when the opportunity to place a good trade arises and your preparation will be the catalyst that will drive your trade. Unfortunately, there are no shortcuts. The key here is to take as much mystery out of the stock market as possible, to break it down and analyze it.

Active Trading Periods

Good trading requires good volume. While activity within the trading day is no perfect science and there are no formal rules to divide the day based on volume, the trading day is generally divided into three periods:

Opening Period—First 2 to $2^1/_2$ hours

Midday Period—Second 2 to $2^1/_2$ hours

Closing Period—Final 2 to $2^1/_2$ hours

The majority of volume is traded during the opening and closing periods. During these periods, intraday trends are generally established and the trading ranges are wider. Because the ranges are wider and liquidity is higher here, there are many more profit opportunities for the day trader during these periods. These are prime times for scalp and swing trades.

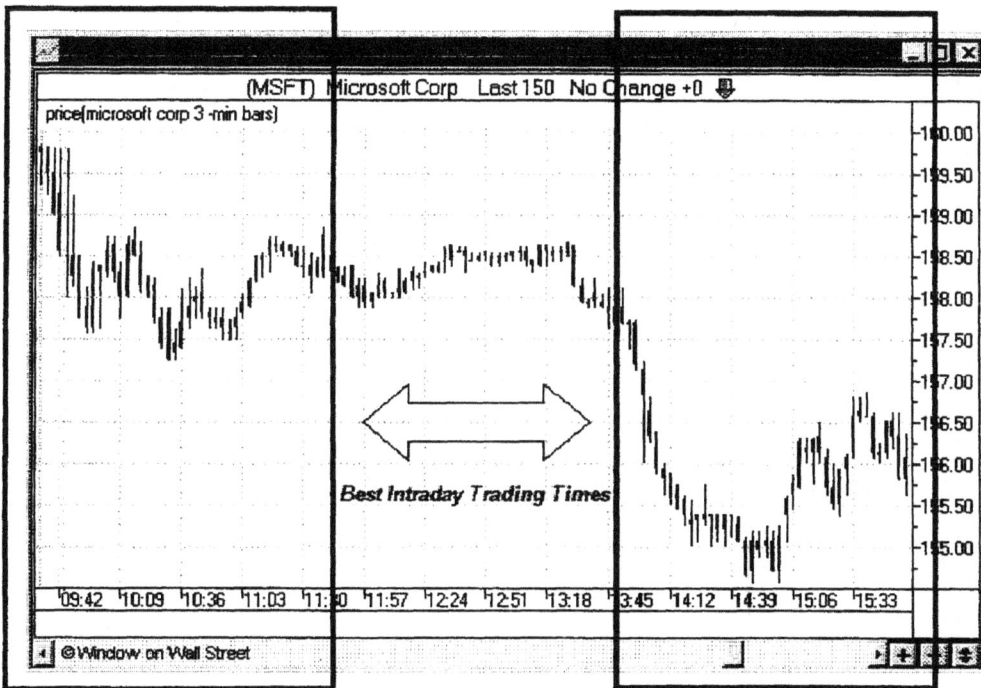

Figure 3-1. Best trading times.

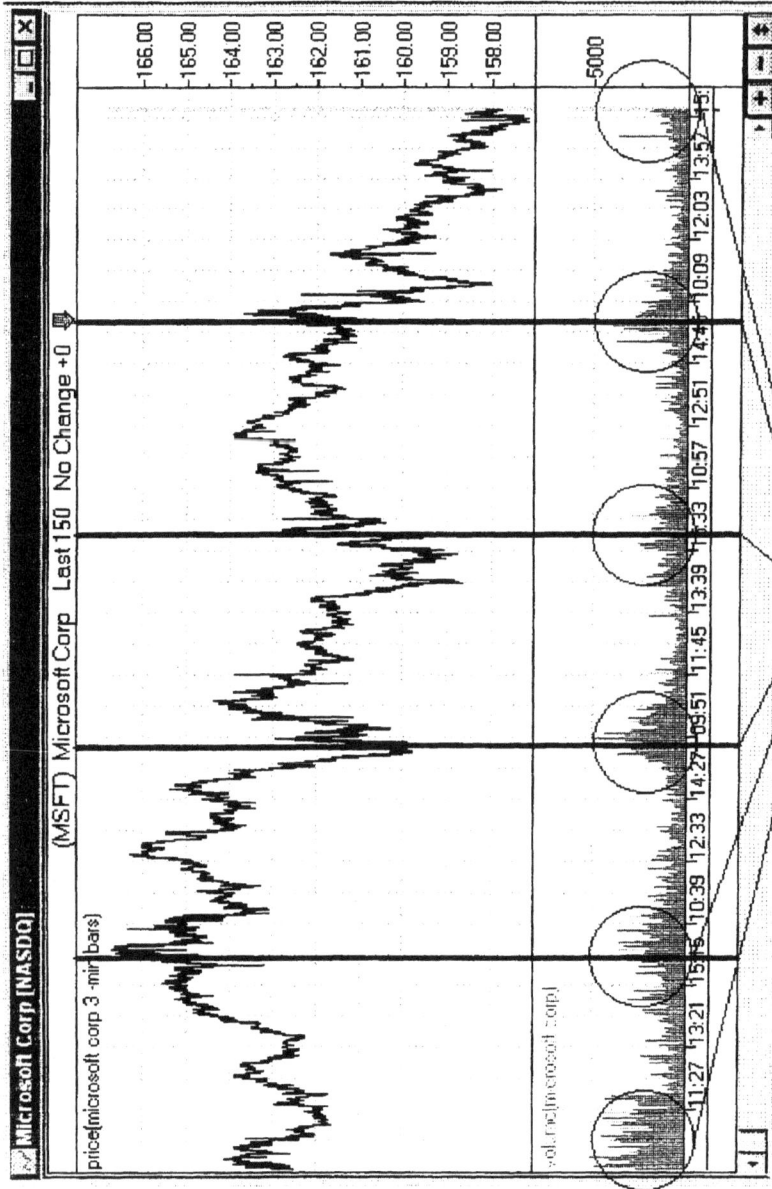

Figure 3-2. Intraday 5-day chart with volume depicting most active periods

On the contrary, the midday or "lunch" period is often made up of false breakouts and narrow trading ranges. This is the time of day that is quieter. The opening period is quite a stressful time, and the lunch period is the time when the market rests, reassesses the open, and gathers energy for the volume that will be coming in during the closing period. Because of the frequency of narrow ranges here, this is the time when scalp trading is poor and the commission risks run high—traders often find themselves spinning wheels and getting nowhere.

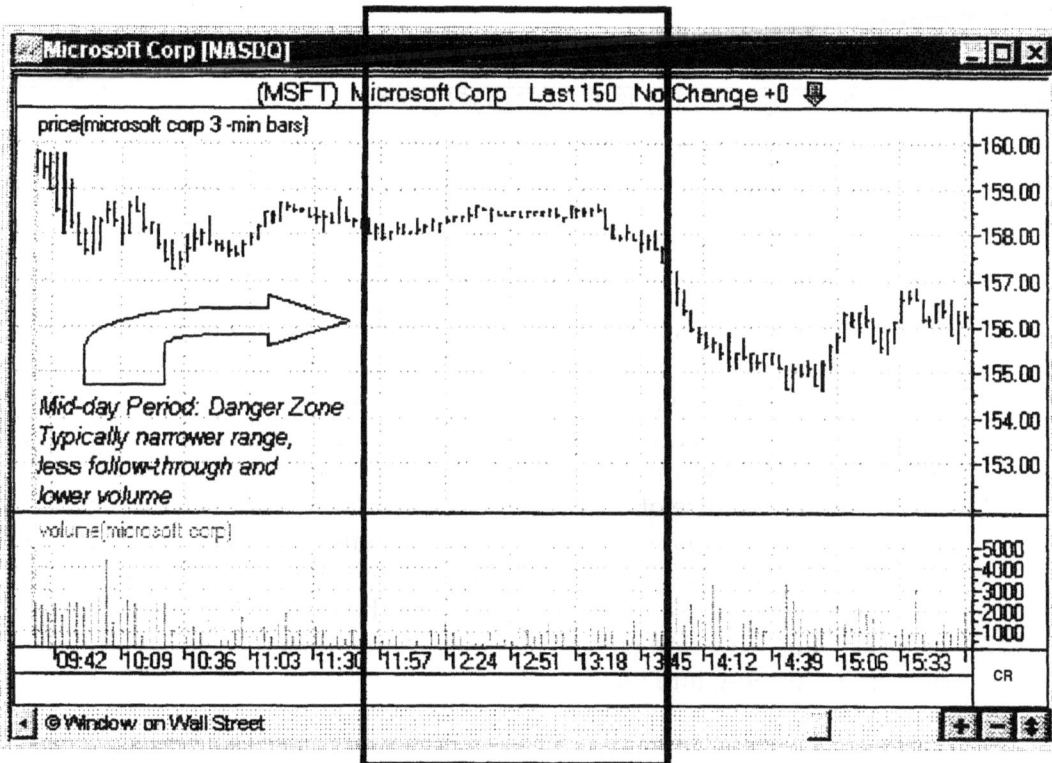

Figure 3-3. The midday period.

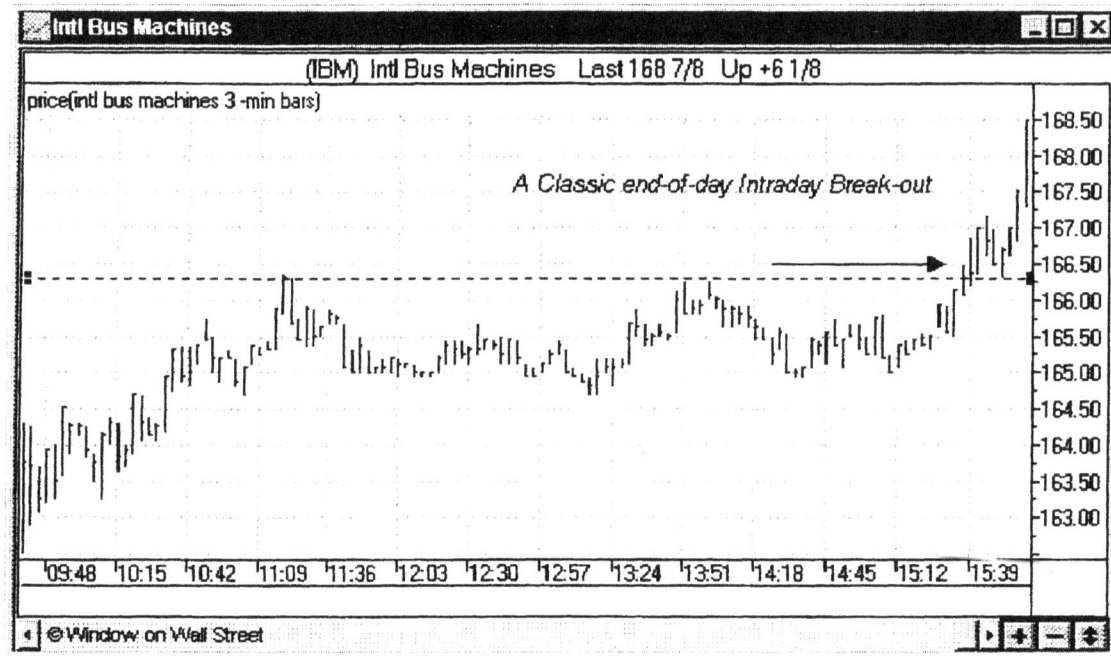

Figure 3-4. End-of-day breakout.

The closing period is an exciting time for trading. The follow-through on trends during this time is the best, for a couple of basic reasons: the deadline to place orders before the closing bell and the fact that the day's news and trends have been established during the open and midday periods. Intraday breakouts and new intraday highs and lows are great scalp opportunities because of the urgency to fill orders before closing time.

When the market is coming in to the close with an extensive trend, look for a brief reversal just before the close, due to profit taking. For example, on a strong up trend, look for a small sell-off before the close and the converse for short covering on a weak close. While these are simple concepts, do you build these into your trading day?

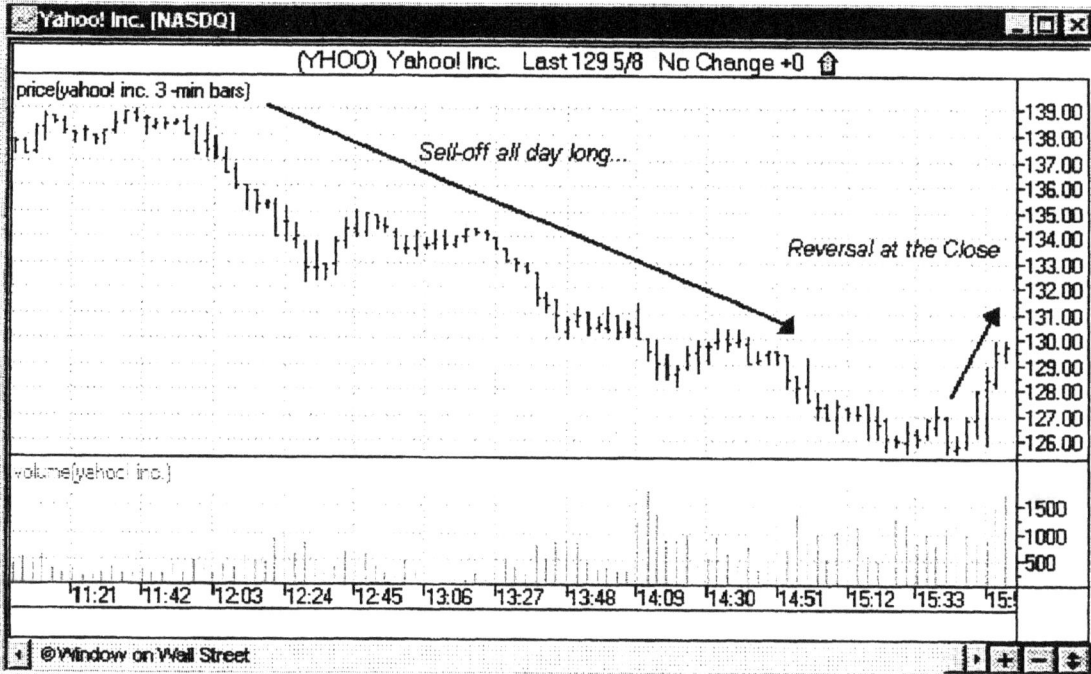

Figure 3-5. Closing reversal.

Assessing Market Conditions

Assessing the market's general sentiment and potential direction is the first order of the trading day. In this process, the day trader prepares scenarios, either mentally or in written notes, in order to prepare for the day's activities. With the mind-boggling advancements in networking technology, the market moves at such a rapid pace that as the day progresses, there is often little time to think. Having a prepared scenario helps the trader through the day. The key is to remain objective and avoid too much bias in one direction or another. This allows for flexibility, a key trader quality. Traders must allow the market to tell them what to do and must have the ability to reverse opinions instantly. Surfers approaching the beach look at the types of waves coming in, realize the likelihood that they will change, and acknowledge that the strength or weakness of the waves will directly affect their performance. More importantly, however, they accept the fact that there is nothing they can do to change the nature of the waves. If the waves are weak or unpredictable, the surfers stay on the beach until a better pattern of waves develops. Traders should also stay on the sidelines until they have a sense for the pattern of the day's trading.

In assessing market conditions, there are three basic factors that traders must consider: sentiment, breadth, and relative strength.

Sentiment. In day trading terms, sentiment is first defined as the sum of today's and any recent news put together—positive and negative, good and bad, bullish and bearish. In the early morning, pay attention to all factors, eliminate the obvious, and begin to plan different scenarios in your mind. These scenarios should consist of what can realistically happen today, or during a specific period. This is one of the most difficult tasks in trading and it does require an experienced viewpoint. If you have limited experience, make a habit of doing this early in your trading. Keep in mind that the goal is to be prepared to react rather than stop short when a market event occurs. Also, you must try to get in sync with today's order flow. The investing public sends orders with heavy emphasis on today's sentiment, so getting an early grip on sentiment is a great advantage. Many day traders start off the day without a clue to today's sentiment, often being too caught up in counting how much money they want to make or are afraid to lose today. Don't make that mistake.

Breadth. The market's amplitude or breadth is indicated by the number of advancing stocks versus the number of declining stocks. We hear it every day in the news, for example: "Dow Jones is up 118 points today; 2,168 stocks advance, 1,234 decline, and 426 remain unchanged." Remember one fact about the equities market: Stocks, in general, move in the same direction at the same time. It should be fairly clear to day traders that monitoring and anticipating the general market's next move is important, because the general market's direction usually determines the direction of most individual stocks. What better time would there be for a strong stock to advance than in a positive market, or for a weak stock to decline than in a negative market? Quite simply, if the general market is down, odds are in favor of the bears; the reverse is true for the bulls.

Relative Strength. We refer here to a stock's relation to other factors, such as prices of larger stocks within the same sector or its response to a general rally or sell-off. Those are clues to a stock's relative strength or weakness. Market breadth tells us that stocks have a tendency to move in the same direction at the same time; this holds true especially for stocks within the same sector. Smaller stocks within a group or sector tend to follow the price activity of larger stocks in the same sector. Some stocks, such as Intel, Microsoft, Cisco, or IBM, are powerful enough to initiate rallies or sell-offs in the entire technology sector. So long as there is little or no news about a specific smaller stock within a group, it will have a strong tendency to trend along with the other stocks in that batch, particularly the larger stocks.

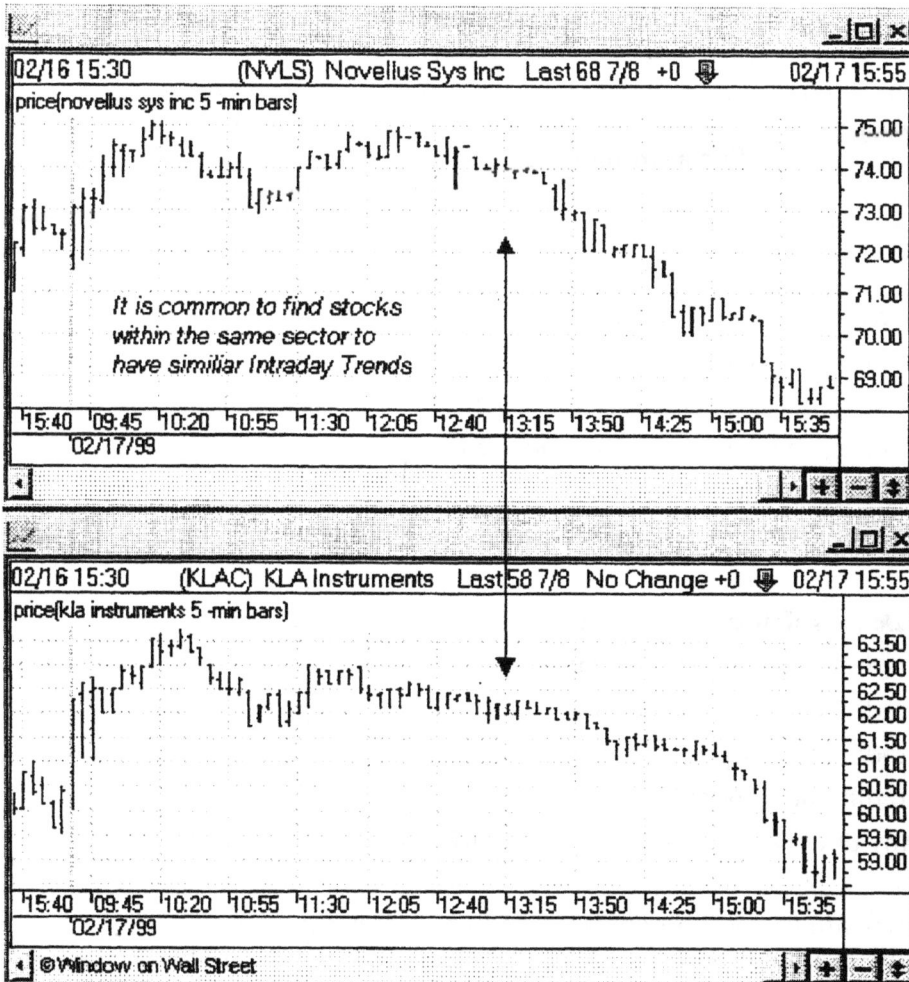

Figure 3-6. Stocks within the same sector.

The larger stocks (so long as there is no individual news) often trend along with the general market. The key here is to identify how a stock responds to intraday rallies of the general market (Dow, S&P 500 futures, or Nasdaq 100) and its response to intraday sell-offs. This is critical in assessing relative strength. Looking out for these details increases the odds of a trader's ability to pull in profitable trades. This is the stock speaking to you; listen to it. The day trader must target strong stocks on strong periods to the long side, while targeting weak stocks during the weaker periods for the short side. While "Buy low, sell high" is smart advice, "Buy high, sell higher" is an exhilarating challenge. This is not to say you must always buy highs and short lows, but rather, it is a surprising phenomenon to find that it is often very easy to convince somebody to buy something cheap, while it is difficult to buy something expensive. In the stock market, when an equity is selling cheap, there is usually a good reason for it: Nobody wants it.

How do we define a strong stock or market and a weak stock or market? There are probably a million different interpretations, but in day trading, the rule of thumb is as follows:

Strong Stocks and Markets
- Trading above today's open
- Trading above previous session close
- Trading above previous session high
- Trading near today's high
- Any of the above with a bullish market sentiment

Weak Stocks and Markets
- Trading below today's open
- Trading below previous session close
- Trading below previous session low
- Trading near today's low
- Any of the above with a bearish market sentiment

There are many different ways to assess strength or weakness, including the examination of support and resistance areas, moving averages, and popular chart patterns. These are examined in greater detail in Chapter 6.

Assessing the Open

The opening period frequently experiences heavy volume and can be the most exciting time of day. The influx of orders during the market's open is massive. The investing public places orders overnight or before the opening bell for a variety of reasons, but often in anticipation of the effect of any news that developed prior to the opening bell. For professionals, the heavy volume often creates a frenzy. Add to this the fact that quote problems are more frequent in the opening period. This is a time when Market Makers and Specialists really have the upper hand, because they are the only ones who see the order flow. Especially on active days with big news, when the opening bell rings, the market is often like a wild animal released from a cage. It is seeking direction and the most astute traders are watching closely. Observing Market Makers, Specialists, and price activity during this time is critical. Intentions are revealed by behavior and price action.

The first half hour of the trading day is so critical that it sets the tone for the day, or at least for the morning session. The strength of the first trend the market takes, as well as the measure of the subsequent retracement, is crucial to strategy building and forecasting. The trading pattern in the first half hour is the foundation for the day's session. Traders should watch:

- first half hour highs and lows;
- strength or weakness of the initial retracement (pullback or profit taking) from these highs and lows; and
- any gaps formed between yesterday's close and today's high, not only for individual stocks, but for market indicators such as the S&P 500 futures, the Nasdaq 100, or a composite.

During the first half hour, the market seeks direction. Often, the majority of the price action during the day is traded during the opening period. Being attuned to the strength or weakness of the trend and subsequent retracement provides clues to the undercurrents driven by order flow. For example, an up-trending market at the open with a shallow pullback and a subsequent breakthrough of the early morning high is a persuasive indicator of strength.

In a gapped market, especially with a large difference between the close and opening prices, the gap looms throughout the day and often acts as a magnet for trading. Here the opening price is critical and sets a key support or resistance level for the day.

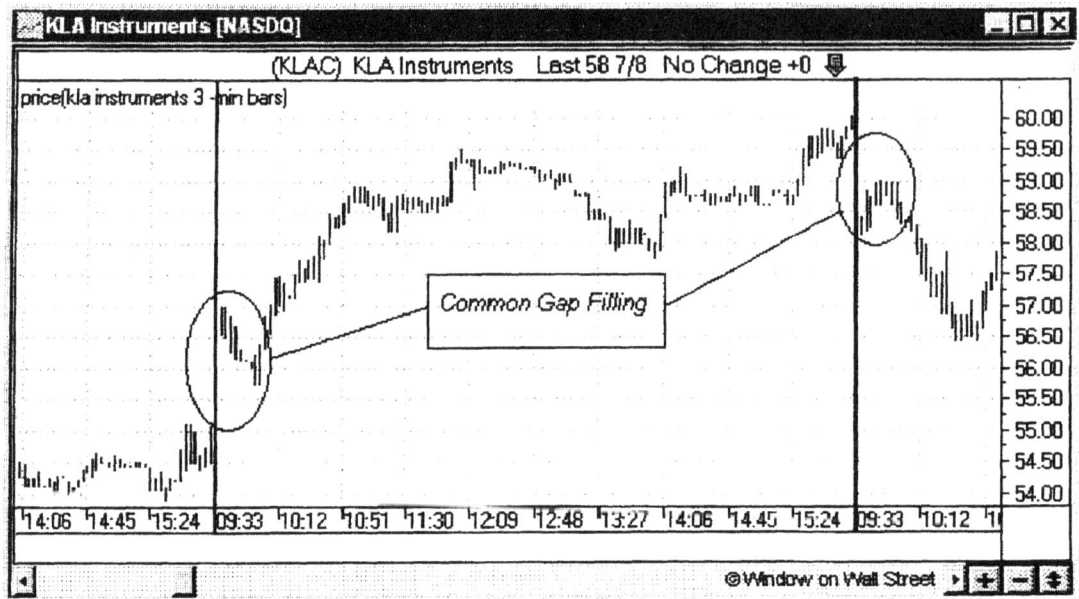

Figure 3-7. Intraday gap filling.

Daily Mental Preparation

One of the most neglected factors in trading is the daily ritual of mental preparation. Professional trading will require your total concentration and clear thinking. If you did not get enough rest or there is a matter on your mind that will distract you from trading, either trade with less aggression, or don't trade at all. Your lack of preparation might cost you more than you think. Start off your day with energy, concentration, and focus. Leave your problems at the opening bell.

Market Indicators for Day Trading

As an active day trader, you must always keep an eye on the health of the market. The last thing you would like to do is take positions on the opposite side of the general market's direction. While there are some exceptions, such as strong news on an individual company, the majority of the profits to be made are on the side of the general market's direction; conversely, most of the money that will be lost will be against the market. Like a doctor who is constantly monitoring the health of a patient, a trader is constantly looking at the health of the general market.

It is best to view market indicators in chart form. This allows the trader to view the trail of the market's progression, to help quickly identify support and resistance points. The following are the most used indicators for day trading:

S&P 500 Futures. Rather than watching the actual S&P 500 index, the S&P 500 futures contract is the most watched indicator for active day traders. Institutions and the best traders trade the S&P 500 futures contract on the floors of the Chicago Mercantile Exchange, as well as electronically, taking positions (or hedging positions) based on the technical price progression of the contract and fundamental factors of the economy that affect the future prices of stocks in the S&P 500 index. There are several stocks, particularly large-caps, that have an astounding, almost mirrorlike, intraday reaction to the price of the S&P 500 contract. The high-volume scalpers of the NASDAQ watch every tick of the S&P 500 contract, even down to having somebody read the Bid and Ask hand signals and transmit the roar of the futures traders on the Chicago Mercantile Floor.

There is more than one S&P 500 futures contract being traded at any time, based on expiration date. Active day traders watch the trading on the most liquid contract—the contract that is going to expire soonest. These contracts expire every three months, in March, June, September, and December. In January, we watch the S&P 500 contract that expires in March. Around the second week of March (without waiting for actual expiration), we begin watching the June contract, and so on.

Keep in mind that S&P 500 futures contracts most often trade at a premium to the actual S&P 500 index today. In other words, it is usually assumed that stock prices in the future will be more expensive than they are today. If the S&P 500 futures contract is selling at a discount to the actual index, that is a very bearish signal for the market.

Active S&P 500 futures traders trade primarily on technicals. Intraday movement in the contract is heavily motivated by technical price pattern forming. Watching the S&P 500 contract on a technical basis is of extreme benefit to the day trader. It is surprising to us, especially since stock prices are so sensitive to the S&P 500 futures, that many day traders ignore the technical price progression of the S&P futures. Futures traders also keep close tabs on the progression of influential stocks, bonds, and key headlines. Watch for support and resistance levels on the futures, measure the strength and weakness of its retracements, and keep an eye out for basic technicals like moving averages, trend lines, double tops or head and shoulders tops, and gap trading. Doing this will give you a tremendous advantage in day trading. Watch the S&P 500 futures as if you were trading them.

NASDAQ 100. There are some days when the technology sector has a mind of its own. What we mean to say is that if the high-techs in the market are trending differently from the S&P 500 futures, the NASDAQ 100 indicator comes in very handy. The NASDAQ 100 is comprised of the NASDAQ's top 100 stocks. According to NASDAQ data to date, the 100 has a 94 percent correlation to the NASDAQ composite (all NASDAQ stocks). This is to say that NASDAQ indicators are comprised mainly of its top stocks, that the large technology stocks such as INTC, MSFT, and CSCO have great influence on technology stocks in general. If you are day trading, the probability of your involvement in tech-related stocks is very high. Watching how NASDAQ's top stocks are trading, especially on days when the tech sector is diverging from the general market, is of great advantage. While watching the NASDAQ 100 is not as technically precise as watching the levels of the S&P 500 futures, you should still keep an eye on its support, resistance, and basic technicals.

Dow Jones Industrials. The Dow Jones Industrials Index is the traditional indicator that measures the prices of 30 stocks traded on the New York Stock Exchange, each representing a major U.S. industry. It is the most watched stock market indicator in the world.

The antiquated Dow Jones Industrials is terrific for measuring one thing: market psychology. While most believe it is not the "true" reflection of the market it used to be, we watch it for its milestone numbers (for example 9,300 or 10,000). Its support and resistance levels are watched and reacted to very closely by the investing public and institutions. Make no mistake: Despite its antiquated approach, we closely watch and don't argue with the numbers on the Dow Jones index.

When tracking the intraday Dow, however, you must note that because there are only 30 stocks in the index, one or two stocks that are bucking the general trend may throw off your timing. Rely more on the S&P 500 Futures or the NASDAQ 100 for intraday tracking.

Tick Indicator. The Tick indicator is a measure of upticking versus downticking stocks. While there are two major types, one for the NYSE and the other for the NASDAQ, we primarily watch the NYSE Tick, due to the unreliable nature of the NASDAQ Tick indicator. The uptick in the NASDAQ is based on Bid; the uptick on the NYSE is based on print.

The gravity of a rally or sell-off is measured by the movement of the Tick toward its extreme levels, at plus 1,000 or minus 1,000. Trend reversals are usually due when the Tick hits these levels. The Tick is best viewed as a chart in order to measure its support, resistance, and trends for the day. There is not much meaning when the Tick is closer to zero. It is commonly viewed as a leading indicator of trend, not only for intraday purposes (especially in scalping), but also for gauging strength or weakness for a period longer than one day. Typically, when the Tick hits very extreme levels beyond plus or minus 1,000 (toward 1,400, for instance) when preceded by a series of up or down days, this may be indicative of a washout, and a reversal of the previous trend is due in the coming days.

We also stay attuned to the Tick's response to rallies and sell-offs in the S&P 500 futures. A strong response by the Tick to a rally in the futures may indicate broad (thus solid) strength, while a strong negative response to a sell-off on the futures may indicate broad weakness.

Market Leaders. Gauging the market is not limited to watching indices, the Tick, or the S&P 500 futures contract. Keeping a close eye on the leaders of the market is indispensable in measuring general market strength or weakness. On a big up or down day, these stocks are at the forefront of the market and lead the rest of the herd in that direction. Because we are day traders, we want to be very specific as to what we identify as market leaders, so, it is important to group the leaders by major sector. For example, in technology-related issues, keep an eye on the kings of the tech stocks such as Microsoft, IBM, Intel, Cisco, Lucent, Dell, and Compaq (among a handful of others). In the financial sector, keep an eye on J.P. Morgan, Citigroup, Merrill Lynch, and other large-cap plays of the group. Strength or weakness in a particular group is usually confirmed by the same symptoms in its leaders. There are many days in the stock market when trends among different groups or sectors do not correspond with one another. Keeping an eye on the market leaders in each major group will help tremendously in your decision-making process.

4
Forces That Move the Market

There are many forces that affect price movement. However, it all comes down to supply and demand of the stock. Fundamental factors affect the intrinsic value of the stock, and therefore give justification of buying and selling pressure toward one direction over another. Many times the market discounts a fundamental factor in anticipation of what the news may be. It is important for any trader to understand the fundamentals. Fundamentals determine what the underlying value of the stock, and the market as a whole, should be in relation to the economic cycle.

The nation's output, or the Gross Domestic Product (GDP), reflects the overall health of the economy. In turn, the growth of the economy reflects the health of the nation's businesses and their prospective growth for the future. Stock prices rely on the growth of underlying companies and the earnings associated with this growth. Therefore it is imperative that any investor understand and keep abreast of the current economic conditions that influence these companies' stock valuations.

Economic Indicators

Economic indicators showing the health of the economy are reported periodically by different government agencies and by the nation's central bank, the Federal Reserve.

Most of the data are reported on a monthly basis, and they include the following:

1. **Nonfarm Payrolls and Unemployment Rate.** Issued by the Bureau of Labor Statistics the first Friday of every month, this report gives the

number of nonfarm jobs created in the nation, net of jobs lost through attrition. The unemployment rate is the count of unemployed workers who are actively seeking but unable to find jobs, as a percentage of the total labor force. These two numbers are widely followed because of their significant impact on the public's understanding of the strength of the economy. These numbers are also big market-moving numbers. However, the strength or weakness of the job market is a reaction to the economy by employers and therefore is a lagging indicator.

2. **Producer Price Index (PPI).** This number measures the change in prices on the wholesale level, or to manufacturers, at different stages of production. Also reported by the Bureau of Labor Statistics, this number usually comes out in the middle of the month for the previous month's data. There are actually two numbers reported—the overall PPI and the core PPI, which excludes food and energy because these two commodities are highly seasonally affected. Because any changes in price will eventually be passed on to consumers, PPI gives advance notice of price changes and inflationary pressures. Therefore, PPI is a leading indicator.

3. **Consumer Price Index (CPI).** Also reported by the Bureau of Labor Statistics, this index indicates the change in prices on the consumer level. The U.S. Department of Labor measures a basket of goods and services, and uses it to give an indication of the cost of living to the public. The CPI is also broken down into two categories: the overall CPI and the core CPI, excluding food and energy. The CPI is one of the most significant numbers to the public, because many adjustments in salaries, Social Security payments, and other pensions are based on the CPI. Because changes in price to producers are passed on to consumers, this is a lagging indicator.

4. **Gross Domestic Product (GDP).** This number shows the nation's total output for a given time period. It is the sum of all final goods and services. This is an important number because it is the broadest indicator of whether the nation's economy is expanding or contracting. The U.S. Department of Commerce calculates it on an annual basis and reports every quarter. There are two numbers—real GDP in constant dollars and nominal GDP in current dollars. Real GDP measures GDP in relation to a base year to take inflation into account, while nominal GDP does not adjust for inflation. Because the number is compiled for three months past, then reported, this is a lagging indicator.

5. **Retail Sales Report.** Because about two-thirds of the nation's GDP consists of durable and nondurable consumer spending, retail sales is an

important number to gauge the strength of consumer expenditures. The U.S. Department of Commerce reports this number in the middle of the month for the previous month's data.

6. **Durable Goods Orders Report.** Durable goods are any nonperishable goods that last for more than three years. Reported by the U.S. Department of Commerce, this number is also broken down into an overall number and a number excluding defense, because defense spending is not related to the business cycle. Transportation is also often excluded, because a large aircraft order can create large swings in the durable goods number and skew the perception of the economy. This number indicates the willingness of businesses to invest capital spending for future needs, because change in demand affects the need to purchase durable goods to increase capacity. Therefore, it is a leading indicator.

7. **Industrial Production Report.** Reported by the Federal Reserve, this number is an index of the physical output of goods, excluding services. Because this number focuses on such a narrow sector of the economy, it is sensitive to any change in production and reflects those changes quickly. Therefore, it is a leading indicator, and in fact is a component of the Leading Economic Indicators.

8. **Capacity Utilization Report.** Also reported by the Federal Reserve, this number measures the rate of operation for U.S. factories. When the capacity utilization number (CU) is low, the economy is in recession and unemployment is high. When the CU is high, the economy is in expansion. However, when the CU gets to a certain level (about 90%), there is a diminishing rate of return because in order to keep up with demand, factories incur higher costs and increase in capacity does not translate into higher earnings. At this point, prices must rise to meet demand, and inflation kicks in.

9. **Index of Leading Indicators.** Reported by the U.S. Department of Commerce, this index is issued monthly and is a compilation of leading indicator data that suggest the direction of the economy three to six months into the future.

10. **National Association of Purchasing Managers Index (NAPM).** The NAPM indicates the direction of the economy three to six months in the future, based on a survey of purchasing managers at 300 major companies. Growth within the manufacturing sector is indicated when the index is above 50, while contraction is indicated when it is below 50. This information is released on the NAPM's monthly business report.

11. **Consumer Confidence Index.** This number is calculated by conducting a monthly survey to gauge consumer outlook on the economy, personal finances, employment, and plans to purchase big-ticket items in the near future. The consumers' optimism or pessimism is directly reflected in their expenditures and in the economy. Therefore, this is a leading indicator.

12. **Housing Starts and Building Permits.** These numbers include any homes or units within a building that a permit is issued for, and are very sensitive to consumer confidence levels because homes are so expensive. Historically, housing starts drop six months before the rest of the economy, so this is a leading indicator.

There are many other reports of economic data that are released weekly, monthly, and quarterly. Depending on the market sentiment, certain indicators become more sensitive to the market and will have more impact than others. Sometimes, the same data showing the same weakness or strength in the economy will have opposite effects due to a shift in focus by the market.

In December of 1998, the market was concerned about a slowdown in the economy, as the world financial crisis at the time would eventually affect the U.S. A strong nonfarm payrolls number eased much of the concern for the day, and the market rallied. In February of 1999, the myriad of strong economic data previously reported changed that sentiment to one of concern over a stronger than expected economy and the consensus that the Federal Reserve would no longer need to ease interest rates. Instead, the bias may now be on the tightening side. A stronger than expected nonfarm payrolls number reinforced this fear and the market reacted in the opposite direction with a sell-off.

There is no sure way to determine what number will trigger a rally or a sell-off. The market decides depending on the sentiment at the time and its concerns. It is up to the individual to decipher the significance of each piece of data, so each bit of information should be absorbed and pondered. Keep a close eye on the market's reaction to the data.

Due to the speed of transmitting information, the globalization of our economy, and the integration of governments and demography that make up the arena of financial markets, the perceptive trader must be constantly aware of both political and social events that affect the global and domestic economies. Economic progress cannot be immune to political instability or ignore the state of mind of the population. Keep abreast of current events, because they affect the financial markets directly or indirectly.

Inflation

Inflation is perhaps the most frightening word in the stock market. As prices rise, every dollar earned becomes incrementally less valuable as its purchasing power diminishes. If left alone, inflation will ultimately kill an economy. Therefore, the number one priority of the central bank of any nation is to fight inflation through monetary policy—interest rates and money supply. Germany's Bundesbank and the U.S. Federal Reserve are the most revered central banks by the world's financial institutions as premier fighters against inflation. Much of the previously mentioned economic data reflects the state of the economy. As the economy heats up rapidly, prices increase due to supply and demand of goods and services, thereby creating inflation. Interest rates measure the borrowing cost of anything from overnight Fed Funds to the benchmark 30-year Treasury bond. As the Federal Reserve raises interest rates on overnight Fed Funds (the rate at which banks lend to one another on an overnight basis), the effect on the 30-year Treasury Bond is magnified due to the longer duration of the debt investment period. The longer duration creates a steeper yield curve. Because of the long time frame, the action of the 30-year bond must also factor in any uncertainties in inflation—and thus interest rates—that can plague the economy in the future. As inflation becomes increasingly evident, bonds fall in price, and thus increase interest rates at the long end of the yield curve. Stocks are also susceptible to inflation, for three reasons:

- Inflation means every dollar earned by the underlying company has less buying power, so each dollar is worth less.
- Rising interest rates crimp the economy and add borrowing cost to the companies' debt structure. The future growth of the company will be affected by higher interest rates.
- As bond prices fall, the attractiveness of the secured investment backed by the U.S. government makes it more competitive with stock prices. Investments other than equities will become attractive options.

Corporate Profits

The price of a stock measures the ability of a company to earn profits now and in the future. Some companies have stable but slow growth consistently, and therefore their stock's price volatility is low. Others have great potential growth in the future, and their prices reflect the company's ability to grow and the potential for higher profits in the future. The ability to earn profits and grow is usually factored in by the market and is reflected in the price to earnings ratio (P/E). Any violent reactions to a disparity in the relation of price to the reported earnings are the result of surprises to the market that have not been factored in.

A day trader must be able to understand the movement of prices as a reaction or anticipation of the market—as a consensus on the stock's performance or lack of it. If INTC is expected to show good earnings, the stock will most likely trade higher before the earnings announcement in anticipation of the good news. However, how the stock trades after the announcement is determined by how good the news is, and by the market environment. If the earnings come in better than anticipated, the stock will attract even more investors, while an expected earnings announcement may trigger profit taking as investors who bought the stock in anticipation now sell for profits as they look for other plays. The good news has already been factored in prior to the announcement. Thus the phrase, "Buy the rumor, sell the fact."

Analysts

In addition to earnings announcements, keep abreast of the analysts' upgrades or downgrades. Analysts who cover certain stocks or sectors forecast future strengths or weaknesses in earnings by upgrading or downgrading the stock or sector, based on their outlook for the future. Upgrades and downgrades often have an immediate and significant effect on stock prices. However, a day trader should be cautious in taking day positions based on these reports, because prices are often gapped to factor in the change in opinion.

Fiscal Policy

As previously mentioned, certain discretionary government policies have both direct and indirect fiscal impact on the economy. Through government spending and changes in tax rates, the Treasury can have a big impact on consumer spending. If consumers are allowed to keep more of their hard-earned dollars, they will eventually spend more. In turn, the growth in consumer demand leads to business investments through the depletion of inventories, and economic expansion occurs. However, the effect on stock prices lags in time—the time it takes for the impact of the policies to be felt—as opposed to the direct stimulus that occurs as a result of monetary policy.

Options Expirations

The third Friday of every month, options on stocks expire. The third Friday of every third month (March, June, September, and December) is a triple witching day, so called because of the expiration of futures contracts, options on stocks, and options on futures. When options expire, option players, arbitrageurs, and institutional players try to square their positions. This sometimes creates abnormal volatility in the market. As expirations get closer, price moves are sometimes incoherent and illogical. Because option strike prices are traded in round numbers, prices often gravitate toward those levels on expiration dates.

Institutional Orders

When institutions execute large buy or sell orders, that usually affects the price of a stock for the short term. This gives short-term day traders a great trading or scalping opportunity if they can see the order flow whether to buy or sell. Market makers try to mask these huge orders as much as possible, but the skilled day trader can sometimes uncover the opportunity and make a nice bonus. Here are some clues:

- Watch the Market Maker activity in relation to time and sales. If MLCO is the last one to leave consistently, and there is good volume at that price, the Market Maker is trying to get in (or out) with momentum. This may suggest that momentum will shift soon. Once again, consider the supply and demand for this stock. If the institutional player soaks up the supply, increasing demand with temporarily limited supply will be reflected in rising prices. Higher prices will then induce more sellers to increase supply.

- Watch the order flow from the ECNs. Because institutions can move large orders anonymously through ECNs, many traders follow the direction of the order flow of the ECNs. Again, the supply or demand that is soaked up will affect the future direction as supply tries to keep up with demand or vice versa.

- Watch the block trades (10,000 shares or more). The same principle of supply and demand applies here.

PART II
Building the Trade

5

Price Action and Momentum

A professional trader is no less than a master of pricing, which is the heart of the profession. As traders react to movements in price, they profit when they are correct and sustain losses when they are wrong. Professional traders can profit from different kinds of movement in price, ranging from microscopic teenies (1/16ths) to hundreds of points. We believe that understanding these many types of price movements opens a day trader to more opportunities, adds to your body of knowledge, and fine-tunes your perception of the laws of supply and demand. In this chapter, we study the different movements in price that a day trader is exposed to, beginning with very short-term movements. In Chapter 6, we discuss prices in longer-term movements. For the sake of discussion, we divide the different price moves into three basic types: *price action (noise), momentum,* and *trend.* Price action and momentum are related to very short-term price movements, while trend is established in longer-term time periods. Figure 5-1 depicts the difference between the three. We begin with an in-depth discussion of Level 2 data.

Interpreting Level 2 Data

Correctly interpreting Level 2 data is no easy task. In contrast to NASDAQ Level 1, Level 2 data allows you to see more detail of the stock's current price quotations, including current momentum. For the day trader, it is the advantage of seeing a clearer picture of the stock, at one particular moment, that differentiates Level 2 from Level 1. Many newcomers mistakenly believe that having access to NASDAQ Level 2 will make them

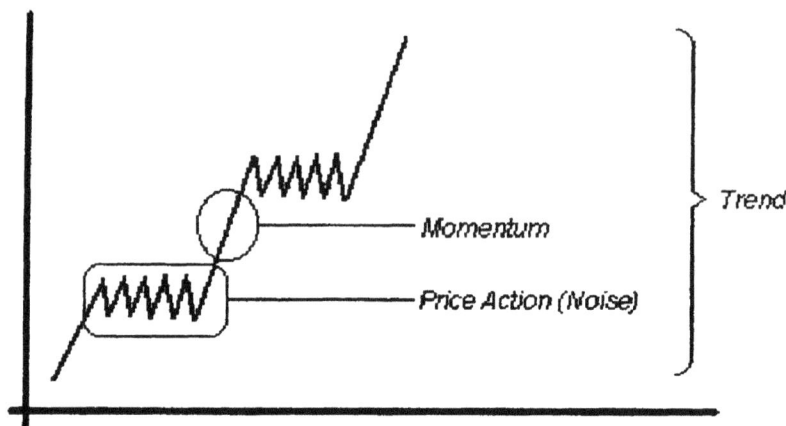

Figure 5-1. Price action, momentum, and trend.

better traders. For newcomers, this is almost totally false. NASDAQ Level 2 is simply a sharper tool for pinpointing data and executing orders faster, as well as receiving better quotations. If you gain enough experience and speed and if you are so inclined, there are also opportunities in scalping. Level 2 by itself, however, will never tell you with absolute certainty whether the price of a stock will go up or down. You must always remember that nothing will forecast market activity with certainty.

To use Level 2 to your advantage in anticipating price direction, you must cross-reference Level 2 data with other facts. Every skilled NASDAQ trader is unique and has a singular method or style. One of your objectives is to develop a style that is unique and suitable to your personality type, background, and especially risk tolerance. Some NASDAQ traders cross-reference by using charting and technical analysis; others simply use Level 2 cross-referenced to the futures, or to whatever is in the news. Many go by the seat of their pants, using a concoction of market feel, experience, and various random data.

On the Level 2 screen, you will be able to identify the posted buyers (on the Bid) and sellers (on the Ask) for the stock. As prices rise or fall, the Bids and Offers are cleared and subsequently reveal higher or lower prices. When the price rises, as confirmed by the Time and Sales report, the Bid and Ask will go up in tandem. The Bid rises as buyers step up to reflect their intentions to pay higher. Consequently, the Ask rises as well, as sellers retreat to higher prices by raising their Offers in the hopes of selling higher. A more solid price move to the upside is evidenced by a well-supported Bid (as buyers step up) and weak Ask (as sellers retreat to higher prices). The reverse is true when the price is falling: The Bids are weak and retreat to a lower price as the Ask price declines to reflect the sellers' strong intentions to sell lower.

Skilled NASDAQ traders have a certain way of watching the Bid and Ask on Level 2. We take note of the displayed Bids and Offers, the thickness of Bids and Offers, and their corresponding order sizes. We make a special note for changes in the high Bids and low Offers (the inside market) and *who* in particular is stepping into that inside market. Is it a Market Maker, INCA, or some other ECN? Does it have size to buy or sell? Does the Market Maker, INCA, or ECN keep buying? Do they keep buying at a particular price? At what price are transactions occurring? These are some questions that race through a NASDAQ trader's mind while reading Level 2.

Many beginners mistakenly believe that *all* participants in the stock are posted at the Bid and Ask on Level 2. Nothing could be further from the truth. In addition to displayed participants, one must also consider the other, *undisplayed* participants in that market, who, collectively, are a formidable force. They may be other day traders in the wings or institutional players. Regardless, you must first accept that there are numerous others ready to transact now but not yet posting their intentions. As a day trader, you must acknowledge that there are others staring at that very same Level 2 screen you are looking at, all with the same objective—profits. The more popular and liquid the stock is, the more people are watching it. More likely than not, they are not watching for amusement. On very liquid stocks like Microsoft, Cisco, or Intel, the Level 2 screen is an abstract of the price. There are hundreds of undisplayed participants willing to take advantage of the price moves, from scalpers to swing traders. On stocks like these (and innumerable others), hundreds of millions of dollars in equities are exchanged every day. This is one of the many times when your cross-referencing and trading skills will come into play. Many of these techniques are discussed in this book. Not being aware of the powerful order flow that comes from the undisplayed market is a common weakness of the inexperienced NASDAQ trader. It limits the competitive advantage that NASDAQ Level 2 can provide.

How do you find out about the undisplayed participants and their order flow? The answer to that question is quite simple: *You never will*—not with absolute certainty and not through NASDAQ Level 2 alone—*before* the price move occurs. Perhaps there will be an indication during the price move, but never before that. Even the most skilled NASDAQ traders never

> **In observing quotation windows for NASDAQ Level 2 and SuperDOT, you must consider not only the participants who are posting their intentions, but also the significance of participants who are undisplayed.**

> There are undisplayed participants willing to sell to posted bidders at the bidding prices.

> There are undisplayed participants willing to buy from posted sellers at the offering prices.

BID			ASK			TIME & SALES	
MM/ECN ID	Price	Size	MM/ECN ID	Price	Size	Price	Size
ISLD	96 3/8	9	MLCO	96 1/2	10	96 1/2	3
REDI	96 1/4	20	GSCO	96 1/2	10	96 1/2	10
USCT	96 1/8	1	COWN	96 1/2	8	96 3/8	3
BEST	96	10	FBCO	96 1/2	10	96 1/4	25
INCA	96	10	SBSH	96 1/4	10	96 3/8	9
NITE	96	1	INCA	96 1/4	9	96 3/8	10
MSCO	96	10	ISLD	96 1/4	6	96 1/4	2

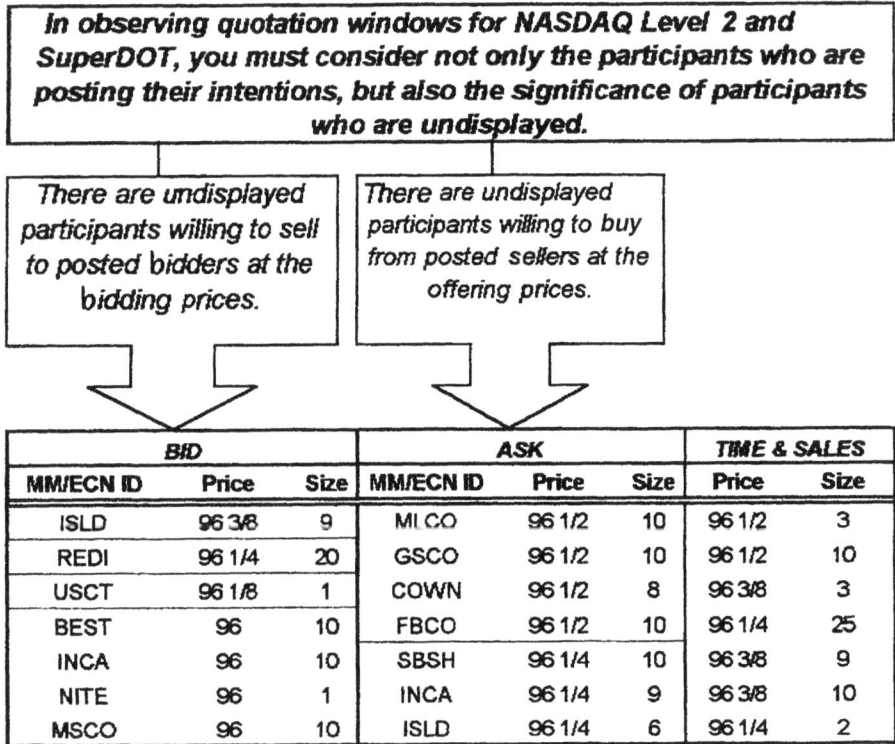

Figure 5-2. Displayed versus undisplayed participants.

know with absolute certainty. While most beginners are instinctively caught up in trying to read the Bid and the Ask, perhaps the most important piece of information on NASDAQ Level 2 is the Time and Sales Report (the *Prints*) at the right-hand side of the window. This is the trail that everybody leaves, without exception. Whether it is an institutional order, a Market Maker, or 80 day traders buying up or selling the stock, everybody's trail, by regulation, is left on the Time and Sales report. You must learn to keep a watchful eye on the Prints and correlate this information with the Bid and Ask. Being aware of where the trades are occurring, whether at the Bid or at the Ask price, is of key importance in understanding the momentary pressures of order flow. Prints at the current Ask price signify *buying* order flow as aggressive buyers pay Asking prices. On the contrary, trades at the Bid price signify *selling* order flow as aggressive sellers are willing to "hit the Bids" (sell to Bidders at Bid prices). Even with the same Bid and Ask scenario, the price at which the actual trades are occurring may indicate the difference between upside and downside pressure.

In fact, the Bid may reflect a higher number of buyers than sellers on the Ask, which may apparently indicate strength, but the Prints may be telling a different story. Keep in mind that the Bid and Ask are merely price tags, while the Prints reflect the true activity of the market. Figure 5-3 shows differing order flow with the same Bid–Ask scenario.

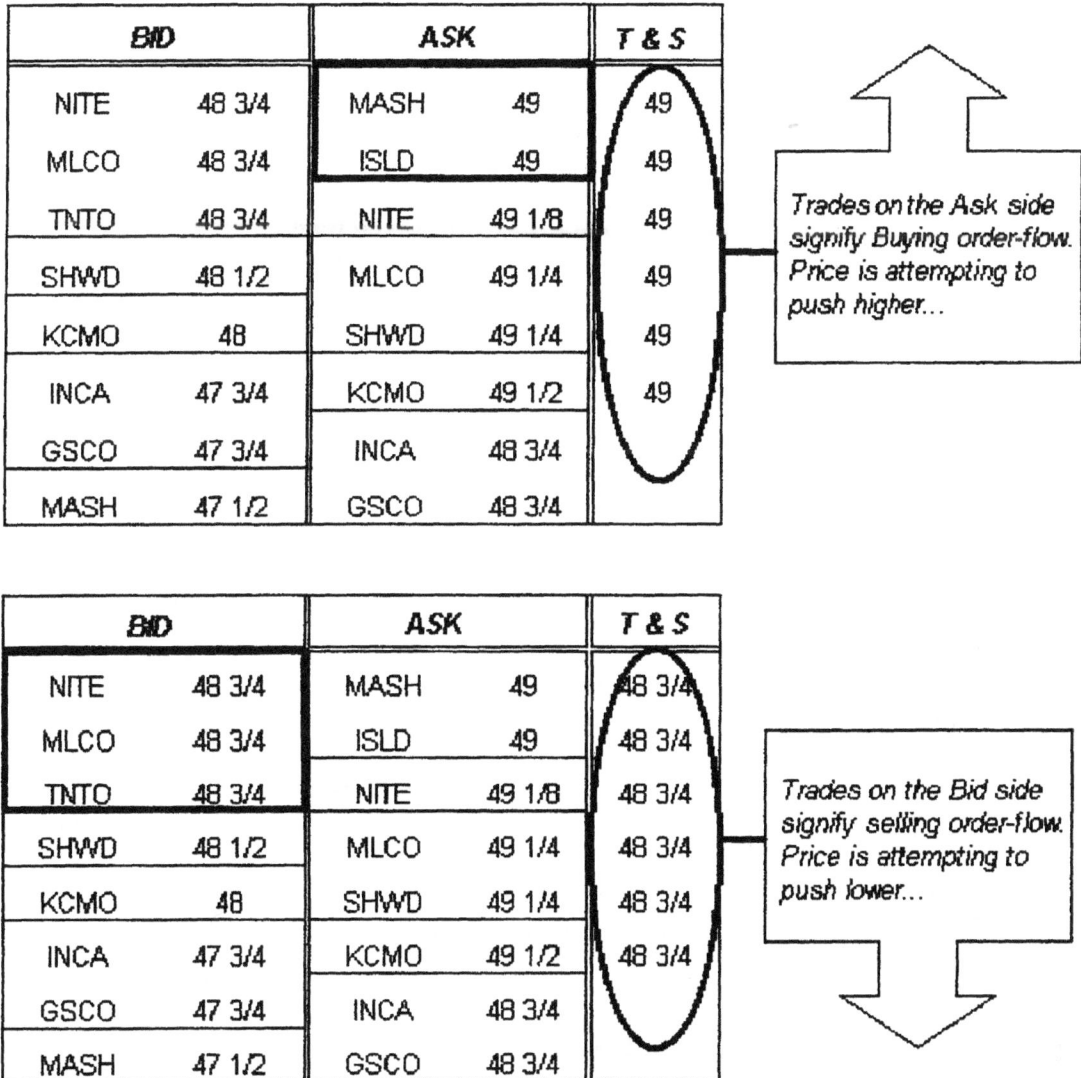

BID		ASK		T & S
NITE	48 3/4	MASH	49	49
MLCO	48 3/4	ISLD	49	49
TNTO	48 3/4	NITE	49 1/8	49
SHWD	48 1/2	MLCO	49 1/4	49
KCMO	48	SHWD	49 1/4	49
INCA	47 3/4	KCMO	49 1/2	49
GSCO	47 3/4	INCA	48 3/4	
MASH	47 1/2	GSCO	48 3/4	

Trades on the Ask side signify Buying order-flow. Price is attempting to push higher...

BID		ASK		T & S
NITE	48 3/4	MASH	49	48 3/4
MLCO	48 3/4	ISLD	49	48 3/4
TNTO	48 3/4	NITE	49 1/8	48 3/4
SHWD	48 1/2	MLCO	49 1/4	48 3/4
KCMO	48	SHWD	49 1/4	48 3/4
INCA	47 3/4	KCMO	49 1/2	48 3/4
GSCO	47 3/4	INCA	48 3/4	
MASH	47 1/2	GSCO	48 3/4	

Trades on the Bid side signify selling order-flow. Price is attempting to push lower...

Figure 5-3. Different order flow on the same Bid–Ask scenario.

The Basics of Identifying Momentum

Momentum is at the heart of efficient order execution and successful scalping. Getting a clearer picture of temporary momentum is one of the advantages of having access to Level 2. For example, a transaction executed at the Bid price reflects a seller who is willing to meet the buyer's Bidding price. This means that the buyer has the upper hand. When the buyer has the upper hand, there is a negative effect on the stock price (selling order flow). This can be compared to the terminology in the real estate market, "buyer's market," meaning that prices tend to go lower. The same laws of supply and demand are practiced on Level 2 (including SuperDOT), but at lightning speed. Consequently, when a transaction at the Ask price is reported, a buyer was willing to meet the seller's price. In this case, the seller has the upper hand and this reflects a positive effect on the stock price (buying order flow or "seller's market").

In trying to anticipate momentum, one of the many things we look out for is the first trade at the Bid or Ask price that is immediately followed by a sequence of reports at the same price—at the Bid or the Ask. In fact, a strong giveaway for solid momentum is the presence of transactions that are beyond the current inside Bid or Ask (override trades). Override trades indicate that there are buyers who were willing to pay *higher* than the inside Ask; conversely, for downward momentum, sellers were willing to sell at a price *lower* than the inside Bid.

The Inside Bid and Ask

Observing the Bid to Ask range and the volume of shares available at both ends allows the trader to get a better indication of where the price is for that moment, and possibly what the future direction will be. However, the *number* of Market Makers and ECNs at the Bid and Ask should not be the only indication of liquidity. One Market Maker refreshing selling quotes at the Ask price is a good indication that this Market Maker has a big order or intends to unload size. The inside Bid may be full of Market Makers and ECNs, but as soon as sellers realize that a Market Maker is selling heavily at a certain price level, these other sellers may begin unloading as well. As the buyers become exhausted, the sellers will start "hitting the Bids" (selling to the buyers at the Bid price) and the Bid to Ask range will move down as the price drops.

A Closer Look at Price Action

Our definition of price action is the participation of the active buyers and sellers at a given price within a moment in time, in reaction to the external forces that influence the stock or the market. Understanding price action is a tremendous advantage to the active participant in the market, particularly direct-access users. It helps increase a trader's awareness of the nature and source of price fluctuations, supply and demand activity, order execution, and scalping techniques.

Many long-term investors consider short-term price fluctuations "noise" and would rather watch the longer-term trends of the market. If we were investors, we would not want to torture ourselves by watching the short-term noise either. Inversely, a day trader cannot rely on a long-term price trend, because a short-term price fluctuation in the opposite direction can ruin your profits. With each level of price action, many factors that cause price changes must be considered, including different indicators, fundamental and technical analysis, and short- or long-term trends. However, all the levels of price action are subject to the supply and demand for the stock at its price level at any given time. For the short-term day trader, the basic concept of supply and demand, or the immediate buying and selling pressure of the stock, is critical to timing the trade for efficient order execution or even a quick profit. It is especially important for day traders with direct access, because of continuous real-time quotes, access to Market Maker activity, and instantaneous executions—thus allowing the opportunity for precise trading. Because of the high-velocity nature of the markets today, extensive technical analysis may be too slow to confirm a price move. By the time you get a confirmation, it is usually too late. Therefore, a proficient day trader must be sensitive to the buying and selling pressures at the microscopic level, or the Bid–Ask level of price action, while utilizing other methods to identify and prepare for that impending move.

Price, without the factor of time, moves in one dimension, or in a straight line. (See Figure 5-4.) The chart in Figure 5-5 shows prices in relation to time, giving price movements a two-dimensional view. However, because scalping and precise order execution are limited to a very narrow time span, the relationship of price to time is sometimes irrelevant. This is not to say that charts and technical analysis are useless. In fact, they are very important. But for the sake of understanding price action, we will eliminate the two-dimensional view. Because price moves in a straight line—up or down—we can now narrow the parameters of the possible direction *right now* to only two paths. While we know that outside factors cause price direction, let us narrow our focus to just the momentary buying and selling pressures that create volatility.

Bid and Ask

We know that the Bid is the price the collective group of buyers is willing to pay for a particular stock, and the Ask is the price the collective group of sellers is willing to sell the same stock at (Figure 5-6). When the market is

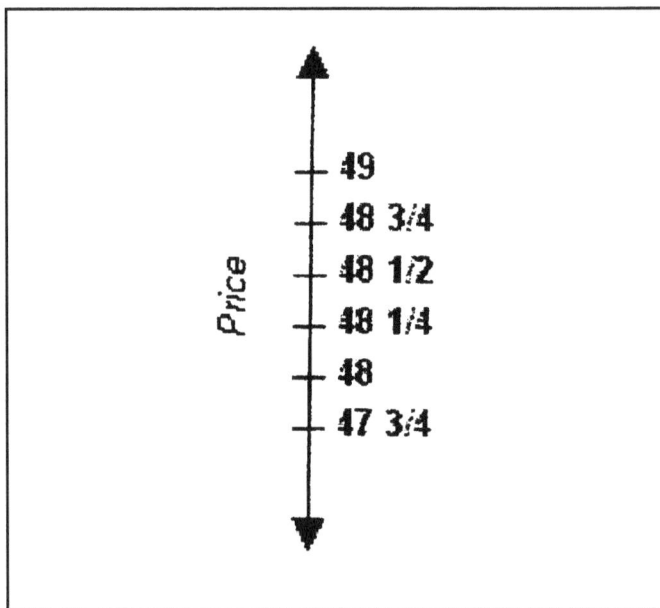

Figure 5-4. One-dimensional price action.

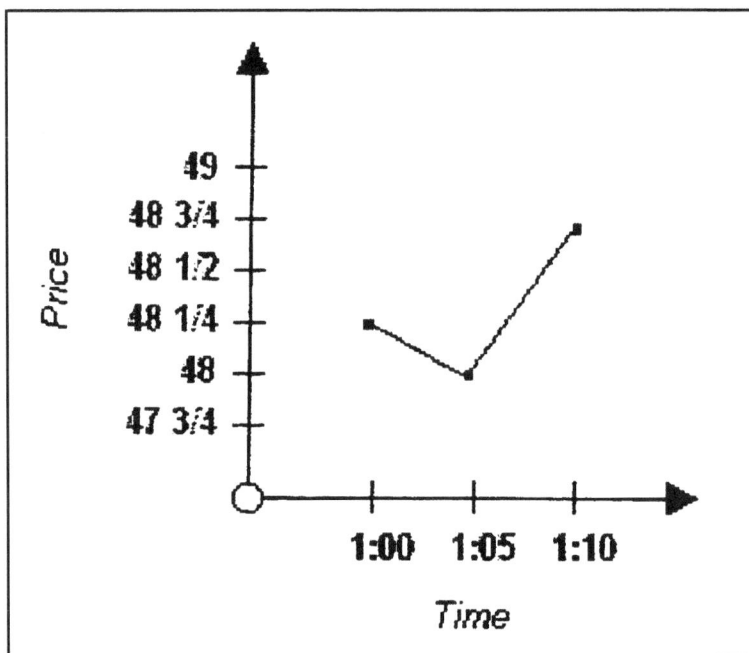

Figure 5-5. Conventional price movement.

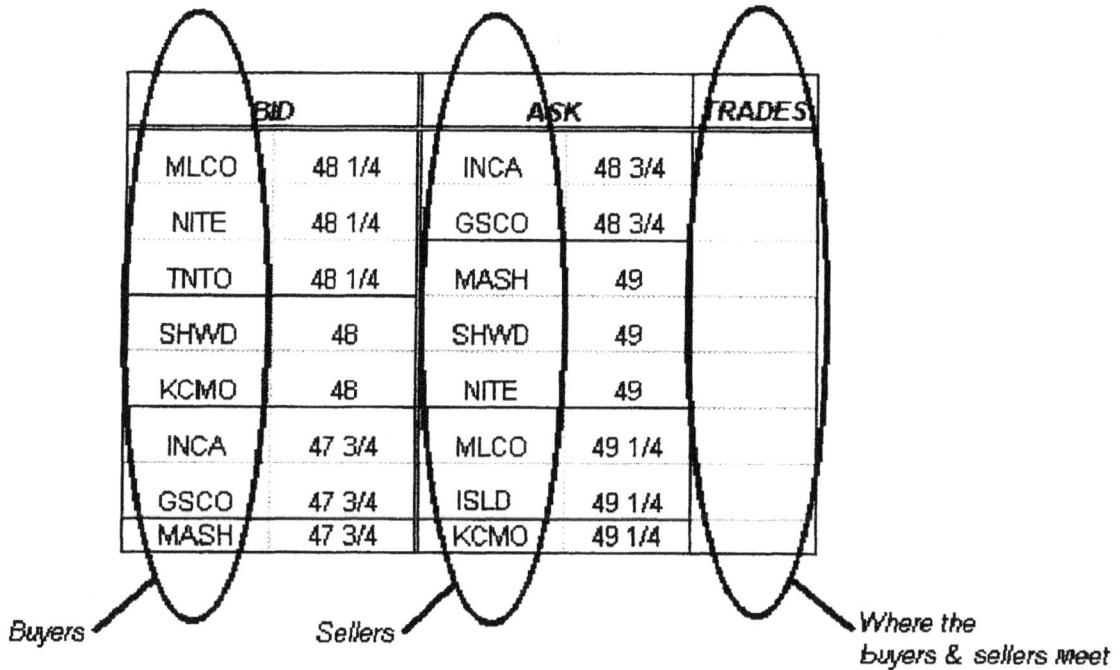

	BID		ASK		TRADES
MLCO	48 1/4	INCA	48 3/4		
NITE	48 1/4	GSCO	48 3/4		
TNTO	48 1/4	MASH	49		
SHWD	48	SHWD	49		
KCMO	48	NITE	49		
INCA	47 3/4	MLCO	49 1/4		
GSCO	47 3/4	ISLD	49 1/4		
MASH	47 3/4	KCMO	49 1/4		

Buyers   Sellers   Where the
buyers & sellers meet

Figure 5-6. The basic Bid and Ask scenario.

inactive, nobody steps up to buy or sell at a better price. But one participant (Market Maker or trader) who wants to buy the stock may want to avoid the competition from the other buyers at $48\frac{1}{4}$, and step up to Bid the stock at a higher price. As soon as one buyer posts a Bid at $48\frac{1}{2}$, this creates a new high Bid (Figure 5-7). But has the buyer really bought anything? As of yet, a buyer and seller have not met to consummate a transaction. Also, how many shares is this buyer willing to purchase at that price? The buyer may be willing to purchase more than is being posted. If there is no participant willing to sell at $48\frac{1}{2}$, or if the buyer wants more than sellers will sell, other participants who are willing to buy may take notice and join the first buyer at the new Bid of $48\frac{1}{2}$ (Figure 5-8). There may be other buyers who have more urgency to buy the stock, bypassing the option to Bid $48\frac{1}{2}$ and opting to meet the sellers at the current Ask price of $48\frac{3}{4}$. You can see from the chart that the price just jumped half a point, from $48\frac{1}{4}$ to $48\frac{3}{4}$ (Figure 5-9). If there are more sellers than buyers at $48\frac{3}{4}$ and the Bid stays at $48\frac{1}{2}$ or even moves lower, take note that the price based on the Ask level still does not change. A day trader who buys by paying the sellers at the Ask price is caught with the stock at $48\frac{3}{4}$. The price action will only be completed if the demand for the stock exceeds the supply, in this case the supply at the Ask $48\frac{3}{4}$, forcing the sellers to retreat to a higher price and thus force a new high Bid at $48\frac{3}{4}$. The trader who bought the stock at $48\frac{3}{4}$ can now join the sellers by offering to sell at the higher Ask price for a profit (Figure 5-10). While the chart reflects a move from $48\frac{1}{4}$ to 49, the price action only occurred between $48\frac{3}{4}$ and 49. It is important to note in this case that in order to profit, the spread on Level 2 had to be cleared first.

Charts factor in time horizon, which gives the price movement two dimensions. This allows the individual to see, from historical price movements, peaks and valleys, the systematic patterns associated with investors' psychology. But by understanding the Bid to Ask level, the day trader can see the picture on a chart from a different perspective and understand the behavioral patterns of the price action. Price action is determined by supply and demand of the stock, or the buying and selling pressure at each price level. When a stock appreciates too much, buyers no longer find the stock attractive enough to pay the higher price. Therefore, the sellers now must discount the stock by selling at a lower price level in order to unload the stock in their inventory. A chart attempts to organize the randomness of price fluctuations through technical analysis of price patterns over time. However, understanding the Bid and Ask allows the trader to see that the price moves instantaneously, and this makes the trader more aware of the buying and selling pressures within each price level. This enables the trader to take advantage of the price action, either by scalping or simply by using a highly efficient method of order execution. A chart that reflects a price move may indicate a profit opportunity in hindsight; however, could you have taken advantage in real time?

BID		ASK		TRADES
NITE	48 1/2	INCA	48 3/4	
MLCO	48 1/4	GSCO	48 3/4	
TNTO	48 1/4	MASH	49	
SHWD	48	ISLD	49	
KCMO	48	SHWD	49	
INCA	47 3/4	MLCO	49 1/4	
GSCO	47 3/4	NITE	49 1/4	
MASH	47 3/4	KCMO	49 1/4	

Figure 5-7. NITE posts high Bid at $48\frac{1}{2}$.

BID		ASK		TRADES
NITE	48 1/2	INCA	48 3/4	
MLCO	48 1/2	GSCO	48 3/4	
SHWD	48 1/2	MASH	49	
TNTO	48 1/4	ISLD	49	
KCMO	48	SHWD	49	
INCA	47 3/4	MLCO	49 1/4	
GSCO	47 3/4	NITE	49 1/4	
MASH	47 3/4	KCMO	49 1/4	

Figure 5-8. MLCO and SHWD join NITE at the high Bid.

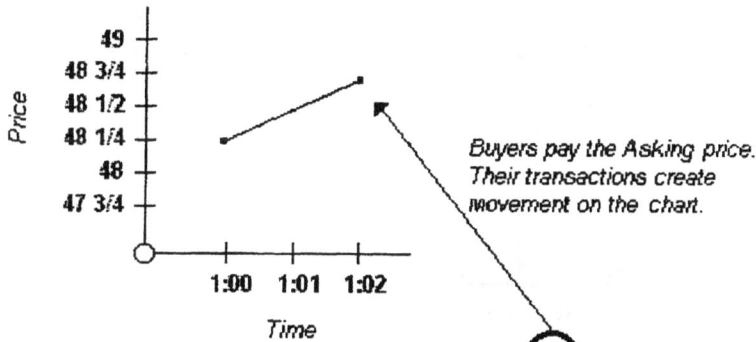

Buyers pay the Asking price. Their transactions create movement on the chart.

BID		ASK		TRADES
NITE	48 1/2	INCA	48 3/4	48 3/4
MLCO	48 1/2	GSCO	48 3/4	48 3/4
SHWD	48 1/2	MASH	49	48 3/4
TNTO	48 1/4	ISLD	49	
KCMO	48	SHWD	49	
INCA	47 3/4	MLCO	49 1/4	
GSCO	47 3/4	NITE	49 1/4	
MASH	47 3/4	KCMO	49 1/4	

Figure 5-9. Buyers pay the Asking price.

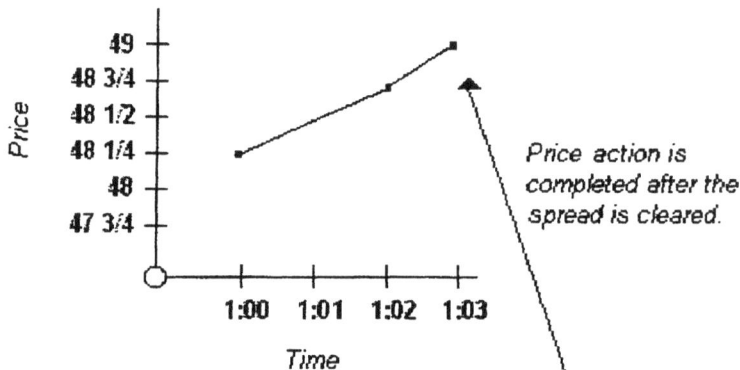

Price action is completed after the spread is cleared.

BID		ASK		TRADES
NITE	48 3/4	MASH	49	49
MLCO	48 3/4	ISLD	49	49
TNTO	48 3/4	NITE	49 1/8	49
SHWD	48 1/2	MLCO	49 1/4	48 3/4
KCMO	48	SHWD	49 1/4	48 3/4
INCA	47 3/4	KCMO	49 1/2	48 3/4
GSCO	47 3/4	INCA	49 3/4	
MASH	47 3/4	GSCO	49 3/4	

Figure 5-10. Price action from $48^1/_4$ to 49.

A Closer Look at Momentum

Understanding price action allows the trader to recognize momentum. Momentum is the force of buying or selling pressure that keeps the price action in motion until the opposite force becomes overwhelming. Thus, this causes the direction of price action to shift, the same way a ball that is thrown will stay in the same motion until some opposing force eventually brings it to rest. Similarly, a stock in motion to the upside attracts buyers until it rises enough to be more attractive to sellers and thus causes that upside motion to pause or reverse. The momentum is identified by constant buying pressure, as demand stays consistent through the higher price levels. Depending on the criteria or the significance of the information that caused the force or buying pressure, a pause or sell-off will consistently attract more buyers and limit the selling to the downside as the buyers continue the motion to the upside. Recognizing the degree of momentum helps the trader to anticipate further price moves and therefore to get in and out for profits with each successive move to the upside (or downside, if that is where the momentum exists). From day to day, and even within the trading day, momentum can shift from one direction to the other depending on various factors that affect the price of the stock. This does not necessarily change the longer-term trend of the stock, but only justifies the trading activity for a given part of the day. Therefore, day traders can consistently fine-tune their order executions and even make money playing both sides of the market, as long as they properly recognize the momentum and price action of a stock given a certain time span.

Observing Market Makers' Activity

While your main focus when trying to identify momentum is the level of activity of trades occurring, it is imperative that you also pay close attention to what the Market Makers are doing. Just as you should try to get out of positions with momentum in order to scale out (locking in part of your profits in increments to reduce risk exposure) or to save in the spread, Market Makers who have extensive positions or large institutional orders to process will also scale out of positions with momentum, rather than wait for the top or bottom. Think of yourself as a Market Maker or an institutional trader with a huge long position. The market is running in your favor and you think the top is near. Quite obviously, you want to avoid the top, because there is no demand there. You may have unrealized profits, but as you try to unload your exposure and take profits, others will compete with you to sell. This selling activity sends the stock tanking as you frantically try to book your profits. Instead, intelligent traders should unload in increments as the market continues to run in their favor. Market Makers and Specialists behave this way. This type of professional activity is important to watch for because it can signal that Market Makers or institutional traders are starting to unload, and at least an intermediate top may be near. As demand diminishes and supply builds, others join in to start taking profits. Remember that most people do not sell at the high; they sell after the high is established and when the stock begins to trade down. More people start to sell as the top is more confirmed, and the momentum is established to the downside. By being alert to Market Maker activity, you may be able to identify the high point approaching and to scale out of your position closer to the high point, rather than waiting for the crowd to confirm the top for you.

Identifying price action and momentum is fairly obvious. If you are scalping and you jump in late, you will probably be the last fool and the price may not extend enough for you to get out safely, let alone get out with a profit. Therefore, timing and anticipating price action and momentum are crucial to judging entry and exit points for profit. Anticipating a price move is basically visualizing the future buying or selling pressure, given the appropriate situation. As easy as this may sound, this is a major problem for novice traders and may mean the difference between profitable traders and losers. You can visualize as much as you want, but if the price moves in the opposite direction, the market is proving you wrong and you will lose money. As in any sport involving hand-eye coordination, timing is a skill that comes with experience. Through practice and more practice, you will learn to judge the threshold where one force will overcome the opposite force and the buying or selling pressure will sustain continuing motion.

One day in December of 1998, the market was rallying, while CPWR (Compuware) was lagging. Twice we bought CPWR at 73 in anticipation of a late rally, and twice we were wrong and sold out for a small loss. However, we took note that MLCO and MSCO were buying the dips at $72^3/_4$ and would not let the stock drop below that price. So the next time CPWR tried to break 73, we let it go and waited for the pull back to $72^3/_4$, where we bought 1,000 shares on the Bid price of $72^3/_4$ with a stop at $72^1/_2$. Once again, MLCO held the stock at $72^3/_4$. A short time later, the stock moved up again, but this time the urgency of the buyers seemed stronger, so we put in a market buy order at 73, to add to our position. Suffering some slippage, the buy order got filled at $73^1/_4$ as CPWR vaulted to 74 in a matter of seconds. We sold 1,000 shares at $73^7/_8$ and 1,000 shares at 74 for a profit of $1,875. Had we waited for the confirmation of a breakout, it would not have been possible to buy even at $73^1/_4$ and we would have missed the opportunity for the profit, despite having a strong indication of what the stock would do. Our anticipation on the first two attempts was wrong, but our timing the third time proved correct, and we were able to profit from it. Our risk on the first buy of $72^3/_4$ was a $^1/_4$-point loss, but our potential for gain was far greater. Although the trade seemed scary at the time, we defined the risk and jumped in. Timing and anticipating the move were vital for getting in at the right time and price. Waiting for a confirmation may have been safer, but it would have cut our profit drastically and the risk, in case we were wrong, would have been far greater for a smaller return.

A market in motion carried by momentum is virtually unstoppable by a single market participant, especially by a day trader. Therefore you must learn to leverage the momentum of the market in your favor by first antic-ipating the impending move, then timing your entry in order to carry you along with the current of the market's tides. By becoming more sensitive to price action, we can see and almost feel the urgency to buy or sell a stock and the competition involved in buying or selling that stock. A good day trader can anticipate this impending buying or selling pressure and exe-cute before the frenzy begins. With experience, you will become more sen-sitive to price action, and almost see the support and resistance levels with-out the confirmation of charts. This is when your gut instincts will help you to anticipate and recognize breakouts and reversals. Learn to act on anticipation of the impending price action and what others will do—not merely reacting to what others are already doing. However, you must also be objective and let the market show you the signals. Being sensitive to the market requires patience and experience. Through practice you will not only learn to recognize the price action and momentum, but develop the timing and the ability to anticipate future price moves. Experience will allow you to refine this skill and make that skill instinctive. Then you can broaden your focus to include other indicators that will help you to gauge your market awareness. Anticipation of price movement requires accuracy of processing various data, and extrapolating from it the correct market environment that prices will follow. Timing the price change requires pre-cision, and is a skill that can only come from experience. Both anticipation and time are necessary in order to surgically get in and out of the market quickly, to maximize your profits without incurring any damage from choosing bad entry points.

6

Patterns, Trends, and Gaps

Knowledge of technical analysis—the study of price behavior, price relationships, and volume—is indispensable to day trading. It differs from fundamental analysis, which takes into account factors that affect the actual valuation of a stock. Fundamentals are factors such as earnings and growth potential; management; factors within the accounting statements (earnings, expenses, assets, and liabilities); and macroeconomic, social, and political influences. In the study of price behavior, we eliminate fundamental factors and concentrate purely on the patterns established by price movement, relationships, and volume. Technical analysis can be extended very far indeed, to include complex mathematical logarithms. However, it is astounding to see, on a daily basis, the significance of its most basic concepts. Familiarizing oneself with the many basic concepts available in technical analysis and using them to cross-reference one another (and even to cross-reference your fundamental analysis) is a powerful approach to tackling the challenges of short-term price movement. In this chapter, we examine these basic concepts. The knowledge and application of elementary theories in technical analysis, as opposed to complicated concepts, satisfies a few important issues that are critical to day trading:

- Because we are students of mass psychology, we must understand that the majority of participants do not engage in technical analysis but rather engage in fundamental study. Of the participants who do engage in technical analysis, the majority do not get involved in complicated approaches, but are more familiar with basic, easy-to-understand theories. Quite often, you will find that rudimentary approaches to technicals, such as support or resistance levels, create self-fulfilling patterns in price—often just due to sheer popularity.

- The predominant guide or indicator to the day trader is the S&P 500 futures. Like stocks and other commodities, fundamentals govern the dominant trend of prices for futures. However, the order flow of futures contracts on the short-term to intraday basis relies heavily on technical price behavior. This is because fundamentals take a longer time period to change, while fluctuations that are analyzed by price activity are reflections of short-term supply and demand. Familiarity with basic concepts of technical analysis help day traders anticipate the short-term direction of the futures.

- Finally, awareness and application of basic technical concepts suit our philosophy of simplicity in trading. We find that getting involved in complicated analysis distracts the trader from the basic factors that govern supply and demand for the day. Especially for a novice, engaging in complexity can be a distraction from the indispensable basics of discipline, psychology, equity preservation, and big-picture awareness.

Short-Term Price Basics

Price can only behave in three ways: go up, go down, or shift laterally. In our market, prices of stocks reflect the sentiment of the participants at any given moment. Price fluctuations are governed by the current order flow. A predominance of buyers causes the stock price to increase, and a predominance of sellers causes the price to decline.

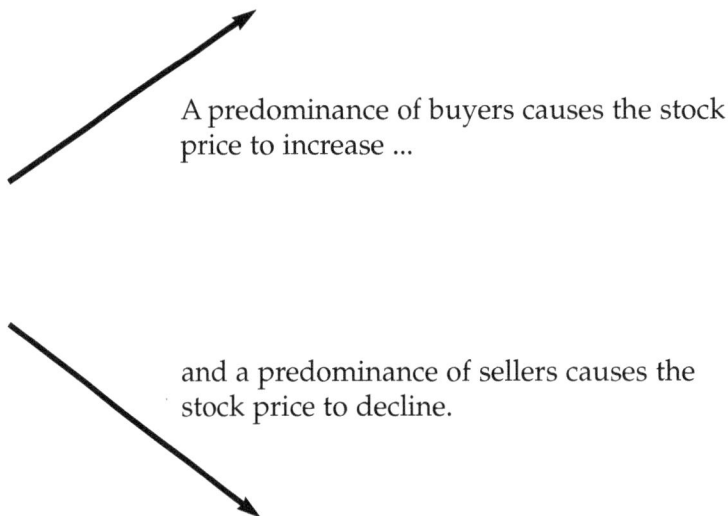

A predominance of buyers causes the stock price to increase ...

and a predominance of sellers causes the stock price to decline.

Figure 6-1. Basic price direction.

A market, as we know, does not go straight up as much as it wants to, but instead rises in stages. A rising market has to contend with gravity that is caused primarily by adjustments in valuation and profit taking. This is what causes corrections, reversals, retracements, or pullbacks. Conversely, a declining market does not go straight down, but rather has a tendency to decline in stages, also due to adjustments in valuation, profit taking (short covering), and "bottom fishing."

While a declining market may appear to be as simple as a mirror image of a rising market, prices behave differently when they are rising compared to when they are declining. Stock prices reflect sentiments of confidence, optimism, or greed versus the sentiments of suspicion, pessimism, or fear. In analyzing human psychology, fear is a stronger sentiment than confidence. As a result, stock prices have a tendency to fall sharply and at a faster rate than they rise, as they move up in stages. As a day trader, you must be familiar with this behavior and build it into your anticipation technique. Profits are taken quicker on the short side than they are on the long side.

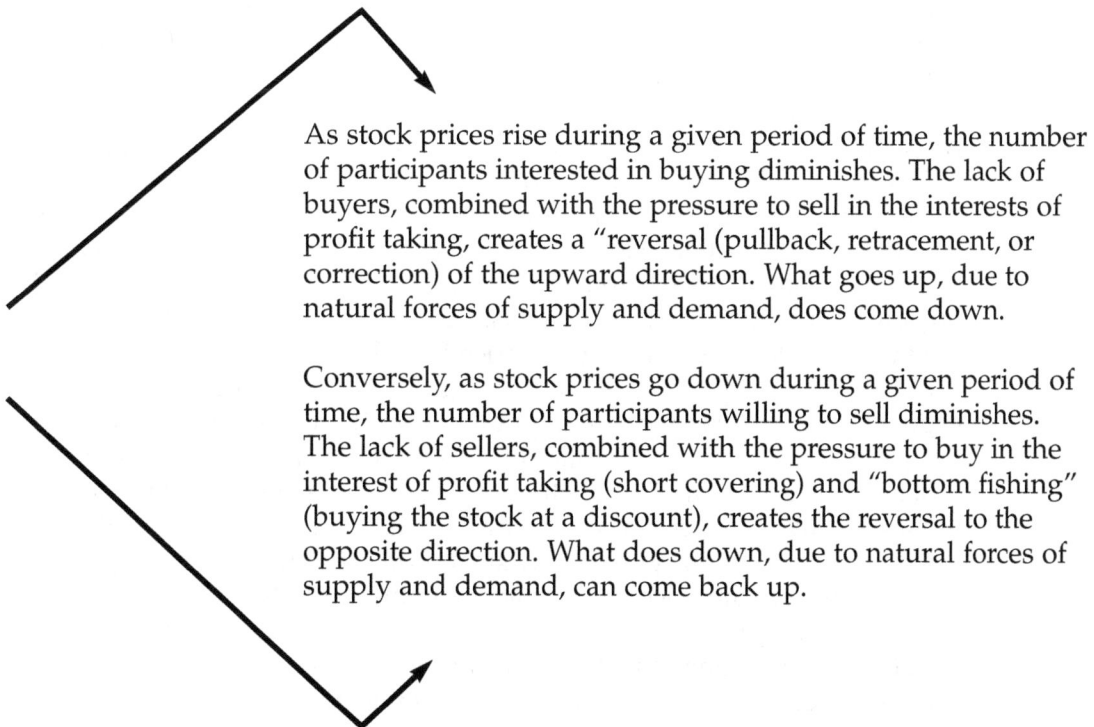

As stock prices rise during a given period of time, the number of participants interested in buying diminishes. The lack of buyers, combined with the pressure to sell in the interests of profit taking, creates a "reversal (pullback, retracement, or correction) of the upward direction. What goes up, due to natural forces of supply and demand, does come down.

Conversely, as stock prices go down during a given period of time, the number of participants willing to sell diminishes. The lack of sellers, combined with the pressure to buy in the interest of profit taking (short covering) and "bottom fishing" (buying the stock at a discount), creates the reversal to the opposite direction. What does down, due to natural forces of supply and demand, can come back up.

Figure 6-2. Retracement basics.

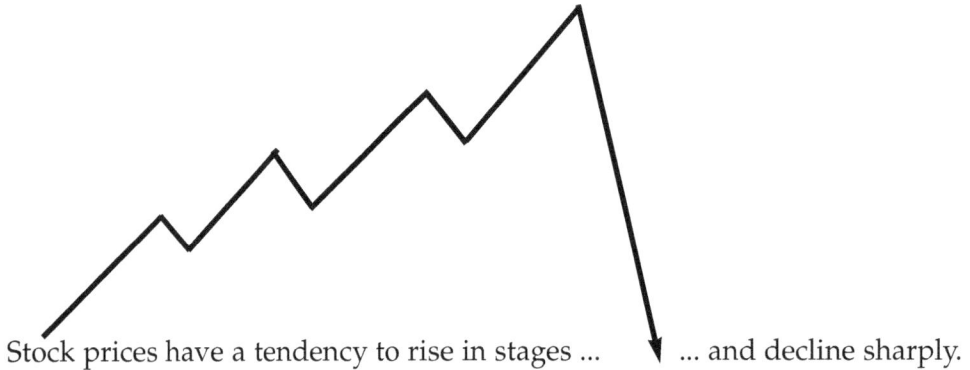

Stock prices have a tendency to rise in stages ...   ... and decline sharply.

Figure 6-3. Stock price behavior.

The Short-Term Price Cycle

Most people like confirmation. This is reflected by the fact that most people would opt to take money that is for certain, such as a steady paycheck, or in the case of putting money to work, interest on savings accounts, CDs, or bonds. The same applies to participants in the stock market: Confirmation of a price move is the strongest motivator to send buy or sell orders. Now we must acknowledge that during any period of time, only a finite number of buyers or sellers are in the market. As the stock price increases due to buying pressures, the dominance of buyers diminishes, and is eventually conquered by the sellers. However, because most people seek confirmation or proof of a price move before orders are sent, the majority of buyers send buy orders after the stock has demonstrated a move to the upside. It works the same way for the sellers, as the price is declining.

In a short-term price cycle, if the majority has bought near the top, a slight reversal in direction would put the majority in negative territory. As the price moves down, the majority begins to panic, and because most order flow is based on emotion, the sell orders come in fast, and nobody is willing to buy. The fact that the majority, in its fear, accelerates the downward pressure explains in part why stocks sell off sharply. The steeper the sell-off, the more the price is confirmed, and the majority sends a final rush of sell and short orders until the last of the remaining sellers throws in the towel. The dominance of the sellers becomes exhausted and the stock reverses direction, to repeat the cycle all over again.

In the short-term price cycle, the majority is always caught in the extremes...

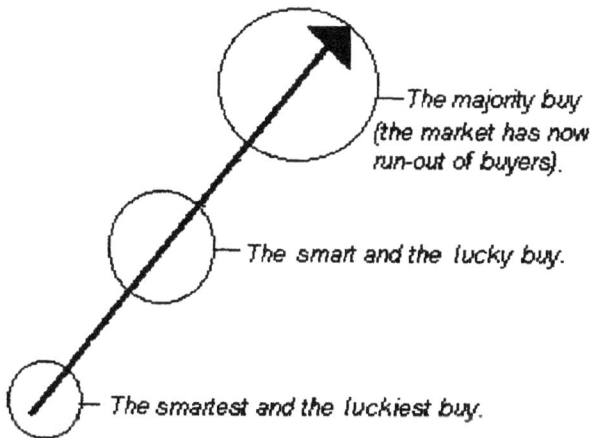

—*The majority buy (the market has now run-out of buyers).*

—*The smart and the lucky buy.*

—*The smartest and the luckiest buy.*

Figure 6-4. Short-term price reaction.

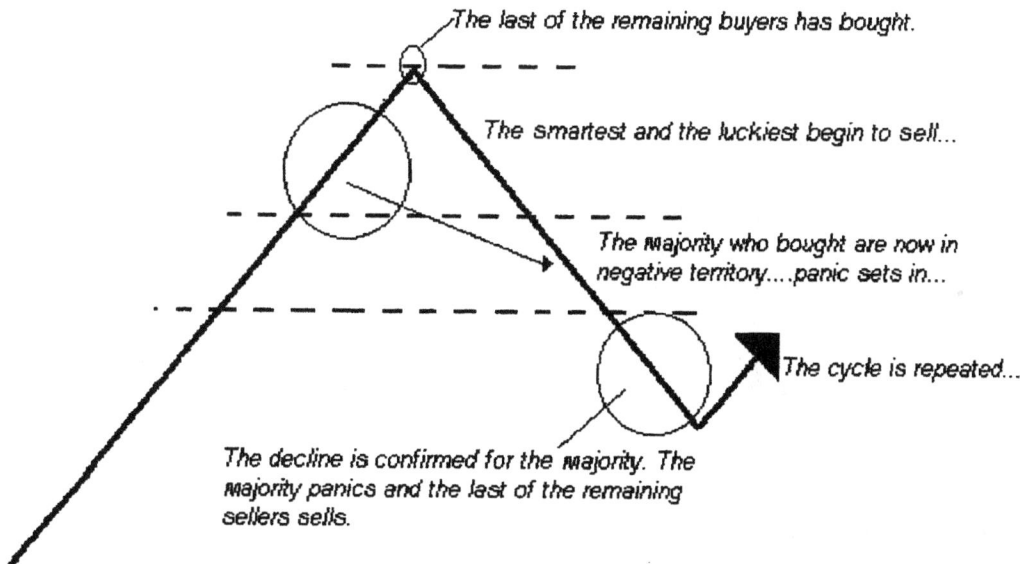

The last of the remaining buyers has bought.

The smartest and the luckiest begin to sell...

The majority who bought are now in negative territory....panic sets in...

The cycle is repeated...

The decline is confirmed for the majority. The majority panics and the last of the remaining sellers sells.

Figure 6-5. Completed short-term price cycle.

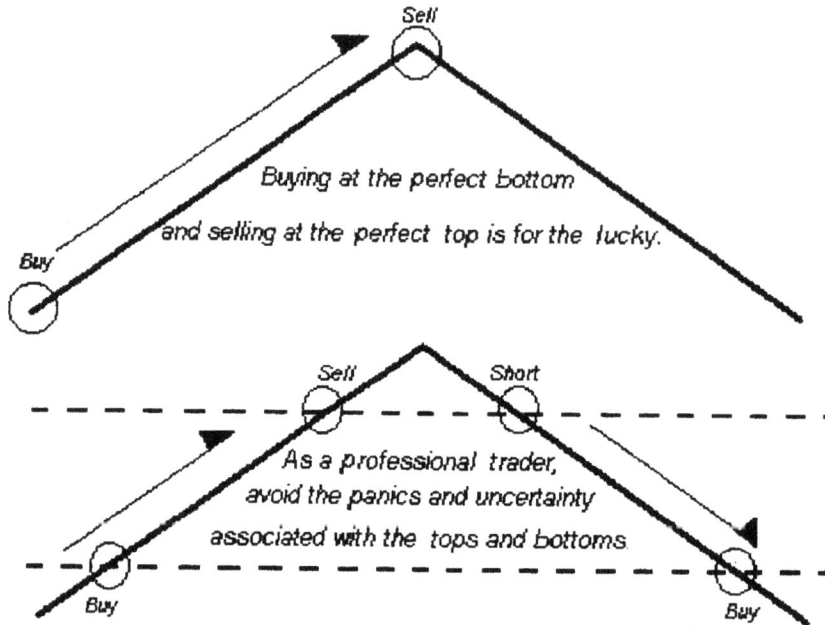

Figure 6-6. Day trader targets.

Perfect Tops and Bottoms

While it is terrific to be able to buy at the bottom and sell at the top, as professional traders we avoid dwelling on the desire to be able to trade this way every single time, because we know it is impossible. The perfect tops and bottoms are for the lucky (which we may occasionally be!). We are usually happy with being in the correct direction and letting winners run as much as possible, while avoiding panic situations. In other words, while taking the perfect top and bottom is nice, we just want as much of the middle as possible. Use the momentum to exit out of your trades while you have the upper hand. Otherwise, you will have to join the rest in panic, and you may lose some or all of your well-earned profits in the process of getting out.

Support and Resistance

While the study of support and resistance is rather elementary, it is also one of the most compelling factors, and the most commonly used, in the process of deciding to take or dispose of positions. It is the heart of technical analysis. A support level is a price area at which a stock finds more buyers than sellers. Conversely, a resistance level is a price area at which a stock finds more sellers than buyers. Support and resistance prices are typically price areas rather than exact prices.

While the analysis of support and resistance areas was historically done using daily and weekly charts, it is an indispensable concept in intraday trading, and intraday chart analysis is governed by the same concepts. Figure 6-8 depicts an example of how important it is to know support and resistance areas in intraday price activity. In day trading, the first important price areas to note when trading a market or stock are:

- today's opening price,
- previous closing price,
- previous intraday high,
- previous intraday low,
- today's intraday high,
- today's intraday low,
- previous support and resistance levels, and
- today's support and resistance levels.

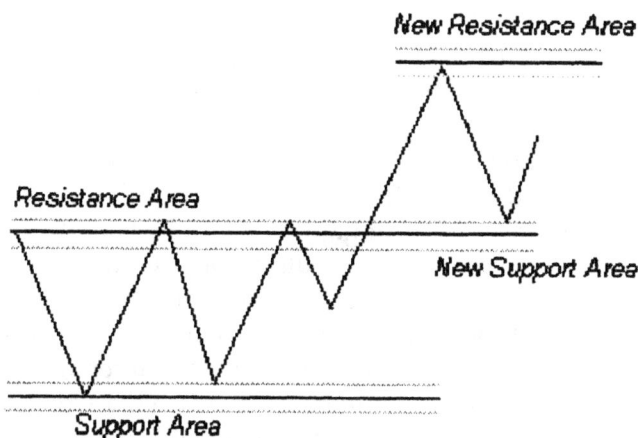

Figure 6-7. Basic support and resistance.

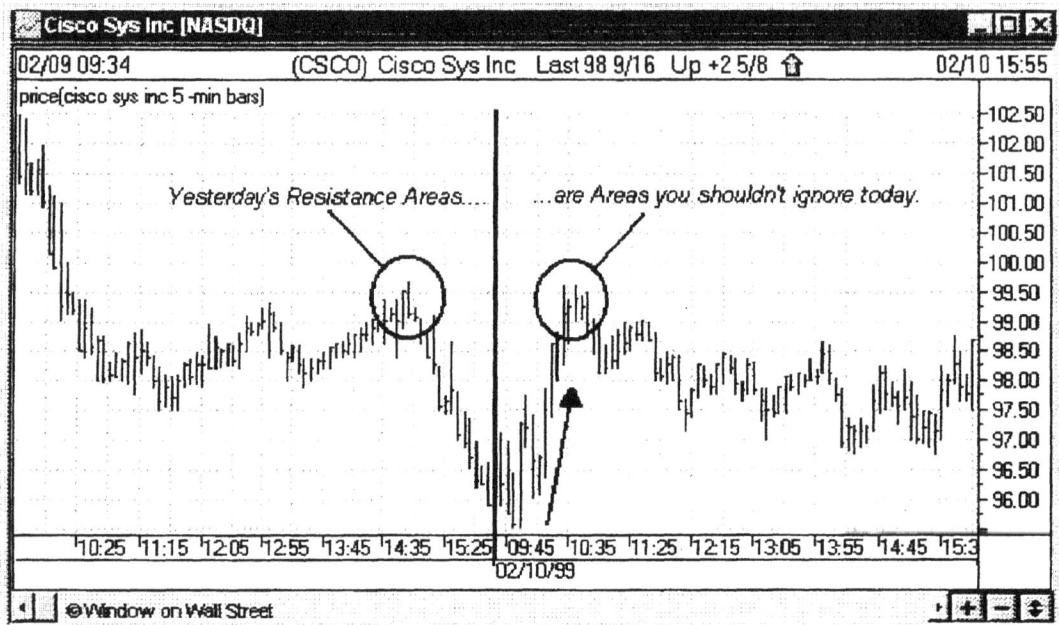

Figure 6-8. Intraday support and resistance.

Each one will represent part of the short-term grid that we are dealing with. If the market conditions and sentiment are suitable, any break beyond these primary grids suggests a search for a new grid, or trading range. In this case, we look further back in time at how this stock or market has behaved previously in the range that it wants to establish today or within the short term. It will be necessary to look at a wider time span.

Chart Views. While knowing recent key price areas is crucial indeed, these prices are often violated in search of new (for new highs or lows) or previously traded support, resistance, or gapped areas. It is highly beneficial for a day trader to know the crucial areas outside of yesterday and today, simply because stocks too often range beyond these points, and when they do, you may run out of time while trying to analyze the historical data. Viewing a stock's or index's price trail in many different "pictures" is advantageous in gauging future direction. This is what we view to either trade the time period, or at least prepare for possible moves, build scenarios, maintain objectivity, and avoid getting caught in too much intraday noise. There are three basic views we take when studying price:

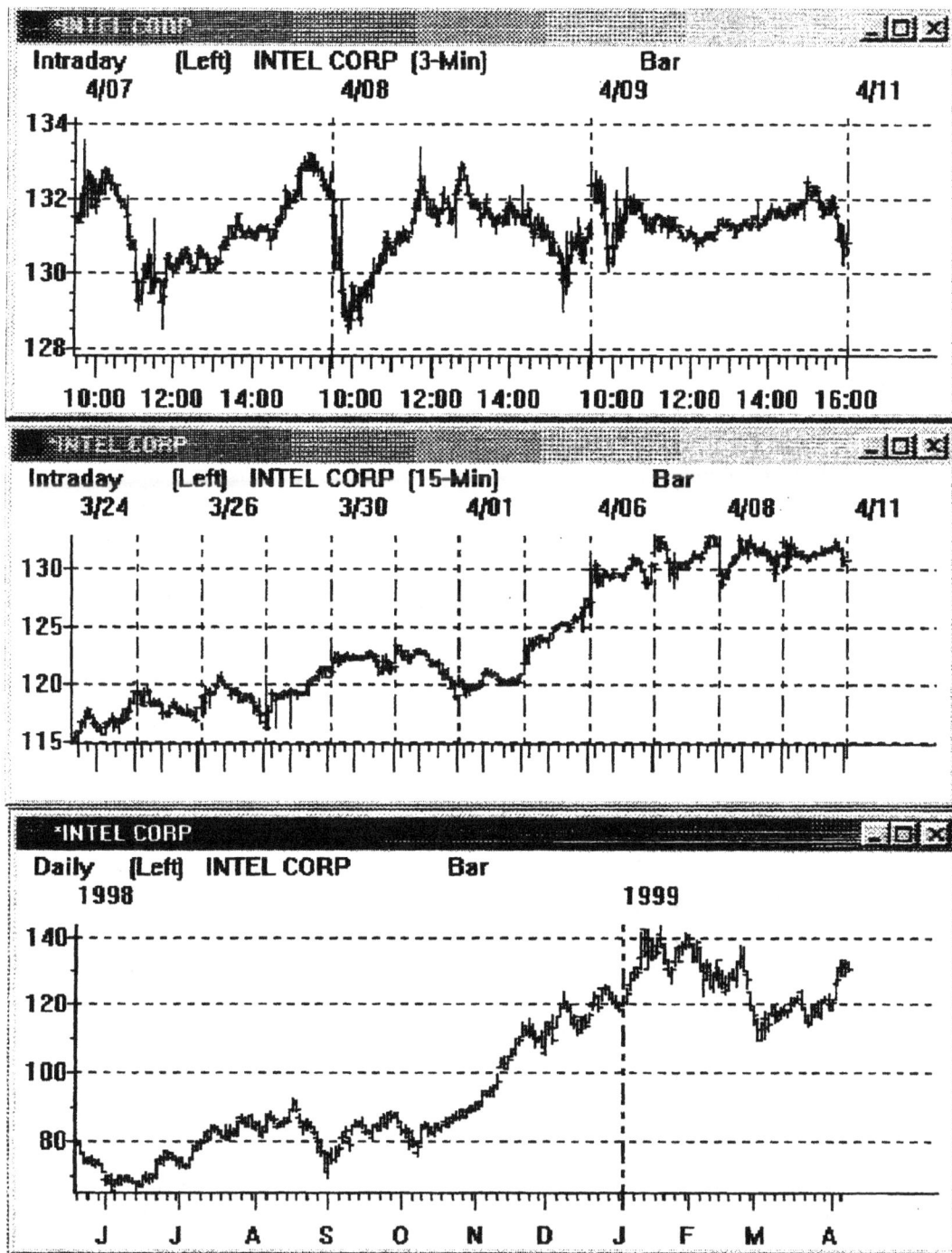

Figure 6-9. Basic chart views.

- short-term intraday
- intermediate-term intraday; and
- long-term daily (usually 300 days).

It is of extreme importance to scale your charts. This means that the entire period you selected must be in view.

Milestone Numbers. After years of watching intraday price activity on hundreds of stocks, one fact is fairly evident: The whole numbers in prices (no fractions) often are convenient areas to mark or round off support and resistance points, particularly when approaching the decade (10 points) and century marks (100 points). These numbers are considered milestone levels for the stock and are active more because of psychological or mental estimations than anything else. Because these price areas are so common to attracting or repelling order flow, but with little fundamental significance, they are good support and resistance levels to use in cross-referencing to other forms of technical analysis, when the evidence may point to the same area. These are also convenient price areas to place stop orders. While this theory is a fairly simple one, it bears enough weight in intraday price action to be considered an indispensable day trading tool. Figure 6-10 depicts an example of intraday price behavior around these numbers.

Breakouts and Breakdowns

Basic technical analysis indicates that when a stock has violated or "broken" a resistance level, the move to seek a new resistance level is extensive. This is known as a breakout. Participants of the market that have established their willingness to pay more for the stock attract a host of new buyers to propel the stock to find a new resistance point. Also, participants who had taken a short position before or at a stock's resistance point in anticipation of a retracement have entered into negative territory and thus need to cover their short positions or reestablish long positions by sending buy orders. As the stock is propelled to higher levels, what was formerly the resistance point becomes the next support point. This basic technical concept is explained by knowing that if the facts have changed to indicate higher value, should it trade to lower levels than before? If participants are willing to pay more now than they were before, the former resistance point becomes a future support area. You will frequently find that when a resistance area is violated, the price can come down to retest that area again, and if it finds enough buyers, the breakout is confirmed and the continua-

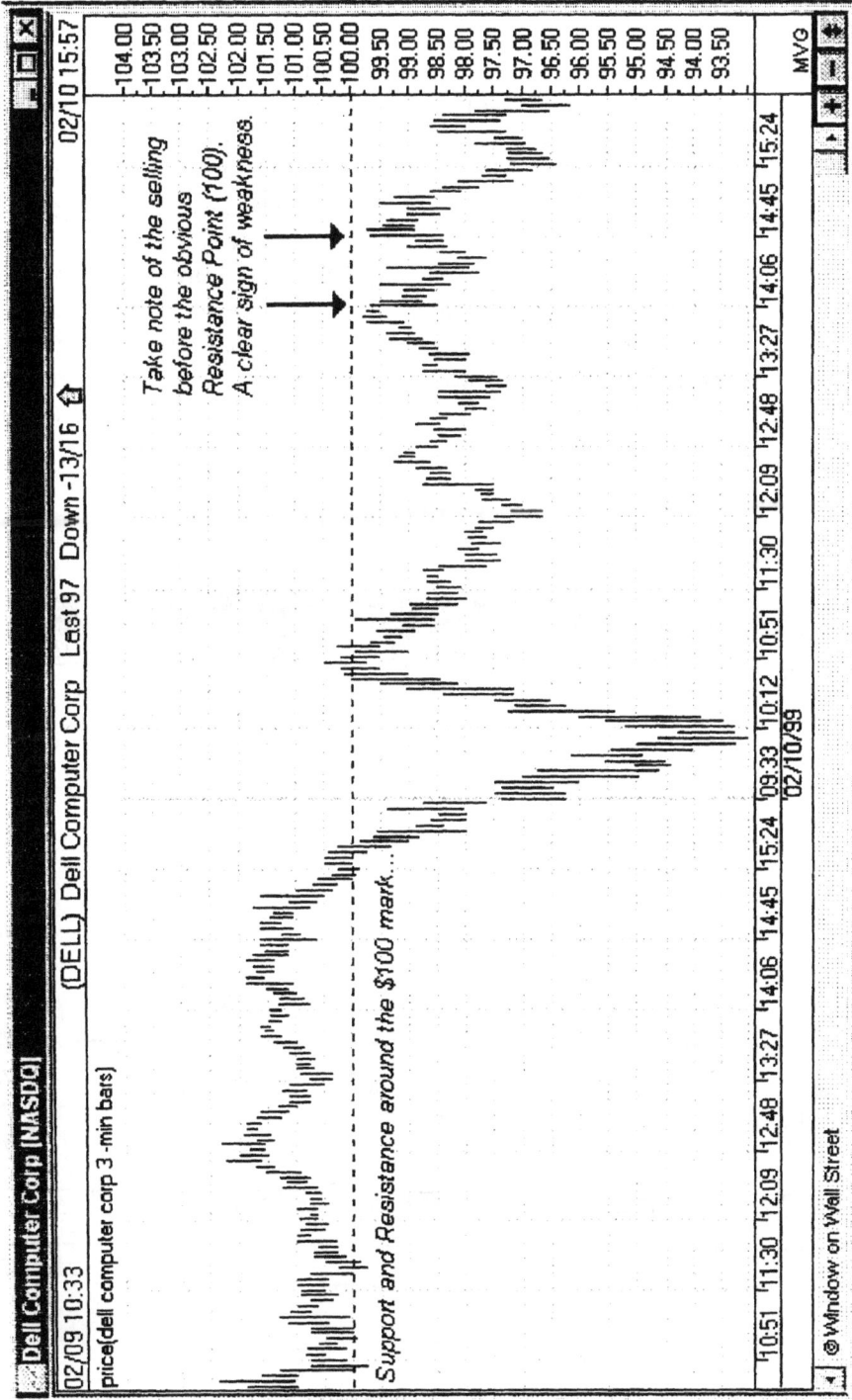

Figure 6-10. Whole numbers, 10's, and 100's are important psychological numbers.

87

tion move to the upside, to raise value, has proven its validity. If a stock could not find buyers at the retest, the downward move is sharp, because it has just proven that the breakout is false. This is where the risk exists in buying breakouts. The participants who committed to the breakout will scramble to unload their risk exposure. In the process, the sell-off is sharp, and the inexperienced day trader is caught with a stock that is probably about to retest the bottom of the original range. The key in trading breakouts is to look first for a successful test of the former resistance area, which will now act as support. If you have bought the initial breakout, you must practice strict risk management in keeping your stop-loss tight, because of the stock's potential to sell off sharply if the test fails. Figure 6-11 gives an example of an ideal intraday breakout. Points *a* show how IBM attempts at the 173 resistance point. First, note the whole number (173) and second,

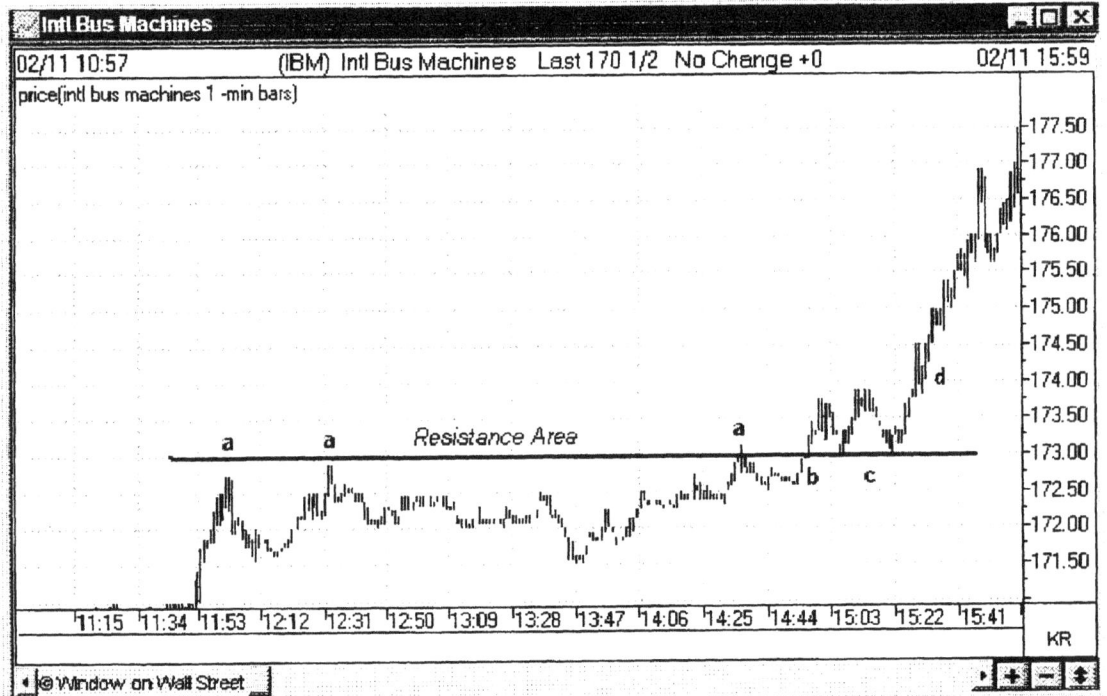

Figure 6-11. An ideal intraday breakout.

note that each attempt is a little bit higher than the previous one. The tech sector was very strong that day. Point *b* is the breakout. While this would not have been attractive considering the false breakouts previously (at midday), this particular breakout was stronger and occurred at the closing period. It established a higher high as the market was in rally mode. The test at the new support level, point *c* (previous resistance), was successful, which justifies a buy at point *d,* the new breakout level, with a stop-loss set below support.

The same theory works in the opposite direction, known as breakdowns. The same rules apply as for breakouts, but all in reverse. What was formerly a support area becomes a future resistance area when that support point is violated. A breakdown below support is typically a strong price move in search of a new (or previously tested) support point. Note that it is more difficult to open breakdown trades because of the uptick rule. If you do have the opportunity, it is prudent to set the stop-loss just beyond the former support point.

Overshooting and Undershooting. Support and resistance points are price areas rather than specific prices. The first violation of support or resistance does not necessarily mean a breakout or breakdown is occurring. A stock or indicator too often appears to overshoot support or resistance levels for a variety of reasons. Typically, if a stock is coming into the area with strong momentum, it is very likely to overshoot. In fact, you will often find that, no matter how strong the momentum, a stock will usually pause and consolidate at the area before following through on a pattern to either break through or retrace. Also, many participants place stop-loss orders at known support and resistance areas, or just beyond. Market Makers have been notorious for taking stocks to these points to trigger these orders, only to take the stock back in the opposite direction if their internal order flow does not point to evidence that the direction of momentum will continue. In tackling breakout and breakdown scenarios, one must be very attuned to the potential for false breaks. A reliable sign of a solid break, as discussed previously, is a successful retest of the former resistance (now support) for breakouts and the former support for breakdowns (now resistance).

When a stock is charging in to an obvious resistance level, *undershooting,* or heavy selling before the obvious resistance point, is a telltale sign of weakness. People who are committed to the long side and other participants who are targeting to go short are coming in early, before the obvious resistance area. Conversely, hard buying that undershoots an obvious support area for a stock that is selling off into it indicates the buyers' motivation to compete by coming in early, a sign of strength.

Dealing with Wide-Spread Stocks. This is perhaps the most common problem in deriving plays from charts. Overshooting and undershooting are more prevalent in wide-spread stocks. Due to the nature of the spreads, Bids and Offers can get hit beyond the actual support or resistance areas, which, on the chart, may reflect a break. A wide-spread stock uses a wide "brush" to paint its picture on a chart. Be very cautious when trading wide-spread stocks based on short-term support or resistance points. This is territory in which even the best Level 2 traders' skills are tested.

There is more than meets the eye in observing Level 2 spreads. An experienced Level 2 trader knows that the technical definition of *spread* does not necessarily apply in practice in today's highly liquid market, compared to how markets behaved before. The spread is known as the difference between the inside market prices: the inside Bid versus the inside Ask. However, you must consider the liquidity of that inside market in judging the stock's price action. For example, stocks like Cisco (CSCO), Dell (DELL), or Microsoft (MSFT) will often show teenie or eighth spreads, but their high daily liquidity and the popularity of the stocks among NASDAQ Level 2 scalpers makes it hard for an inexperienced participant to take advantage of that narrow spread. The inside market in these stocks, despite its apparent safety, is not liquid enough to accommodate all players. Think about it: A stock with 4 million shares of volume in one day trades at an average rate of more than ten thousand shares per minute. Many big stocks trade well over 4 million shares. In fact, we have seen even 100 million shares of one company traded. Only the fastest and most experienced Level 2 players are able to consistently take advantage of that narrow spread. Thus, what is commonly defined as a narrow spread does not necessarily indicate safety in actual practice. Stocks like these behave more like wide-spread stocks that fluctuate more between the *liquid* Bid and Ask, at about one-quarter, three-eighths, or even half-point increments.

Trends

While determining a trend can be as simple as looking at a chart to see whether it points up or down, let us define trend from a technical standpoint. An upward trend is established by a series of combined price cycles that demonstrates a succession of higher highs and higher lows. Con-

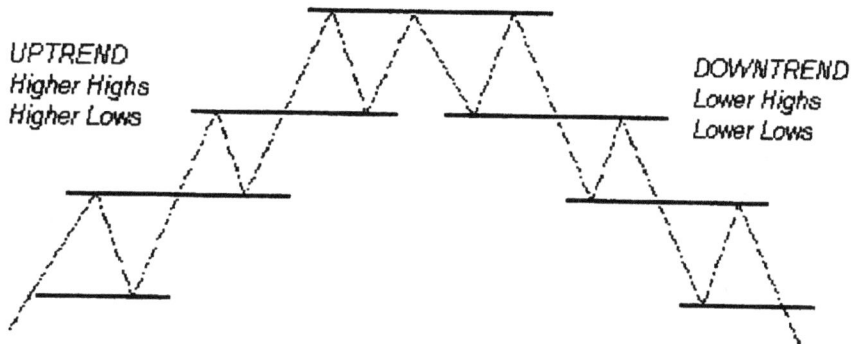

Figure 6-12. Trend basics.

versely, a downward trend is a succession of price cycles that demonstrates lower lows, successful tests of resistance, and lower highs.

Trends can be established and defined in many different time periods. This is a particular source of confusion to many beginning day traders. While "don't buck the trend" is a fairly easy-to-comprehend catchphrase, many traders are confused about what the word *trend* really means. This is because of the serious lack of an objective or target. Because the market can have more than one trend at any given moment, based on time periods, you must know which trend is applicable to a given trade objective. As a day trader, it is important to identify what the trend is on this trading period and the last few days, as opposed to the dominant trend of the market, which may last many weeks or months. Knowing exactly what your actual trade objective is, for a single trade in particular, will put your thinking in line. If you would like to profit from a trade that you intend to open and close today, analyze the trend established first by the stock on this period, then by its market today. In fact, it is important to know that the market is very capable of completely reversing directions within one day, for example, turning from bearish to bullish on a dime. This will help you in practicing your discipline (if you take the wrong direction) and having the flexibility to reverse direction and take advantage of the opportunities that come along with that reversing trend. In trying to capitalize on the trend, technical definitions such as higher highs and lower highs will help guide the trader to determine the correct direction.

The importance of knowing the trend is explained quite simply: The majority of the money to be made is on the side of the trend, while the majority of the money to be lost is on the opposite side. It is no accident that this is one of the Golden Rules of trading. Combining the knowledge of the support and resistance, the trend, and the relative strength of a stock is a powerful approach to day trading. If the market is rising, the winning odds are to the long side of stocks that are exhibiting strength; conversely, if the market is declining, odds are on the short side of stocks that are exhibiting weakness.

Gaps

The volatility of the markets has paved the way for more prevalent daily gaps. Knowing how to play a gap is an integral part of being a day trader. The rules are quite simple. A trading gap is a series of price levels that have been skipped due to changes in fact or sentiment. Gaps occur after trading in a stock is halted due to an imbalance in order flow usually caused by the announcement of news. More commonly, gaps occur between the time the market closed yesterday and the time the market opened today. The difference between the last closing price and the most recent opening price is the gap. These untraded levels are caused by a variety of reasons, but mostly by fundamental developments in the stock or the market in general that occurred after the close or before the next opening. Factors such as earnings announcements, analyst upgrades or downgrades, and market sentiment (often motivated by key economic news, important headlines on influential stocks, or large moves in foreign markets) are a few of the common conditions that cause gaps. Due to larger participation and greater price sensitivities in the market, gaps now occur almost daily.

When faced with a gap opening, three-eighths of a point or less is typically not significant (unless you are dealing with low-priced stocks). As a rule of thumb, the higher the gap, the more it casts a shadow on the trading day. A gap acts like a magnet—it attracts trading. The untraded levels explain the psychology behind gaps. For example, if a stock is gap-opened $2\frac{1}{2}$ points higher than the previous day, active traders who took home long positions will take profit and sell into the strength. Also, because the stock is trading at a higher level, the number of interested buyers diminishes while the number of sellers increases. This causes the stock to tend to trade toward the gapped area, where it might find more buyers. The opposite is true of stocks or markets that are gapped down.

Because stocks tend to trade into the gapped area, that does not mean a gap-down should be bought or a gap-up should be shorted at the open. Keep in mind that there is usually a very good reason for the gap. Some gaps are filled right away, while some may take many hours, days, or even months to get traded. (Make use of your charts.) There are also gaps that are never filled (breakaway gaps). As a rule of thumb, gap-ups tend to get filled quicker when the market is undergoing a bear phase, while gap-downs are traded sooner in bull markets.

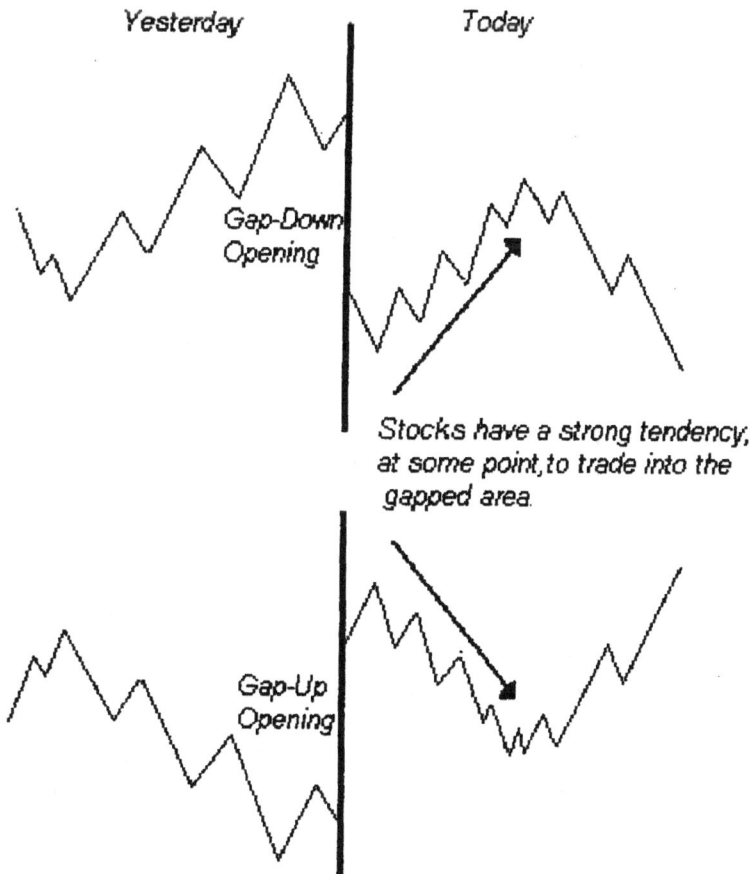

Figure 6-13. Gap basics.

Basic Gap Play. In facing a gap-opening, allow the stock to trade for 15 to 30 minutes, avoiding any play to either side at the open. Observe how it is trading while constantly checking the health of the market. If the stock was gapped-open on no internal news, it is probably due to the gap established by the S&P futures or another stock within its sector. In this case, watch what caused the stock to gap, too. The futures or whatever market factor caused this stock to gap will probably dictate this stock's direction at the open as well. Take note of yesterday's closing price, as well as key support and resistance areas. It is beneficial to look back further as well. If it was a gap-up and the stock drifts into the gapped area, you are looking for support at recent support or resistance areas, as well as at the closing price. You may be short here once the intraday low of the first few minutes is broken, but keep your stop tight—at worst, at any high established today. If the stock reverses and trades to break the high established during that critical 15- to 30-minute period, and better if the market is rallying as well, you are looking to cover short, reverse, and go long. The gap play incorporates a lot of cross-referencing. This is to say that you must use all your knowledge—technical and fundamental—to manage a gap play. You must set stops at the next key levels: recent support or resistance, yesterday's close, today's open, high or low. It is preferable if the gap is above the recent high, or in gap-down cases, below the recent low. Keep in mind that while you may make a play against the direction of the gap (short on gap-up or long on gap-down), you should keep an eye on what caused that gap if the news was not internal to the stock. If it was due to a gap in the general market and the futures or NDX are beginning to turn but your stock has not, it is a good idea to follow who is in charge (the indicators) and cover your position, rather than to wait for your stock to confirm (yet again) that it is following the trend of the general market.

Figure 6-14 is an example of NVLS following through on a classic gap play.

Breakaway and Exhaustion Gaps. Breakaway gaps are trading levels that open *above* a resistance point or *below* a support area. These types of gaps are normally due to very strong news. They are less likely to get filled anytime soon, especially if they occur after a long and trendless period. This is usually confirmed by solid volume. Be very cautious in taking positions that are against breakaway gaps. In fact, we are more likely to take the same direction of the gap as long as it is not too large. In these cases the stops are very tight, usually set at just beyond the opening price or, as a worst-case scenario, just beyond the previous support or resistance level that the gap broke away from.

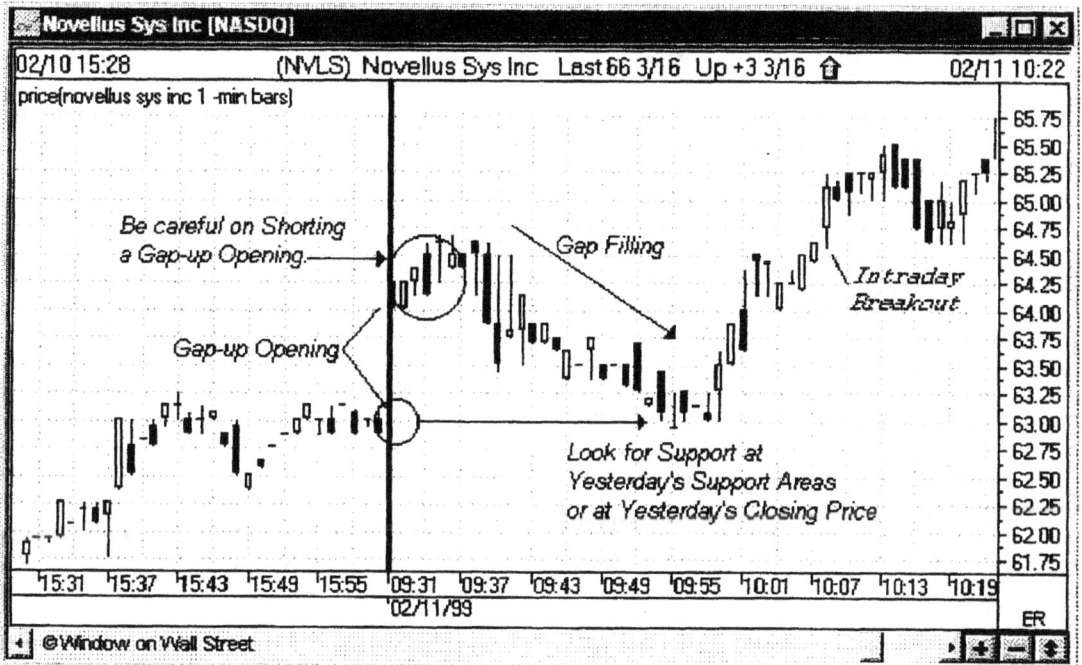

Figure 6-14. Gap filing.

If a breakaway gap fails, the retracement can be very large. This is known as an exhaustion gap, which is prevalent toward the end of a large move (rather than at the beginning of a trendless period). In this case, you must be aware of the daily charts and observe how much the stock or market has moved prior to it. In an exhaustion gap, a large number of participants are already committed and are ready to eliminate risk exposure. In the case of an exhaustion gap-down, it may signal a level at which the price has become cheap enough to warrant further selling. While the profit potential in a breakaway gap can be large, keep in mind that there are significant risks attached if the breakaway develops into an exhaustion gap. As with any play that involves higher risks, keep your stop-losses tight, and use the important technical areas (opening price, former resistance, etc.) to guide you as to where to stop out to protect your equity.

Simple Moving Averages

Moving averages (MAs) act like support and resistance areas, and also confirm for you what your chart is already telling you. MAs merely smooth out the noise of any given period and are usually calculated simply by

Figure 6-15. The 200MA daily as resistance.

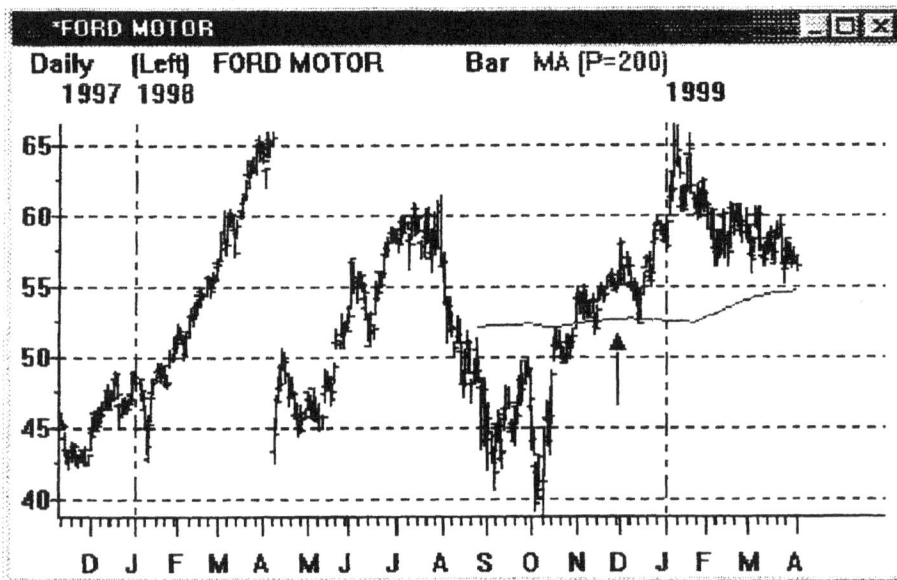

Figure 6-16. The 200MA daily as support.

averaging closing prices for the given chart scale. Thus they are lagging indicators. A rising MA confirms an uptrend and a falling MA confirms a downtrend. A stock that is declining and approaches a rising key MA is expected to find some support at that level. Conversely, a rising stock that is approaching a declining key MA is expected to find some resistance at that price. The MA is not an automatic number that acts like a wall; rather it travels depending upon how well it is acted upon or responded to by the market's participants, just like support or resistance. Also, it is more likely to be an area rather than a specific price.

There is more than one kind of MA. In this book, we only refer to the more popular type used, and in fact, the one we use the most: the simple moving average (SMA). There are many SMAs that are used in day trading: the 10-, 20-, 50-, and 200-period moving averages. These MAs are used in intraday as well as daily chart scales. The shortest MA that offers any type of reliability is the 5-minute, 200-period intraday scale, while the longest is the daily 200-period scale. The longer the time period, the more significant the MA is; the shorter the time period, the more likely it is that the MA will be broken. Thus, the most significant MA for day trading is the daily 200-period MA (200-day moving average). As the stock price approaches these MA price areas, especially if they are going in opposite directions (declining price into rising MA), you can find some support or resistance in this area. Note again that you must adjust your trade objective, expectations, and stop-losses based upon the relevant scales of time and price on the chart you used for analysis.

Figure 6-15 is an example of a stock that experienced resistance at the 200MA daily. Figure 6-16 is an example of the 200MA daily acting as support.

Retracements

When a stock or market is experiencing retracement, particularly after a significant move, the measure of its retracement hints at whether it will more likely continue that previous move or not. As discussed in Chapter 3, observing the stock's relative strength in comparison to the market is key in day trading. A rising stock that is experiencing a correction on account of a sell-off in the general market or the S&P 500 futures rather than because of internal profit taking or an internal sell-off, is a target for when the market stops selling off or reverses direction. This works conversely for a declining or apparently weak stock. This may happen in 15 minutes or it may happen in three days. Your ability to sense market dynamics (experience) comes into play.

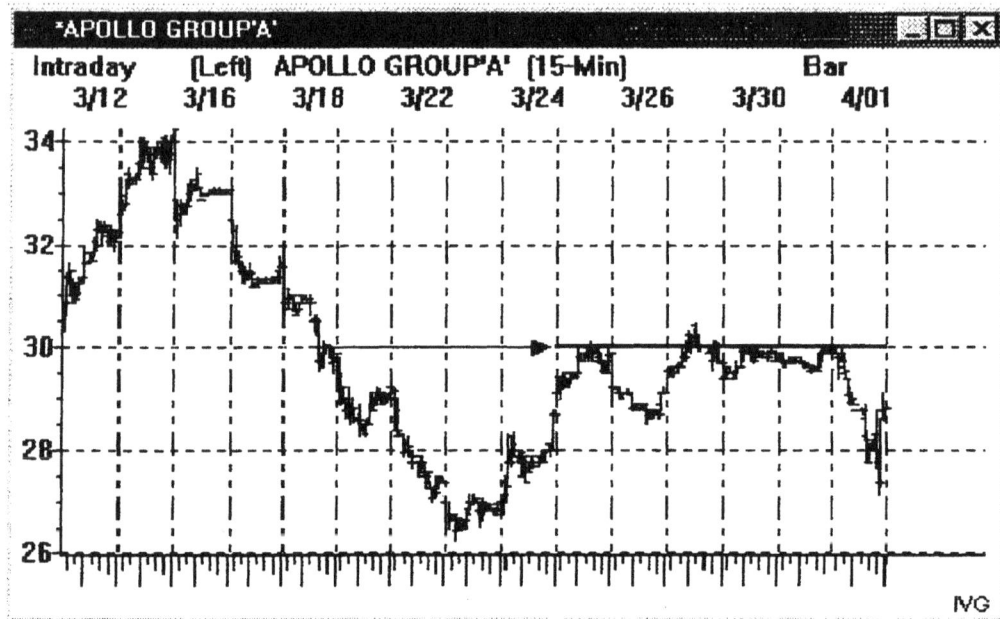

© Executioner

Figure 6-17. Fibonacci 50% retracement.

For individual stocks that are experiencing an internal price move, particularly a large price move into a totally new price territory, technicians of the market use what are known as Fibonacci numbers to measure the strength or weakness of a retracement. The numbers are characterized as a 38 percent, 50 percent, or 63 percent retracement from the origin of the price move. Use these price areas as a guide for setting entry, exit, and stop-loss points. This may be applied to any chart scale after a large price move. Figure 6-17 is an example of a 50 percent retracement, at the area around the round number 30. It is halfway between the origin of the sell-off at 34, and its bottom at 26.

Volume

The higher the volume during any given price move, the more important it is. Less volume suggests a price move that is less significant. Lower volume may even suggest danger or an impending reversal. Volume indicates the number of participants who are committing to that price area. If there are more participants committed to any given price area, their bulk can dictate the movement in price, as they react in concerted effort to control or add to their risk exposure. A heavy volume entry may also be indicative of more coming. Thus, if a stock is experiencing a breakout away from its usual price range on heavy volume, this may indicate more strength to come. The converse holds for breakdowns. If you are watching a stock that is trending up, it is normal for volume to stay steady or even rise. However, declining volume on a trend may signify an impending reversal.

Unlike analyzing price and time, we give less consideration to intraday volume, but more on the daily scale. This is because intraday trends in volume may be too sporadic to warrant any validity (unless there is news). Keep in mind that a large trade is both a buy and a sell transaction and that it may not necessarily indicate direction. Thus, we would rather track volume on daily charts and leave intraday volume for later analysis.

Knowing and Adhering to Your Trade Objectives

If you have identified a price pattern on a 10-day, 15-minute intraday chart, you must adjust your objectives and expectations accordingly. A pattern on a 15-minute chart can take a few or more 15-minute periods to follow through. A pattern on a daily chart may take many days or even weeks to follow through. If a stock has a usual three-point range, it is very likely that you will take at least three points of "heat," probably more, before your pattern is complete. In other words, it is very likely that you will not begin to make money the minute you open your position, unless it is a scalp trade (which carries normally higher risk). More important yet, if you have identified a price pattern on an intraday chart today and you take the position accordingly, this is a trade that may not be suitable for a long-term hold. *Your actions and reactions must always conform to the parameters of your original analysis.*

We are often asked, "What do you think of MSFT or EMC or SRSL or HWP or the market?" Our response is always another question: "What is your objective?" The reason for this is twofold: First, we don't know what a stock is going to do. Second, we pose the question to coax traders into getting used to thinking and deciding for themselves. The lack of objectives and failure to adhere to a trading plan are evidence that the market is in control of the trader. Those traders' reactions will only be dictated by the bait of large price moves, which will quite frequently put the trader in a situation of buying at the top and selling at the bottom. In that case, they are left with only two good choices: Stop trading and buy some good mutual funds, or take the time to get educated.

We encourage you to be patient, observe the market, and train before trading. Technical analysis is always a good starting point, and acts as a means to create a price grid to mark limitations. Developing a specific trade objective for every trade and for every trading session is good risk management. In fact, combine this with discipline and you will be on the road to safe and successful trading.

7

Efficient Order Execution

We begin this chapter with a simple mathematical calculation to point out the importance of efficient order execution in active equity trading. Here are the assumptions:

- You trade only **once** a day: one buy and one sell order per day.
- Your typical order size is 500 shares.
- You waste one teenie (1/16th of a point) for every order, as a result of inefficient order execution.
- You take a one-month vacation every year and do not trade.
- By the end of the year, you have thrown away about **$14,000.00** in poor order executions.

The money that is theoretically wasted here grows exponentially as you consider larger share size and more frequent trades.

Most of us tend to focus on commission costs and fail to see the merits of order execution. While commissions and other trading costs are a crucial factor in active trading indeed, highly efficient order execution is too significant to ignore. All active participants must take full advantage of the new ways to send orders and the added liquidity in our markets that have been catalyzed by the new technologies and a strong market. Casual investors did not care about the teenies and eighths (and more) tacked onto their execution prices. This was not because they lacked intelligence, but rather they did not know how much money it represented, nor did they have an alternative anyway. One must ponder the incredible value that the entire investing public sacrifices because it is unaware of the significance of teenies, eighths, quarters, or halves to professionals. *Your orders are so valuable that they are, in themselves, a commodity.* There is tremendous profit to be made in the sale of non-direct-access customers' order flow. The profits come as a result of knowing exactly when and where the orders to buy or sell are. While this may be quite all right for many long-term investors, active market participants must take control of their own orders, especially now that we have direct access to the markets.

The stock market today has opened up to the small investor in many ways. In the highly competitive and liquid market we have today, fractions of stock price belong to the most competitive participants. No longer are those fractions reserved to the institutional players, or Market Makers; now they are available to any individual willing to take advantage of them. Learn the concepts that govern momentary supply and demand and learn how the system works. In other words, learn to execute your own orders like a true professional.

As discussed previously, learning to send the correct orders can be confusing and overwhelming. This chapter, in conjunction with the techniques outlined elsewhere in the book, will help you understand how to send the right orders in a methodical manner. It is critical that you master your trading tools to benefit from the advantages they can give you. Not knowing what to do in the crucial moments before executing is the equivalent to fumbling for your keys if you are in a rush to enter the door. While we have already discussed a few basics about Level 2 in Chapter 5, let us begin to learn how to use this tool by studying the different order execution types on the NASDAQ.

Level 2 Order Execution Methods

There are three basic order execution methods on the NASDAQ for Level 2 day traders:

- Small Order Execution System (SOES)
- SelectNet System
- Electronic Communication Networks (ECN)

Small Order Execution System (SOES)

The SOES system is one of the two electronic methods that Level 2 participants utilize to communicate their buy and sell orders to Market Makers. While it was established in 1985, it became popular after the market crash of 1987. Here are some facts about SOES:

- SOES is a means for a Level 2 trader to directly communicate a buy or sell order to Market Makers. Only Market Makers have the ability to see and respond to your SOES orders. They are not displayed on either the Level 1 or Level 2 screens for other participants to see. In other words, another day trader or investor cannot directly respond to your SOES order.

- Market Makers cannot use the SOES system to execute their own orders.

- SOES orders can be sent as market or limit orders.

- Market Makers are obligated to fill all open SOES market orders. This does not mean that whenever you activate your SOES button, your order will get filled instantly. While SOES is very fast, it is still limited by the number of shares available at a certain price given the current supply and demand scenario.

- SOES orders are filled on a first come, first served basis. You will frequently find that in a fast-moving market, SOES market orders are terrific, if you sent your order in early. Since SOES will be the first system to get clogged with orders during this time, yours may be filled at the extremes of a price move.

- The maximum order size for SOES is 1,000 shares. (Some less liquid stocks may be limited to 500 and 200 maximum shares).

- SOES market buy orders are filled by Market Makers on the Ask, while SOES market sell and short orders are filled by Market Makers on the Bid side, at their posted prices.

- If you have an open SOES order that is waiting to get filled, you may cancel it without any time restrictions.

- Market Makers are only obligated to fill orders based on the number of shares they display as available. If you send an SOES order for 1,000 shares to a Market Maker who is only displaying 500 shares available, the Market Maker is only obligated to fill 500, his quoted share size.

SelectNet System

The NASDAQ SelectNet system is another electronic alternative for Level 2 users to communicate with Market Makers. Here are some important SelectNet facts:

- Market Makers also use the SelectNet system to trade among themselves.

■ Unlike SOES, there is no order size limit on SelectNet. If you have a buy or sell order that is larger than the allowed maximum SOES order size (typically 1,000 shares), use the SelectNet system as an alternative.

■ Also unlike SOES, you can use the SelectNet system to buy from or sell to ECNs.

■ You must specify a *price* and *order size* for your SelectNet Orders.

■ Your SelectNet order must be available for *at least ten seconds.* You may not cancel your order before this time. This is a system that will teach you how long ten seconds in the NASDAQ can be.

■ Like SOES, SelectNet orders are not displayed on the Level 2 screen. They can only be seen by Market Makers.

■ Your SelectNet order must be within the limits of the current trading activity. *Never send Bids or Offers that are out of the money:* This is an abuse of the SelectNet system. You may get fined or banned.

■ There are two types of SelectNet orders: *Broadcast* and *Preference:*

1. SelectNet Broadcast: Untrue to its name, your Broadcast SelectNet order is only seen by Market Makers. However, it was termed prior to the advent of the ECN, and thus was called Broadcast because it is seen by *all* Market Makers. Any Market Maker can respond, but is not always obligated, to fill your order.

2. SelectNet Preference: In contrast, a SelectNet Preference order is sent to a Market Maker or ECN of your choice. It will only target a specific Market Maker or the ECN that you select, and will not be broadcast to other markets.

■ SelectNet Preference also provides a means to buy from or sell to ECNs. For example, if you identify an ECN such as ATTN (Attain) and your brokerage account does not provide direct access to the ATTN system (see next section) you may buy from or sell to that ECN utilizing the SelectNet Preference method.

ECN Orders

The ECN is a Level 2 trader's best negotiating tool in the NASDAQ market (and perhaps soon to include listed issues). Let us examine some basic but important facts about using ECNs:

■ The ECN is your tool to display your Bids or Offers directly to the entire market. (This is not possible using SOES or SelectNet.)

- Only the best prices for each ECN will be displayed on Level 2. While there may be numerous orders at different prices, a specific ECN can only display the single most competitive Bid or Offer. All other orders will not be displayed on Level 2 until they become the best single Bid or Offer for that specific ECN.

- If you do not see a specific ECN on your Level 2 screen, that usually means there are no Bids or Offers for that stock on that ECN to display.

- Each brokerage house may Offer a Level 2 trader different types of direct ECN access. In other words, if your Level 2 brokerage subscribes to the ISLD (Island) ECN System, your Bids and Offers can be displayed on the Level 2 screen as "ISLD" alongside Market Makers and ECNs. Some direct order entry firms even provide more than one direct-access ECN to their customers.

- If your brokerage house does not subscribe to a particular ECN, you can still buy from or sell to that ECN using the NASDAQ SelectNet Preference System.

- You are not allowed to lock or cross the market using your ECN. The only exception is when you are targeting a matching ECN (the same as yours) on the opposite side. For example, if you want to buy and you see an ISLD Offer at the Ask, you can "lock," "match," or "cross" that order by Bidding at a price that is equal to or greater than the Asking price *using the ISLD system also.* If you are first to send the order to that ISLD Offer, your execution will be instantaneous at that posted price. The same is true when you are selling. You cannot do this against a posted Market Maker or a posted ECN that is different from yours; your order will be rejected if you try. To specifically target a Market Maker or a different ECN, use SelectNet Preference.

- When using the ECNs, you are more susceptible to partial fills. This is not necessarily a disadvantage, because you are frequently able to compensate by getting better prices than the Market Makers'.

- Some ECNs do not allow odd-lot orders (fewer than 100-share increments). Check with your Level 2 order entry firm.

- If you are Bidding or Offering using a direct ECN system, your order can be matched by another trader, but only on two conditions:
  1. The other trader is using the NASDAQ SelectNet Preference System to specifically target your ECN and price.
  2. The other trader is using a direct ECN system that is the same as yours. For example, a trader using TNTO direct cannot communicate an order with a trader using BTRD direct.

	SOES	SelectNet Broadcast	SelectNet Preference	Direct Order ECNs
Order Types	Market buy, sell, or short Limit buy, sell, or short	Limit buy or sell only	Limit buy or sell only	Limit buy or sell only
Display on Level 2	Not displayed	Not displayed	Not displayed	Displayed if best bid or offer on that ECN only
Filled By	Market Maker only	Market Maker only	Market Maker or ECN	Matching ECN only
Cancel	Any time	Must wait 10 seconds	Must wait 10 seconds	Any time
Size Limit	1,000 shares	No limit	No limit	No limit
Your Target	All Market Makers	All Market Makers	Specific Market Maker or ECN	Matching ECN only
Partial Fills	Uncommon	Uncommon	Uncommon for Market Makers Common for ECNs	Common
Odd Lots	Allowed	Allowed	Allowed for Market Makers Not allowed for some ECNs	Not allowed for some ECNs

Figure 7-1. NASDAQ Level 2 order execution methods and their basic characteristics.

This ends our discussion of the different order execution methods. It is not easy to learn how to use them; in fact, it can even be confusing. However, with practice you will gain familiarity and expertise. Figure 7-1 summarizes the characteristics of each order execution method, and will serve as a guide as you familiarize yourself with them.

Order Execution Techniques

When you are on the verge of sending your order, it is important that the decision to buy, sell, or short right now has already been made—and with conviction. Indecisiveness before executing is a common trader sickness, especially among the inexperienced. At this moment, there should be no hesitation. Hesitation can cost a trader a lot of money. If a trader who has doubts is faced with a tough situation, it causes panic and often leads to bad decisions, which then lead to losses.

The only decision that is left to be made at the moment of trade is whether you will:

- Bid to buy—Bid in (limit order)
- Pay the Asking price to buy—Hit the Ask (limit or market order)
- Offer to sell—Offer out or Offer short (limit order)
- Sell to the Bidders—Hit the Bid (limit or market order)

Momentum is the key. In Chapter 5, we discussed the basic ways to identify momentary buying and selling pressures. The level at which the market is trading *right now* dictates the basic philosophy to employ in order execution. If the market has no momentum, perhaps the way to get your order executed may be as elementary as selling to the Bid or buying from Ask. However, when there is momentum, you must take advantage of the extra teenies, eighths, and quarters that we mentioned in the beginning of this chapter. The best way to do this is to observe the Time and Sales report. While the status of the Bid and Ask reflects significant information, nothing gives away temporary momentum more than the Time and Sales report. Too much focus on the Bid and Ask without regard to the trade reports may even be detrimental to your correctly judging momentum (see Chapter 5).

The movement of the Bid and Ask in correspondence with the trades is indeed important to solidifying the price move. However, knowing exactly where the buyers and sellers are meeting is key to your order execution technique. For example, in Figure 7-2, the Ask may be showing an abundance of sellers at $45\frac{1}{4}$, which may give the illusion of downward pressure in price. However, the many trades reported at $45\frac{1}{4}$ confirm the abundance of buyers willing to transact at current Asking prices. Here, the sellers have the upper hand, as buyers are willing to pay more than their option to Bid on the Bid side. As mentioned in Chapter 5, the Bid and Ask scenario does not necessarily reflect all participants in the market; it only reflects displayed participants. Let us say that in our example, you are about to send an order to sell. If the trades continue at the quarter, and especially if displayed sellers at the current Ask are retreating to higher prices (disappearing), you may send an Offer to sell (through an ECN or SelectNet) at the quarter or somewhere reasonably close to it. There is no need to send a market order (SOES) to take the Bid price ($45\frac{1}{8}$), because it is being demonstrated to you that current buyers are willing to pay Asking prices at $45\frac{1}{4}$, and Sellers at that price are ready to retreat and display higher prices. The Time and Sales report will be your guide. If the stock is experiencing momentum in the other direction, then the strategy will be different. The Order Execution Guide in Figure 7-3 will suggest your order execution technique, given the different directions of momentum. Memorizing and understanding the theories outlined here will sharpen your order execution techniques.

BID			ASK			T&S	
MM ID	*Price*	*Size*	*MM ID*	*Price*	*Size*	*Price*	*Size*
ATTN	45 1/8	10	MLCO	45 1/4	4	45 1/4	3
LEHM	45 1/8	10	SBSH	45 1/4	10	45 1/4	10
USCT	45 1/16	1	INCA	45 1/4	8	45 1/8	3
AGIS	45 1/16	10	FBCO	45 1/4	10	45 1/4	10
NITE	45	10	COWN	45 1/4	10	45 1/4	9
BEST	45	1	GSCO	45 1/4	10	45 1/4	10
INCA	45	10	ISLD	45 1/4	6	45 1/4	6
MASH	44 15/16	5	TNTO	45 5/16	20	45 1/8	1
SELZ	44 7/8	1	RSSF	45 3/8	1	45 1/8	1
DEMP	44 7/8	4	LCVG	45 3/8	1	45 1/4	10

Figure 7-2. Level 2 window with upward momentum.

	Direction of Current Momentum		
Action	**Increasing Price** Sellers have the upper hand.	**Decreasing Price** Buyers have the upper hand.	**No Momentum** Equilibrium
BUY	Pay the Ask (or a level higher in fast markets). SOES market buy SelectNet preference Aggressive bid on ECN	No need to use SOES. Bid the Bid (or better) using ECN.	Bid the Bid using ECN Bid in between spreads using ECN. SOES or SelectNet buy
SELL	No need to use SOES. Offer the Ask (or better) using ECN.	Hit the Bid (or a level lower in fast markets). Offer low Market sell	Offer the Ask using ECN. Offer in between spreads using ECN. SOES or SelectNet sell
SHORT	Do not use SOES. Short offer the Ask (or better) using ECN.	Good luck! Keep an eye out for upticks. SOES or ECN short on upticks.	Offer short at the Ask using ECN. Offer short in between spreads (ECN) or market short on uptick.

Figure 7-3. Order execution guide.

As illustrated on the Order Execution Guide, you will be faced with the decision to send either market (SEOS) or limit orders (Bidding or Offering through your ECNs). The basic idea is that if the priority is very high, you should use market orders; in lower-priority situations, you should use limit orders. As much as possible we want to avoid using market orders, and maintain the majority of orders to limit. There are however, some exceptions.

Market Orders

SOES market orders only come into play when you do not have the upper hand. This is when the price is rising and you need to buy, or when the price is falling and you need to sell. In scalping, for example, the frequency of using market orders will be higher due to the nature of the trades. Scalps are quick, in-and-out types of trades that ride on visible or impending momentum, and the urgency to enter and exit early is higher. Scalps usually follow the format of market order in (priority to open the position) and limit order out (getting out with the momentum, when you still have the upper hand). For example, referring to Figure 7-2, if you need to buy at $45^1/_4$, your priority is very high, because the stock is already in motion and trading at that price (the Ask). If you Bid in (using your ECN) along with the displayed buyers at $45^1/_8$, or even halfheartedly raise the Bid to $45^3/_{16}$, your chances of being able to open a long position for a scalp will be minimal. The stock is already trading ahead of your Bidding price. You will be a witness to history rather than a participant in it. In fact, that may even be the last time the stock ever trades at that price.

Market orders should always be used with caution. Whether you are scalping or merely sending an order to open or close a longer-term position, be especially sensitive to price extension when you have an open Market order. If you have sent a Market order and believe that the price has extended too much, be ready to cancel and wait, or replace it with a Limit order. While there is clearly a risk here, you must use your best judgement with respect to all conditions we discuss in this book. The point is, never leave an open Market order alone, especially when attempting to open a position on a volatile stock.

Use SelectNet in high-priority situations. SelectNet Broadcast is not a good option to use in high-priority situations. As an alternative to SOES Market Orders however, you can use SelectNet Preference. What is important is that you target the correct Market Maker at the correct price. If the stock price is rising rapidly, odds are that the SOES queue is clogged with orders. If you opt to use SelectNet Preference, target a Market Maker who is displayed on the Ask, at the price he displays. Choose the Market Maker who appears to have been selling frequently today or, if you have not been watching, target the one who is staying at the Ask and refreshing displayed intentions more than the others. It is also advised that you choose the bigger, more active Market Makers such as Goldman Sachs (GSCO), Merrill Lynch (MLCO), Morgan Stanley (MSCO), or Knight (NITE); there is a number of others that you will gain familiarity with as you go along. While SelectNet is an excellent way to pick up or dispose of stock quickly, remember that it is very widely used by NASDAQ scalpers as well. Note also that Market Makers are obligated to fill SOES orders, and that they may fulfill their obligation to honor their quotes by automatically responding to SOES orders over SelectNet. Market Makers use a combination of all these methods in order to place large orders by collectively filling both SOES and SelectNet. Which would be better, SOES or SelectNet? As an absolute for high-priority situations, a SOES market order is better, because a Market Maker will always eventually fill your order; using SelectNet, the possibility exists that your order will never get filled. In less critical circumstances, it depends on the situation: If you are targeting a Market Maker who is obviously an aggressive seller (or buyer, when you need to sell), it is probably better to use SelectNet Preference.

Limit Orders (Bidding and Offering)

Your first priority in trading is to avoid going with the herd whenever possible. You are constantly trying to be ahead of the rest of the market. This concept also applies to pinpointing your orders. As much as possible, you want ease in executing your orders rather than having to use a market order. You constantly want to be buying or selling when you have the upper hand (with momentum), unless you really want in, right now. In exiting, using limit orders with the correct momentum is always ideal. For example, let us say that you own a stock and it is approaching your target, which may be at a previously tested resistance point. Use your ECN to Offer out of your long position while the momentum is there, rather than waiting for the stock to confirm for you what you already know. You may end up having to sell (or buy to cover short) when everyone does—especially if the stock is coming into a blatantly obvious resistance level. Thus you may lose some of your profits because of your hesitation (or greed). By not getting out with the momentum in your favor, you will pay the spread. Employ the techniques in the order execution table (Figure 7-3) to take full advantage of your ability to trade directly in these markets, especially if you have access to NASDAQ Level 2.

Do your Bidding and Offering on ECN, rather than SelectNet. The general approach is simple: Use your ECNs as much as possible. When you are about to announce your intention to buy or sell, would you rather announce that to a limited group of Market Makers (on SelectNet) or to the entire world for that stock (on an ECN)? Think advertising: You reach a larger audience with your ECN. Your odds of getting a hit by using an ECN are far better than by using SelectNet. In addition, Market Makers know more about the stock's order flow than we do. What they choose to do or not do with your SelectNet orders usually has very good reasoning behind it—and they are not about to give you free money. In fact, nobody in the market will do that knowingly.

The next question is, to Display or not to Display? There is a lot of power in your ECN's ability to display your order. The ability to manually display your orders is one of the great advantages of direct access to the markets today. However, it may also serve as a disadvantage when used incorrectly. As a rule of thumb, you want to place your ECN or SelectNet orders only on the last few moments before your price is being traded. The general idea in sending your orders efficiently is to conceal your intentions from the market until the last possible moment. This is especially true if you have a sizeable order, which brings us to a very important point: *The more you display or reveal your intentions, the more other participants will have the upper hand.* This is especially true of stocks that are trading with lower volume or liquidity. For example, let us say you are an inexperienced trader who needs to sell out of a position because the stock is acting weak. It is a lower-volume stock and the Bid is at $61\frac{1}{4}$ while the Ask is at $61\frac{3}{4}$; there is a half-point spread. Because you are willing to sell, wanting to get the best price possible, and have the ability to Bid and Offer like a Market Maker, you send an order to Offer the stock at $61\frac{3}{4}$. You wait a few seconds, then a few minutes, with no result. You notice that nobody is willing to buy the stock you are Offering at $61\frac{3}{4}$, so you cancel your order and sends a new, more attractive order to sell at $61\frac{5}{8}$. The same thing happens; You wait and wait. You get frustrated, so you cancel your open order to Offer at $61\frac{5}{8}$ and replace it with a new, more attractive order to Offer $61\frac{1}{2}$. You have just narrowed the spread from half a point to a quarter of a point. That is terrific, except that in the process, you have:

1. increased the number of sellers at the Ask;
2. announced to the world that nobody wants to buy at $61\frac{3}{4}$;
3. announced that nobody wants to buy at $61\frac{5}{8}$;

4. announced that nobody wants to buy at $61^1/_2$;

5. displayed your frustration, desperation, and willingness to lower your price, which may represent the position of other, undisplayed participants (you are not the only one who noticed the stock was acting weak);

6. displayed a pattern that suggests that in a few moments, you are about to send an order to take the current Bid price if nobody wants to buy at $61^3/_8$—the price you are only about to Offer, based on your pattern;

7. made other participants nervous by the possibility of the current Bid getting hit, and the possibility of retreat by the current buyers, who also happen to be watching;

8. triggered other sellers to act ahead of you by hitting the Bid before you do;

9. alerted other skilled participants that both the Offer (by desperate sellers) and the Bid (by retreating buyers) were lowered; they have also confirmed the downward momentum with Time and Sales at the Bid price.

The participants in item 9 now begin the rush to sell and short the obviously weak stock. In the end, you are at the back of the herd.

This is a common example of an inexperienced trader using powerful tools in a faulty manner. The idea is to use the stock's momentum. If the stock is not in motion, your power to Bid or Offer must be balanced by the advantage of concealing your intentions. In our example, you had no need to establish and display the pattern of lowering the price. You should have quickly taken notice that your Offer was not getting taken at the current Ask or between the spread, and opted to sell to the Bid while it was still there. After all, you were right in your intuition to sell the stock's weakness; but a callow approach with a powerful trading tool caused you to lose money. Worst yet, you may repeat the process if you don't learn from this experience.

When sending Bids and Offers, be reasonable! This caveat applies whether you have a highly liquid or low-volume stock. Again, your best clue will be the Time and Sales report. Make an attempt to Bid or Offer (using ECNs or SelectNet) at a price that is at or within sensible proximity to the current Time and Sales. Bidding too low or Offering too high may result in lost opportunities: The stock may pull away in the opposite direction, and if you have to execute an order, you want to avoid the frenzy of that pullback. This is when you will be fighting your inherent greed to take the best possible price; if a stock is going up, it is easy to Offer higher prices because you may believe it will keep going higher. Be reasonable with your

Bids and Offers. If you experience Offering a stock, getting executed, and subsequently watching the stock push higher, it does not matter anymore—you already got the price you wanted at that time. This will happen to you many times in trading. As we discussed in Chapter 6, while it is nice to get the perfect tops and bottoms, as a professional trader, you should be content with the middle. Acknowledge the higher levels of risk and panic associated with wanting perfection every time.

Use ECNs in high-priority situations. If you *must* execute an order now, go ahead and Bid higher or Offer lower. Do not be afraid to pay the next level if the market is moving fast, even if the current inside Bid or Ask has not moved away yet. One of the strongest clues of a fast market is seeing others pay more, so in these situations pay special attention to the prints. Be quick to find a matching ECN on the Ask (if you are buying) or on the Bid (if you are selling); this is one of the best ways to get the next levels. If you want something that everyone apparently wants too; get ready to pay up for it.

Take a last glance at the futures. Despite making it a habit to constantly monitor the condition of the general market, you must take a final glance at the futures or at the Tick before you execute your order, especially when you are in a liquid stock and scalpers are in the wings. For example, if you are going to sell and the futures surged one or three points (or the Tick surged 200 or more points), you may be able to sell at a slightly higher price if the general market is in rally mode. What if the futures or the Tick is starting to tank? Then you must probably be more aggressive to sell. This often happens when you are day trading. Take advantage of the opportunity.

Think fast. Your ability to quickly analyze a situation and to let your hands act as an extension of your thoughts (not having to think about which button to push) is critical to your success. This is most true in volatile situations. While the entire concept of using momentum in efficient order execution is rather simple, the actual application relies heavily on your ability to think and act quickly, maintain objectivity, and control your greed and fear. The markets have become so efficient that your competitive nature to get in and out first will be challenged. The skills of the new day traders as well as the experienced Market Makers are very sharp, and if you want to take full advantage of the new technology, you must learn how to use it and apply it in swift fashion.

Notes for Non-Direct-Access Participants

If you do not have access to Level 2 or only trade occasionally, there are a couple of pointers we would like to discuss that may help your trading.

Placing Market Orders Overnight

The danger in placing market orders overnight lies in the overnight risk of both gap-ups and gap-downs. The market digests all news as it comes in and, significant news, in fact, is often announced in the morning, before the market opens. The news may be significant enough to gap the entire market. To send a market order the evening before strong positive news would expose you to the possibility of paying the highest prices of the day. For example, in Figure 7-4, placing an overnight market order would have meant that the shares you bought, among the millions of shares exchanged of that stock on that day, were at the most expensive prices—almost four points higher than the lowest point the stock traded at that same day. If you had placed an order for 500 shares, your overnight market order may have caused you to pay $2,000 more than the person who bought at the lowest price for that day. While there are indeed some days when this will work in your favor, the decision to place an overnight market order usually amounts to a gamble. It is always better trading practice to wait until the trading day has begun.

Let us now consider the opposite scenario: a gap-down. Bad news about a company or market may be announced prior to market open, and the vulnerability of an open market buy order is increased. In fact, the funda-

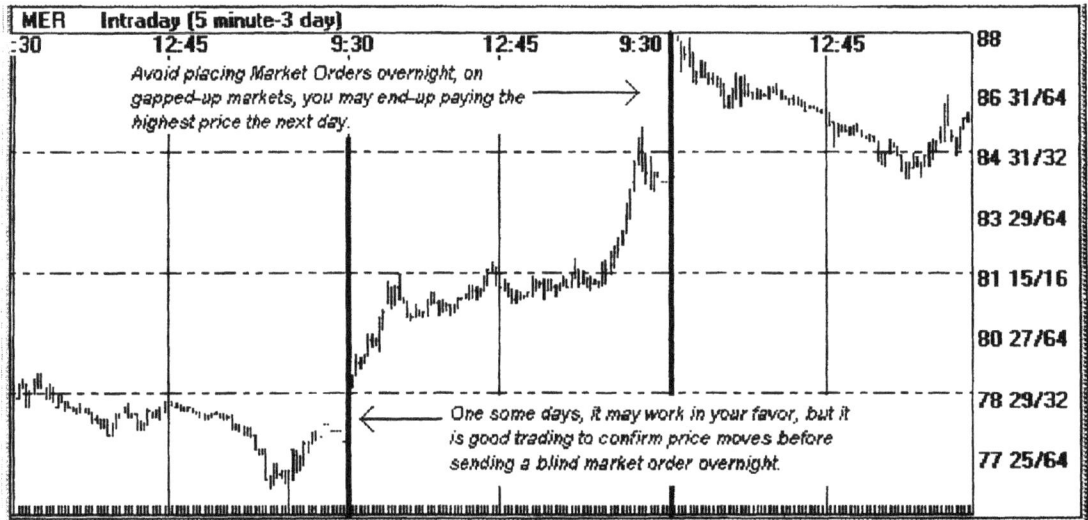

@ CyberCorp 1999

Figure 7-4. Gapped-up markets.

mentals or technicals may have changed so badly that you no longer want a long position on the stock by the time you find out your buy order is filled. If you must send orders overnight, always use limit orders as the preferred alternative.

Using Limit Orders to Protect Longer-Term Positions

Unless you consider yourself a true investor in a particular stock, meaning you will stay with that stock through thick and thin, you must always have a predetermined stop-loss point, without exceptions. If you are an active market participant, but do not have the ability to constantly watch your positions, good-till-cancelled stop-orders will be the best tool to protect your position in your absence. While there is power in using them, you must use carefully selected areas in setting stop orders. If you will be watching your positions, at least set a mental stop that may correspond to a market indicator, a leading stock, or the actual stocks you are trading. Otherwise, if you are unable to keep vigil, always place a stop-loss order on the actual stock. For example, if you are trying to protect a position, you must set your stop-loss at a point that is not too obvious to be taken out on a shallow overshoot. In other words, if the stock is showing obvious support at 42, it is common to find the stock overshoot that price before bouncing off again. There are many reasons for this. Perhaps the momentum coming in was too strong or participants who knew there where are a lot of orders at a certain level colluded to take the price there, only to revert as soon as the stop orders had been taken out. Perhaps it is a wide-spread stock and the difference between Bids and Offers can create a wide support area. Eliminate the obvious by setting your stops slightly beyond the obvious points. Carefully orchestrate the various risks in setting your stops. Often the choice is between protecting your equity as much as possible and giving the stock the benefit of the doubt. Adjust your individual risk tolerances and use your best judgement. The point is that you must always set your stops on longer-term positions at reasonable support or resistance *areas,* and you must always maintain a protective stop-loss in all your trades, especially if you are unable to keep an eye on your positions.

8

Trading Styles

We hear it all too often: The stock market is dynamic. Exactly what does dynamic mean? Energetic, powerful, ever-changing, unpredictable. As much as we all dream of having the power to predict the tides of the market with one hundred percent certainty, let us leave those traits to the immortal. While loss-taking is an inherent part of professional trading, consistency in being able to extract profits that supersede losses leads to the ultimate objective: to build equity. Consistency in this dynamic market also means flexibility. A flexible trader is a powerful trader. Because the market may behave a certain way today and react differently tomorrow or next week, traders must have the ability to adapt themselves and their trading styles to suit different market conditions. Keep in mind also that the market may react a certain way to given news one time and react differently at another time to the very same news. Some days are great for trading and others may not be. Regardless, you must first acknowledge that the market is always changing and that you must take the market day by day, and build yourself a pool of knowledge that you will call your experience or instinct. With experience you will develop a "style" to your liking, suitable to your personality and risk tolerance. In this chapter, we break down the three basic styles of trading that, used in combination, make up for a complete approach to trading stocks in this market. They are: scalping, swing trading, and core trading.

There is more to these basic styles than meets the eye. While we divide these styles to different lengths of time and different kinds of analysis (technical or fundamental), we emphasize the fact that trading based on diversified objectives keeps us more attuned to all kinds of price swings. Each style complements the other. For example, a greater understanding of price movement in all time spans through actual trading and an excellent fundamental knowledge both greatly help a trader in developing scalping technique. On the other hand, a trader's scalping techniques in order exe-

cution and last-minute entry and exit pinpointing would greatly comple-
ment a position-taking method for core trades. Often we find that a good
scalping day makes up for a pull-back in our core positions, or a good
swing of trades makes up for a tough scalping session. Whether in interpreting breaking news, trying to forecast price extension, or extracting
every teenie possible, knowledge of a diversified group of techniques
makes for a much more powerful approach to trading. It will help you
increase your odds of success, boost discipline, and take advantage of
numerous opportunities in equity trading.

In dividing the trading styles into three basic types, we are not seeking to
draw lines that say, "This is a scalp trade, and that is a core trade" as much
as we want to have the flexibility to take advantage of different price
actions. There are no solid lines that divide one type of trade from another,
but rather overlapping areas that help us differentiate the psychology and
technique used in one type or another. There are two goals for every trade:

- To profit from all price swings; and
- To learn from all price swings.

Flexibility also entails knowing when to trade and when not to trade.
Learn to quickly identify whether the type of market is suitable to your
style or not. Keep in mind that you don't have to be sending orders to be
working. You could be participating in the market just as much while you
are not trading. Your lack of participation has an effect on the market in
itself. Avoid nurturing the belief that nonparticipation is not working. This
leads to overtrading or compulsion, which, in trading terms, is the practice
of poor risk management. Upon starting the trading day, you must be convinced to trade, with an aggressive and well-planned intent to make
money. If that is not working, keep your hands away from the terminal.
Take as long as you need to gather your confidence. Keep in mind that not
only are you protecting your money, you are also protecting your psychology. A series of losses first eats into your account balance, and then begins
to eat into what is most important of all: your confidence. Trade with confidence, or don't trade at all.

Scalping

Scalping is taking advantage of small intraday price fluctuations with
momentum. Contrary to popular belief, scalping is more difficult than it
appears and scalping full-time is not for everyone.

With the incredible popularity of day trading in the mid 1990s and thereafter, droves of new day traders arrived to take advantage of small price swings and take the quarters, eighths, and teenies that most of the investing public didn't have efficient access to. Here are the factors about scalping that you should consider.

Objective. The target in scalping is to make anywhere from teenies to about half points (sometimes more) purely on actual and momentary imbalance in order flow that drives the stock to move temporarily in one direction or another. The scalper has the ability to recognize an immediate influx of order flow and jump in for a small profit on the price fluctuation. The faster one recognizes this, and the faster the order is executed, the better the odds of success. A scalper will limit risk to no more than the profit that can actually be made. Most scalp trades are done while there is momentum only, either conforming to or violating the trend, and the scalper exits the trade when the momentum is spent.

Time Span. Scalps last anywhere from a few seconds to a couple of hours. Two hours is very long-term in scalping!

Frequency and Commission Risks. Because profits are small, the frequency of trades is higher. More trades mean more commissions, so managing risk in commissions is critical. On top of commissions, one must also build ECN, SEC, interest, or other applicable trading fees into the equation. Not only are you facing the risk of prices moving against you, but because scalping entails a low risk-to-reward ratio, trading costs significantly magnify that risk. Take this into careful consideration.

Order Execution. If you are going to be scalping, your order execution is half the game, probably more—most especially in the NASDAQ. If you do not have Level 2 access, you should not consider momentum scalping too often. Your ability to quickly get in and out of a trade, particularly in a bad situation, may mean the difference between your profitability or lack thereof. The key here is speed, speed, and more speed.

Account, Data, Software, and Network Connection. In scalping, software with NASDAQ Level 2, SOES, Direct ECN access, and intraday tick charting capabilities is almost a necessity, especially in high-volume scalping. Access to the fastest real-time news also opens up numerous scalping opportunities.

Your connection to the market must be the fastest possible. Speed is important not only in your execution, but in receiving data as well. The decision-making process in scalping depends largely on the speed and accuracy of the data, as well as your ability to read the Bid and Ask scenarios and Prints (Time and Sales) and your ability to interpret the charts and any news that is affecting momentary order flow on a stock.

Competition. A crowded market has left little room for the novice scalper. Market Makers and Specialists can see order flow, and there are scalpers in this market who are literally in and out of a single stock 500 times a day (or more), equipped with the most cutting-edge technology. Would you like to compete with them? We often do. And awareness of their existence is part of your preparation.

Most Popular Indicator. There is no more frequently used indicator for scalping than the S&P 500 futures. Scalpers use the ticks on the S&P 500 futures to anticipate the momentary rush of order flow into a stock.

The Short Side Is Difficult. This is because of the uptick rule. While it is great that stocks fall faster than they rise, scalping the downward direction when the momentum has started is made purposely difficult by our regulators—all in the interest of protecting our markets. On downward momentum, those upticks are valuable commodities. Watch out for them, or take your shots at offering to go short on the Ask side (the only acceptable way to open short on a downtick).

The Small Risk Myth. Many people are attracted to scalping because one only incurs a small risk; for the same reasons people get attracted to trading options, because "your risk is limited to what you put in." The problem here is that a series of small risks adds up to one large risk. Add many small losses, commissions, and trading fees and you have for yourself quite a large risk to your capital. Hundreds of would-be day traders get burned by attempting to blanket the market with hundreds of small-risk trades. For those lucky enough to survive and acquire the necessary high-performance skills to scalp full-time, it probably costs tens of thousands in "learning" capital. What are your odds in excelling as a full-time scalper in a short period of time without investing tens of thousands of dollars in learning capital? Very slim. It will take a long time to learn.

Why Scalp?

We like the idea of cutting losses and getting in on momentum moves. If you are a full-time trader, build scalping into your game as a way to take small profits with limited risks. While most people are not suited to a scalping only technique, learning how to scalp gives you a great advantage in understanding price action details. The key is first to know where the highest probability is, and then to have the cutting-edge tools to take advantage of it. There was a time when scalping was as easy as buying MSFT or DELL as the S&P futures went up and shorting them as the S&P futures went down. The market has become so efficient that those who consistently profit from this type of trading are masters of order execution and have developed a truly great sense of order flow. It may take you a full year or more to mature as a full-time and consistently profitable scalper. The key is to be extremely selective in your scalps and not allow yourself to give in to the temptation (and the costs that go with it) to overtrade with frivolous in-and-out transactions. Slowly building scalping into your trading arsenal is a way to take advantage of the small price fluctuations that can be very rewarding in the long run as far as boosting profit potential and market feel are concerned.

Charts. Scalping is not all Level 2. Use charts to set a grid and for potential clues to direction. If you are going to use a chart to guide you in scalping the stock market, a good chart to use is a scaled intraday 2-day, 3-minute chart (or 3-day) that is linked to your stock window. Studying a two- or three-day intraday view will allow you to instantaneously visualize strategic short-term price areas that are very relevant to today's trading:

- today's high and low;
- the extent of any gaps, based on today's opening price and yesterday's closing price;
- yesterday's high and low; and
- yesterday's critical support or resistance areas.

Note that you must be able to view the chart in its entirety (scaled). In addition to being able to spot the critical short-term price areas very quickly, linking your chart to your stock box will let you know, immediately, if the stock has just experienced a major move before you typed the stock name. You may type the stock name and see from your quotes that there is momentum, and this may tempt you to jump in for a scalp. But failure to check back and see what the stock has done on the critical minutes before you pulled it into your Level 2 view may cause you to jump in on the final moments of a major move, when the price is ready to retrace from profit taking. Take the time to choose quality and well-selected trades for scalping. Your knowledge of the price levels the stock has just traded will be critical.

The Do's and Don'ts of Scalping

- **Master your order execution technique.** The speed of your order execution process can make the difference between your profitability or lack thereof.

- **Master the Bid-Ask-Prints scenarios.** Learn to identify momentum. On non-high-volume stocks, read the Market Makers and ECNs like you would count cards at the blackjack table. Their intentions are revealed by their behavior. On NASDAQ, keep a close eye on INCA, and for the size to buy or sell on the other ECNs. When the price is rising, is the Bid well supported? Are the Market Makers on the Ask retreating to higher prices or not? You must also ask yourself the opposite questions when the stock is heading down.

- **Know the trend.** Is the market strong or weak? Quite obviously, the majority of the profits are to be made on the longside in an up-trending market and vice versa. On downtrends the general rule is short the rallies. On uptrends, buy the dips. If you have a position on the opposite side of the trend, keep a tight stop.

- **Know where you are in the day.** Scalping is often poor in the middle of the day because of the market's tendency to trade in narrow ranges. Be aware, especially during the opening session, that the market can turn on a dime. Be aware that the closing session is more trendy (see Chapter 3).

- **Develop a feel for the market's momentary waves of buying and selling pressures.** You will confirm this by viewing the sequence of trades reported on your Level 2, and progression of the stock across different price levels.

- **Know whether a stock is acting strong or weak.** A stock that is positive for the day is not necessarily strong for trading today. A large gap could explain its positive status, but it may be actually trending down today, because it has become too expensive. Ask yourself whether the stock is trading above or below its opening price, yesterday's closing, and yesterday's high and low. Check the stock's relative strength—take note of how strong or weak its response is to the general market (S&P futures, the NDX, or NASDAQ composite) or to similar stocks within the same sector.

- **Watch the Time and Sales reports.** Keep in mind that the activity of the Bid and Ask does not always confirm price action. The Prints (or Time and Sales) confirm a price move in one direction or the other. Observe how aggressively the stock is trading by taking note of whether it is reporting a succession of trades at the Bid side (downward direction) or the Ask side (upward direction). Override trades, particularly groups of them, offer a strong clue as to how aggressively the market is willing to buy (above the current Ask) or willing to sell (below the Bid). (See Chapter 7.)

- **Get in and out like a thief in the night.** When the momentum has dried up and the trend is questionable, and you will know this, don't hang around. Adhere to your stop-loss and take quick profits while the momentum is still there.

- **Have a little bit of a difficult time getting in.** This confirms the momentum move. If you find that you have a difficult time getting executed to open a scalp trade, don't worry—that's a good problem! You are identifying the correct momentum. You have to work on identifying it earlier and improving your ability to pick up stock that is on the move (place the right orders). If you are buying on upward price action, don't be afraid to pay the Ask price (instead of Bidding on the Bid side or between the spread) and expect to have difficulty getting it. On the other hand, if you get stock too easily or get filled too quickly, you are probably about to face a tough scalp situation—as if someone has passed you a bomb with a burning fuse. In other words, if it looks too good to be true, it probably is.

- **Getting out should be a breeze.** Don't wait for the momentum to turn and join the herd in the panic to get rid of your position. A lot of money is lost that way. Use the momentum, and pass the bomb to someone else before it goes off in your hands. Leave the perfect tops and bottoms to the dreamers. Once in a while, you may get filled at the perfect top or bottom. Consider that a bonus for practicing good risk management.

- **Discipline! Discipline! Discipline!** Cut your losses; don't lose more than you intend to make. If you were intending to take a quarter profit, will you hold it one point against you? Remember that you would only have taken a quarter profit had the trade gone in your favor. Use logic. If it's getting scary, don't just stand there and let the gods of trading decide your fate, head for the hills! You can always try to get back in later if the situation warrants. Do not let losers get away from you especially on wide-spread stocks. This is the law!

- **Don't overtrade. Keep a close tab on your trading costs.** The temptation to overtrade is very high, and so is the cost of overtrading. Commissions, although small, add up very quickly. If you are not one hundred percent confident in your ability to consistently make money through scalping, start off slowly. The best scalpers take a very long time to mature and the market will make no exception for you. Look for quality in your scalps, based on the many factors we mention in this book.

■ **Learn to trade both sides of the market.** A short-side scalp is exhilarating. Although more tricky than long-side trades because of the uptick rule, stocks fall faster than they rise and as a result, you make money faster when you are right on a short-side scalp. You must take your profits faster too—short covering can be pretty violent.

■ **Don't be too biased to one direction or the other.** Let the market tell you what to do. If you feel that the market is going to head in a certain direction, try to analyze the factors that are going to prevent it from going in that direction. If the market reverses, you must be prepared to consciously take action or stay on the sidelines until you acquire a firm grasp on what is going on.

■ **Know basic technicals analysis.** While most scalps are based on Bid-Ask-Prints scenarios, this is not to say that you should forget the technicals. It is critical to know support and resistance levels of the stock for bouncing, breakout, or breakdown points. This includes when the stock is approaching common moving average points (10-, 20-, 50-, or 200-MAs) or whether the stock or market is developing a popular technical pattern such as double-tops, bottoms, head and shoulders, bearish engulfing pattern, etc. Your speed will be critical in helping you to respond to the follow-through on technicals. Keep an eye on those gaps too—not just the overnight gap, but perhaps a recent gap that as yet has been untraded.

  If your attention has been called to a stock you are pulling up on your screen for the first time today, are you checking to see what it has done prior to opening a position in it? What if it just moved seven points in the last three minutes? This is to say that you must track where the stock has come from. Do you know it can retrace four points faster than you can say "Hmmm, it appears that the stock is retracing. . ."? If you can't take the heat, stay out of the kitchen.

■ **Know the fundamentals.** If the stock is active, make an effort to know why it is active. If you interpret the fundamentals to mean that a stock can go higher, and you are not certain enough to take a position, scalp it on the next momentum move while keeping a tight stop. If news is breaking on an issue, how quickly can you interpret it? If you guess, the odds are against you. The stock can go in three directions: up, down or sideways. If you take a position randomly, you will be wrong two out of three times.

■ **Don't chase!** Track the progress of the price move. If the stock has moved several levels, you do not want to be the dunce—the last buyer before a pullback. If you have missed the opportunity, forget about it. There will be countless more. Keep in mind that the larger the price move, the more likely there will be a sharp pullback. You don't want to be caught on the wrong side. You may intend to have a tight stop, but this does not mean you will be able to get out in a panic retracement.

■ **Look for "good" volatility.** Avoid stocks with less than a point and a half to two points range for the day. The ideal volatility range is about three to five points. A range wider than five points can set up for some good trading, but can nevertheless be dangerous.

■ **Look for "good" volume.** This starts at around 500,000 usually; any less would make it increasingly difficult to transfer your stock. The higher the volume, the better. While it may be more difficult to pick up momentum stock on higher volumes (10 million or more), it is far easier to get hit on your Bids or Offers to get out if the momentum is still intact.

Spreads on stocks with lower liquidity can be vicious. Keep in mind that while 100,000 volume may be plenty compared to your 500- or 1,000-share trade, this volume is spread out over a six and a half hour period. In fact, it is also common to see that the majority of that volume is done on a few large block trades, and that the majority of the price change for the day can occur during a gap or a very short period of intraday time. These types of stocks are typically dormant for the majority of the trading day and, odds are, you will be a victim of the spread.

■ **Use your share size to compensate for risk.** The typical share size for scalping is 500 or 1,000, because any profits on lower share sizes are consumed by trading costs. On the other hand, increasing the share size would make a trade difficult to manage. While a highly skilled scalper can handle 3,000 shares with relative ease, avoid trying it if you have not developed the order execution speed needed to manage this size. This is particularly dangerous in high volatility situations—you can make a lot of money, but confront the downside. The rule of thumb is, decrease your share size when trading a stock that is demonstrating extreme volatility. You must always be aware of your share exposure and adjust accordingly to fit your risk–reward ratios. Using your share size to compensate for risks is an invaluable tool in trading.

■ **Never take home a scalp trade!** Take your profits or loss today and wait for tomorrow. Anticipating gaps is a whole different kind of game. There is no room for it in scalping.

Swing Trading

Our definition of swing trading is trading to take advantage of a trend or the reversal of a trend in a market or stock. This can last anywhere from about a half hour to overnight, or perhaps even a few days—so long as the trade or the market is demonstrating a positive response, and of course, is within your stop limits. Swing trading is different from scalp trading in that the trader is willing to stay with a trade as the price fluctuates. While scalp trades are quick in-and-outs only while the stock is in motion, swing trades weather the fluctuations to allow the trend to develop. The intensity of swing trading is nowhere near the intensity of scalping. In fact, it is often a real test of patience or, as one trader put it, "like watching grass grow." Make no mistake though; swing trades can be lethal when you are wrong, but extremely rewarding when you have made the right decision. Profits are larger and you are looking for "sticks" rather than the eighths or quarters. The high-velocity scalpers on the NASDAQ popularized the term "sticks" to signify a point winner. Except in the case of extreme volatility, it is not common to see a straight-line move by one point or more without any noise on the way. Scalpers who often shoot for the quarters are usually happy with that and will take profits on the way. This profit taking is a common reason for fluctuations in the stock price. The key in swing trading is to identify the bias—the trend—that lies beneath the fluctuations.

While the market always has a dominant trend, intraday trends and trend reversals are the target of the swing trader. What is terrific—and tricky—here is that the market does not commonly have one single trend for the day. The market usually experiences some sort of trend reversal within the day. The swing trader is constantly in search of these trend reversals to take advantage of price moves that are more than just momentary fluctuations caused by order flow. Keep an eye on shifts in intraday sentiment and on technical signals in order to get out of trades and get into new ones.

Our market indicators—the Dow Jones industrials, the S&P 500, and the NASDAQ composite—signify that the market is either up (by positive numbers) or down (by negative numbers). However, there is more than meets the eye within the confines of the intraday market. Active participants in the market know that the intraday trends may be different from what our indicators are telling us at first glance. Television may be reporting that the market is up today, but another look at the intraday trends in the market may signify down, probably meaning "down from the open." A skilled swing trader must be in tune with the best-odds direction of intraday trends in the market. The best tools in your arsenal are technical and fundamental analysis and your own experience. You must anticipate either a continuation or reversal of the intraday trend regardless of how the market is being hyped or downplayed in the media, or in your own trading environment. In a popular example that occurred in March of 1999, the market had opened for the first time above 10,000 on the Dow Jones industrials. The hype was all over the news and the exuberance that Friday morning was unbelievable. In fact, one analyst had been so bold as to come out on TV to declare that the Dow, for the first time, would undoubtedly close above 10,000 that day. While we built the exuberance into the scenario, our instincts, backed by our technical and fundamental evidence, told a different story. The market was frothy with gains in the previous periods. It appeared to be a perfect time to strike with a short position on the spiders (SPY, the S&P 500 index tracking stock), and begin tracking the progress of the weaklings for the day for possible swing short positions. On the gap-up that morning, one of us had shorted a half-size lot of the spiders with a tight stop in case the futures started rallying above the first half hour high point with momentum. If it did rally, that would be the signal to cover the short and go long looking for a small profit and then take another shot at a short position. The market followed through on the original short, and we added more as key support levels of the futures were violated. We also added more positions by shorting a few others on our weaklings list for that day—all swing trades anticipating a weak lunchtime period and another sell-off into the close to test the Dow 9,900 level. The market sold off all day long, with only one failed rally attempt after the midday period off a bounce on the 1,315 level in the futures. The market sold off even more in the closing period and the Dow in fact had closed a few points above the 9,900 level—100 points away from the exuberant predictions of the morning. What a difference a day of trading makes. While the media (and the bold analyst) were disappointed with the weak market, we locked in some good profits on the swing trades toward the close and went home with a small 500-share short position on the SPY. This was a classic swing trading day because of the trendy nature of the market. While it was also a great scalping day (shorting the rallies and the breakdowns), we were able to extract the entire extension of the sell-off, without having to incur the costs and potential loss of price extension from scalping.

Here are the factors to consider in swing trading:

- **Use the S&P 500 futures as a starting point.** Keep a close eye on its trends and check to see whether it is bullish or bearish for the day and for preceding sessions. Mark the key support and resistance areas, and take a look at different chart views. Watch the progression of trading during the critical times: the open and heading into the close, the last two hours of trading. The last hour, in particular, is when the market typically picks up steam, in part because trading in the 30-year T-bond futures has closed for the day. The activity can get very intense during this time.

- **Chart recent trends.** A good chart to identify recent potential plays and short-term trends is a scaled intraday 3-day, 5-minute chart cross-referenced to a 10-day, 15-minute chart. It is ideal to view the three- and ten-day periods in their entirety on one chart window. View the S&P 500 futures and then chart your targeted stocks. In scouting for swing trades, you may have to go through your stock list several times a day to check the progression of all your stocks, which may open new opportunities. Support and resistance levels, gaps, averages, and breaks on this chart scale are critical. Daily charts will also be key for sighting technical clues, especially the key moving averages, that are out of view for the 10-day chart. Identify the price points here, mark them, and draw lines if your software allows it. Know your support and resistance!

- **Know the fundamentals.** Because we are dealing with a longer time frame here, fundamentals come much more into play. Particularly watch out for news items that may be compelling enough to boost or break a trend (see Chapter 4).The key is to know that headlines or fundamentals may often be played out over a longer period of time—perhaps many hours, the whole day, overnight, or over a few days. When you have marked a stock for a potential swing trade, check its recent headlines. If any headlines are significant, try to estimate whether the stock has already been too extended to make any real response to that news. Keep in mind that your intraday swing play will most likely be a response to a technical signal; do not let fundamentals over-bias you.

- **Make a target list.** A good list to start with is the S&P 100, as well as the Nasdaq 100. Flip through the intraday 3-day, 10-day chart as well as daily charts of each one and segregate the strong from the weak. You will need to scan many times during the day as prices progress and charts reveal new patterns and potential targets that may have not been there a few hours ago. A skilled swing trader may literally flip through hundreds of charts in one day to find gem plays. If you are unsure of any pattern, ignore it and move on rather than force yourself to see something that is only in your imagination. A good pattern will jump out at you. It is tedious work and requires patience in looking for the gems among the dirt. Doing this will prepare you with targets so that you don't need to be fumbling for them while the trading day is in progress. Stocks that are the movers move fast and early, and often do not wait for latecomers. If the market is strong, target your strong stocks; if the market is weak, go for the weak ones. Pay particular attention to stocks that are near support or resistance, and that includes averages and trend breaks. If the market is not showing strength in either direction for the day, look for your stocks to bounce off support and resistance points. Conversely, if the market is trendy, look for breakouts and breakdowns from these support or resistance points in the direction that conforms to the trend. If you are playing the short side on a weak market, check in with your strong stocks to see how well or poorly they are holding up. This is to prepare you further for the strong period that will eventually come. *Make it a habit to constantly look forward, while internalizing what is happening in the present.*

If you have derived a target, adjust your expectations according to the scale of time and price of the chart. For example, if you found a pattern based on a 15-minute chart, it may take several 15-minute periods to follow through. In other words, if 20 minutes have gone by and you have not made money yet, be patient and use logic in your expectations. The same applies for the scales of price extension.

- **Look for volatility and liquidity.** As in scalping, the ideal daily volatility range is about two to five points. If the volatility is higher than normal, use your share size to compensate for the higher risks. Lower your usual share size when volatility range increases above four or five points.

  The desired liquidity for swing trading, however, is different from the ideal for scalping. We tend to ignore average liquidity of less than 200,000 to 300,000 shares.

- **Discipline! Discipline! Discipline!** Always set a stop-loss for all your swing trades. Stop-losses here are more often mental stop-losses beyond key support or resistance points more than anything else. Because swing trades provide a way to participate actively in the market, there is no need to reveal your intentions by giving away your stop-loss point to anyone else. Once you have set your stop-loss, adhere to it—this is where your discipline comes in. Stick to it, get out, accept your loss, and move on. The same goes for your entry point: If you decide to enter a trade because a stock is about to break out of a range, do not enter your swing trade until it does just that. If you take a technical approach, wait for technical confirmation in trading before you decide to participate. An entry point that is too early may mean that you will be the first one to lose money instead of the other way around. Being an early bird may actually work against you here.

- **Use trailing stops.** This is so you never let winners turn into losers. Once your trade has begun to move in the money, begin to trail your stop-loss behind it, moving it a notch for every movement the stock makes in your favor. If you trail it too tightly, though, it will turn into a scalp and you may lose the continuation. Give the stock some room to fluctuate as it follows through on the pattern. Use your scalping skills to get out with the momentum.

- **Don't get greedy.** Just because the stock has moved in your favor, that does not mean that you are making money. You haven't made money until your risk exposure is eliminated by closing out the trade. Take a look at how much the stock has moved in the day; if it has gone beyond or is close to its usual range, don't be afraid to take profit. Just as in scalping, use the momentum to your advantage by Offering out on the way up for long positions and Bidding in on the way down to cover short positions. The last thing you want to do is give up a lot of profit or pay the spread because you have waited for too much confirmation that the trend is over.

- **Scale in and out.** Scaling is a powerful tool in swing trading. The first entry point is usually a test, and you begin to add your exposure as the stock, still within target, moves in favor of your position. The key here is to make sure that the trend is intact and the market is following through on this trend. Use this in conjunction with trailing stops. Two or three entry points are typically enough. The same works for trade exit. When you have become very uncertain of the direction of a winning swing trade (it is always difficult to tell where the top is, especially for all-time highs), take at least half your position off the table, leaving a tight trailing stop-loss for the remaining exposure. If you are heavily exposed on any trade, be quick to pull the trigger on exiting to reduce the exposure in uncertain situations. This is so you can eliminate the possibility of any serious damage to your trading account. As a general rule for the inexperienced, do not add to losing positions either. Be defensive, winning trades will take care of themselves.

- **Overnights.** Swing trades do include, on occasion, taking overnight positions. The key here is to only take overnight positions that conform with the trend of the market and stock and are of limited share size. *Avoid taking home losing trades.* This is the law. Take home only winning trades and make sure the share exposure is not too large. The profits on the trade will help guard against the overnight risk—any gap in the wrong direction. You must realize that facts change very quickly overnight in the stock market. What you are trying to avoid is the painful loss of a large gap against you. Would you have liked to take home a long position on Oxford Health Plans, the high-flying Wall Street favorite, to find it gapped-down over 40 points and continuing to head down? While these types of gaps are not common, they do occur. Overnight gap plays can be very dangerous and are best left to the experienced.

If you are going to take home trades overnight, the best odds are in favor of the trend. In other words, it is preferable to take home overnight long positions on strong stocks in a bull market, and vice versa. In bull markets, be especially sensitive to stocks that are experiencing a breakout. These are more likely take-home candidates if the breakout is still shallow (meaning that it hasn't already made a large move recently). If there is a gap that has gone in your favor, it is usually a good idea to get rid of the position (or a portion) at the gap point and look to reopen it once the gap has been played out and the trend continues.

Because gaps can be very dangerous, leave no stone unturned. Make sure you are aware of any expected announcement prior to the opening. These headlines include, among others, earnings announcements (including earnings of key market players) and important economic data. Do you know, before you take a stock home overnight, that its biggest competitor is announcing earnings after the close? Surprisingly, many fail to look at these simple things that have a great effect on trading. Do your homework, and leave no loose ends.

Finally, while a strong close is ideal before taking home a winning trade for an overnight play, avoid taking home a stock whose price has been too extended today or in the last few days. Lock in your hard-earned profits (or a portion) while they are still there today.

Core Trading

In core trading, you are testing your skills at being a supreme stock picker. Our definition of core trading however, does not conform to the traditional definition that signifies long-term holds for investment that last many years. Our definition of core trades is simple: trades that take advantage of the dominant trend of the market. This is not investment—perhaps just short of it—but because we define an investor as one who has confidence in a company's ability to grow or pay dividends over a long period of time, our core trades are not investment-type. Rather, these are trades that take advantage of a large and impending move in the stock price based on combined solid technical and fundamental evidence. Our confidence, unlike that of an investor, is limited to the follow-through of the price move and nothing else. If it fails, the position is eliminated. Because larger price moves take a longer period of time to develop, our core trades tend to last from a few days to several weeks. This is solely dependent upon two things: that the dominant trend of the price move is still intact, and that general market conditions suit the expected direction of the trade.

The volatility in today's markets has made room for a perceptive trader to take advantage of large price moves in a shorter span of time. The speculation that surrounds the technology sector in particular has made for strong price extensions that historically had taken much longer periods of time—many months, or often years—for other types of stocks to develop. There is too much opportunity in many of these price extensions to ignore. This is the primary goal of our core trading: to extract the entire extension of large price moves to supplement (or hedge) our scalp and swing trading.

The secondary goal in our core trades is to hold positions that help us keep in tune with the overall progression of the market. Our open core positions help us develop a solid feel for the dominant trend and coax us to look forward. This type of big-picture market feel is indispensable to our day trading.

Here are the key factors in core trading:

- **Core trade psychology is different.** You are looking at a longer period of time. If you are taking advantage of a larger price move, it may take a longer period of time with more price fluctuations and more psychological fluctuations. You must adhere to the overall technicals and fundamentals. One of the primary reasons for core trading, besides monetary gain, is to teach the active day trader to stay in tune with the overall perspective and stay detached from too much intraday noise. In other words, panic less and think more.

- **Keep a separate account for your core trades.** The reason for this is twofold. First, if you are actively trading, it will be difficult to keep track of your intraday trades if executions and costs are mixed up with profits or losses for the day on your core trades. Remember that you will be checking your executions and trading costs on a daily basis. If these are commingled with profits and losses on open core positions, reconciling your intraday trading profits, losses, and costs will be more tedious or, worse yet, subject to error.

The second reason is less practical, but more psychological. Keeping your open core positions constantly in front of you can cause you to lose your overall perspective on the core trade in favor of the microviews of the intraday market and the panic and excitement that go with them. In other words, watching every teenie of your open core position may drive you to prematurely exit a good trade—especially when you are facing tough and unprofitable intraday situations or when the market is selling off in a strong way. Doing this will probably drive you crazy as well. Keeping a separate account for your core trades highlights the different objective and psychological criteria that you set for these positions.

- **Know the dominant trend.** Take one look at the market. It can only be in one of three positions: up, down, or sideways. If the dominant trend of the market is up (bullish), where and when did it originate? Check the daily and weekly charts of the S&P 500, the S&P 500 futures, the NASDAQ composite, and of course, the Dow Jones industrials. The uptrend is simple: buy pullbacks and buy breakouts. The downtrend is the opposite: short rallies and short breakdowns. The sideways market is building in uncertainty; keep tighter stops here, and take smaller profits.

- **Know your relative strength.** No, not the RSI (the Relative Strength Index); but if the market is coming out of a bear phase, look for stocks that performed well during the bear phase and are breaking out of a range. These are potential targets for when the market enters a bullish period. This is not to say that a normally strong stock that has sold off simply due to bad overall market situations should be ignored. Quite commonly, the strongest stocks are the last to sell off in a bad market, and their sell-off may in fact signify a market bottom.

- **Bottom picking.** Bottom picking is quite tricky. Remember that in doing this, you are violating the "don't buck the trend" rule. There is a reason why some stocks are at the bottom. The likelihood for many stocks that have demonstrated weakness (especially when they are quick to sell off in bad market situations) to shoot up anytime in the near future is probably poor. In core trading, as in scalp or swing trading, buy the strong and sell the weak. If you are bottom picking, your risks are higher. At least wait for a little bit of confirmation that the stock is holding and rising above a bottom. Blindly buying something that looks cheap is usually a mistake; it probably will be cheaper soon. Why don't you buy it then? Adhere to the technical definitions of trend and manage your risks accordingly.

- **Know the technicals.** The best charts for core trading are the daily and weekly charts. Keep a very close tab on major and minor support and resistance levels, moving averages, trends in volume, and retracement numbers (Chapter 6). Set your stop-losses based on these (along with very unfavorable news) and do not ignore them. The technicals will often give you clues before fundamentals do. Do not argue with your technical analysis. The fundamentals may be telling you that everything is intact, but when your stock is selling off or not rallying along with the rest, there is usually good reason.

- **Know the fundamentals.** While there is no arguing with technicals, fundamentals are very much in play in core trading. A solid trend is usually accompanied by strong fundamentals. Look out for significant news that can throw a wrench in the dominant trend. The key is to cross-reference your technical skills with your fundamental skills, and have check marks on both.

- **Keep wider stops.** It is impossible to consistently risk one-eighth of a point to make ten or fifteen points. Adjust your risk-to-reward ratios and set your stops and exit points based on key support or resistance levels on daily or weekly charts.

- **Keep your bets small.** If you are shooting for a large price move, confront the potential downside. If you want to have a large position, add to it as the trade goes in your favor. If you have a small initial position and the stock has pulled against you, you can exit with minimal damage. If you have jumped on the correct trend, you will be surprised at how much a host of small positions can earn.

- **Keep an eye on technology-related issues.** The large price moves are found in this sector. In picking the best winners of our time, the odds are that they were all technology related.

- **Know your stock.** Make sure you understand the nature of the stock you are taking a position in. In core trades, fundamentals are in play and lack of familiarity with the stock's fundamentals may negatively affect your performance here. Core trades require much more research than scalp or swing trades. Do your homework and plan carefully.

  Inexperienced traders are often lulled into buying a stock that they have never heard of because it came in as a tip or rumor or even to copy an experienced trader's position. Make your own educated decisions, because the risk you are taking will be your own, for better or for worse. The wise words of Warren Buffet apply here too: "Know what you buy."

- **Be precise in your entry and exit points.** While commissions are not as much of a factor here as in intraday trading, your precise entry and exit points are. If you are planning to take a core position on a stock today, keep an eye on the trading for the day. Your knowledge of intraday price swings will help you tremendously. Perhaps you may be able to pick up the stock slightly cheaper if the momentum is down. In addition, what if the market is demonstrating evidence that a sell-off is coming (or a rally, if you will sell)? Even if you are core trading, execution prices are critical when taken collectively, as discussed in Chapter 7. If you have only six executions a month that waste a quarter each, even for small, 300-share lots, you will have wasted over $5,000 by the end of the year.

- **Take quicker profits on the short side.** As discussed previously, stocks sell off quicker than they rise. If you have a core short trade, be very attuned to the down days—these are most likely the days you will be covering your short position. Bounces caused by short-covering and bottom picking in a bear market are vicious. You don't want to be caught trying to cover in these periods; the result may be a loss of a large chunk of profits. Just as in scalping, your short core positions should be covered with ease, while the momentum is down.

- **Don't buck the trend, but most of all, never short a rising market.** No matter that you can't accept the fact that everyone is making money on the long side except yourself. Bucking the trend is a financially painful and potentially self-destructing experience. Taking a position against a stock solely because "it has gone up too much" is for dunces. Many inexperienced day traders have liquidated their trading capital this way, especially on hot stocks. Your core trades are taken to profit from a large price move before it takes place, not after. Note also that most of the money to be made from a strong trend is on the correct side of it, not playing against it. Once the trend has been played out, put your efforts, and your money, into another day. Your best trades are always ahead of you.

A Dynamic Approach

The term *day trader* connotes that our trades are opened and closed within the same day. While this holds true for the large majority of our activities, our awareness of the market in all senses is heightened by our active participation in all types of price movement. Be it a 15-second scalp trade, an overnight swing trade, or an 8-week core trade, countless opportunities for profits abound in the stock market. Be aware of and make use of these opportunities. It will be a great advantage for you.

The value of the lessons learned—both good and bad—from studying and participating in price movement in all scales of time and price is an important aspect of day trading. Your learning curve in trading will never end. Exposing yourself to learn from the market as a whole, rather than approaching it with too many restrictions, accelerates that learning curve. Be patient and flexible in your approach, adjust your expectations according to correct scales of time and price, and learn at a pace you are comfortable with. Define every trade before you enter it. You will constantly polish your skills and style to suit the market conditions. That is a dynamic approach to the challenging tides of a dynamic market.

9
Scalp Trade Examples

In the stock market, scalping is a trading technique that profits from small price fluctuations. Because there are numerous price movements and retracements, even within a short-term trend, this technique can be rewarding for a disciplined day trader. Think of scalping as coins littered on a street in the path of an oncoming bulldozer. How quickly you can get in and out of the bulldozer's way while picking up as much change as possible determines your bread and butter for the day. However, if you get too greedy and can't get out fast enough, you will get run over by the approaching bulldozer of the market. This is where discipline and risk management allow the agile day trader to exit as soon as the momentum shifts the other way. At the same time, it takes confidence to step into the path of the oncoming bulldozer without freezing up like a deer caught in front of approaching headlights.

There are many different types of scalping, depending on the time frame, the market conditions, and the risk–reward relationships involved with different spreads on a stock. For example, a stock that has a $1/2$-point spread between the Bid and the Ask will involve a different technique, or indications to look for, than a stock that has a much narrower spread. However, one criterion remains the same: Don't let any losers get away from you. Most people do not trade recklessly, and they all have the same intention of trading for a profit while cutting losses quickly. It only takes one moment of frenzy and carelessness for a trade to turn into a disaster. Avoiding disaster requires constant risk management and control. Too often, a novice trader will enter a trade to scalp a quick $1/4$ point, but when the trade turns in the other direction the trader decides to hold on to the losing trade as a position for a longer-term trade. Most of these positions will retrace back, but it only takes one of these "positions" to turn into a nightmare. Never risk more than the intended profit potential.

In scalping, understanding price action is critical to developing a gut instinct or "feel" for the market and the momentum that results from a rush of order flow. This degree of intuition takes experience and some trial and error. However, starting with small share sizes will help reduce the cost of learning. Developing this style of trading can be rewarding, and you can keep losses to a minimum. Traders who attempt to scalp should have access to a NASDAQ Level 2 screen and the fastest equipment and connection available, because the speed of execution is critical to a trader's chance of success.

The examples of scalping presented here involve varying degrees of risk–reward, time frame, and scalping techniques. In every case, scalping for a quick in-and-out profit requires precision and speed. A good day trader should be able to execute different types of orders like they were extensions of your thoughts. Practice to the point of automatic reflex, because the last thing you want to do is hesitate over which order to send while the trade is ripping against you.

Example 1: Pacificare (PHSYB)

On February 22, 1999, Pacificare reported earnings of $1.21 per share, after the close of the market, beating the analysts' average forecast of $1.14 per share. The following morning, PHSYB ("fizibee") opened up 2 points (dollars per share) and continued to trade strongly even though the market sold off after the release of Greenspan's text of testimony to be given before the Senate Banking Committee. As PHSYB continued to grind higher, we looked for a point at which the momentum from a rush of order flow would allow for a quick scalp. Normally, PHSYB has a wide spread and scalping it is difficult. On this day, however, volume was high and the earnings announcement attracted many buyers, thus narrowing the spread and giving us a chance to scalp without the normally huge risk of a wide spread.

As PHSYB approached 73, there were many sellers getting out in front of the round number around $72\frac{3}{4}$ to 72 15/16. SHWD had held the stock at $72\frac{7}{8}$ even with an Instinet (INCA) Bid at 72 5/8 (Figure 9-1). With SHWD leaving the Ask, we looked for the first print at 73 to jump in with a SOES at market order and a SelectNet Preference to GSCO at 73. Our risk, if we were wrong about the breakout, was $\frac{3}{8}$ of a point by hitting the INCA Bid at $72\frac{5}{8}$ (Figure 9-2). We bought 1,000 shares at 73, anticipating that the sellers in front of 73 would buy back the shares once the breakout was confirmed. If we had missed the 73's, we would have cancelled our order because the opportunity would have been missed. Taking a higher price level, while not knowing if the Bids would continue to come in strong, would mean a wider spread and a higher risk for a smaller return. GSCO confirmed our anticipation of a

NSDQ: PHSYB								
BID			**ASK**			**T&S**		
MM ID	*Price*	*Size*	*MM ID*	*Price*	*Size*	*Price*	*Size*	
INCA	72 5/8	10	SHWD	72 3/8	10	72 7/8	1	
ISLD	72 1/2	4	MSCO	73	10	72 5/8	15	
MASH	72 3/16	1	GSCO	73	10	72 5/8	10	
MONT	72	1	COWN	73	1	72 7/8	1	
SLKC	71 15/16	1	PWJC	73	2	72 13/16	4	
FBCO	71 7/8	1	SELZ	73	1	72 13/16	4	
MWSE	71 7/8	1	WARR	73	1	72 3/4	5	
SBSH	71 3/4	1	FBCO	73	1	72 3/4	1	
LEHM	71 3/4	1	ISLD	73	1	72 3/4	1	
MLCO	71 1/2	1	BTAB	72 1/8	1	72 3/4	1	

Figure 9-1. PHSYB scalp sequence 1.

NSDQ: PHSYB								
BID			**ASK**			**T&S**		
MM ID	*Price*	*Size*	*MM ID*	*Price*	*Size*	*Price*	*Size*	
INCA	72 5/8	10	GSCO	73	10	73	1	
ISLD	72 1/2	4	COWN	73	1	72 7/8	1	
MASH	72 3/16	1	PWJC	73	1	72 5/8	15	
MONT	72	1	FBCO	73	1	72 5/8	10	
MSCO	72	10	BTAB	73 1/8	1	72 7/8	1	
SELZ	72	1	MASH	73 1/8	1	72 13/16	4	
SLKC	71 15/16	1	OLDE	73 1/4	1	72 13/16	4	
FBCO	71 7/8	1	NITE	73 1/4	10	72 3/4	5	
SBSH	71 3/4	1	SHWD	73 1/4	1	72 3/4	1	
LEHM	71 3/4	1	DLJP	73 7/16	10	72 3/4	1	

Figure 9-2. PHSYB scalp sequence 2.

breakout (Figure 9-3) by jumping from the Ask to the Bid at $73\frac{1}{8}$, while trades were printing on the Ask and some even higher on an override (trades occurring at a higher price than the posted Ask price—the trail of desperate buyers seeking to buy at higher prices to ensure a purchase). Notice that DLJP and ISLD jumped on the Ask at $73\frac{3}{16}$, as the stock was running, to take profits early and to stop the momentum. However, the strength of the break-out, as evidenced by the prints at $73\frac{1}{2}$, overcame the Ask at $73\frac{3}{16}$ and took them out. We held on to the trade as long as the momentum continued to be strong throughout the higher prices. When the stock hit 74 the Bid was only $73\frac{3}{8}$ and the Ask was full of sellers at 74. Because many buyers up to 74 were

| NSDQ: PHSYB | | | | | | | |
| BID | | | ASK | | | T&S | |
MM ID	*Price*	*Size*	*MM ID*	*Price*	*Size*	*Price*	*Size*
GSCO	73 1/8	10	DLJP	73 3/16	10	73 1/2	7
ISLD	73 1/8	15	ISLD	73 3/16	5	73 7/16	6
REDI	73	5	MLCO	73 1/2	1	73 1/2	7
INCA	72 7/8	20	SBSH	73 1/2	10	73 7/16	1
BTAB	72 5/8	1	SHWD	73 1/2	1	73 3/8	1
MASH	72 3/16	1	RSSF	73 5/8	1	73 3/8	1
MWSE	72 1/8	1	CANT	73 3/4	1	73 3/8	1
MONT	72	1	NITE	73 3/4	10	73 3/8	1
MSCO	72	10	FBCO	73 3/4	1	73	10
SELZ	72	1	MONT	74	10	73 1/4	1

Figure 9-3. PHSYB scalp sequence 3.

probably willing to take profit at this point, we offered our 1,000 shares out at $73^{15}/_{16}$ on the Ask through ISLD and got taken immediately for a $937.50 profit before commissions (Figure 9-4). Although the stock could have continued to run a little more before the momentum stalled, we wanted to take our profit while the momentum was on our side. Had the momentum stopped at 74, we would not have been able to sell at the Ask side. We would have had to dump it on the Bid at $73^3/_8$, costing us $^5/_8$ of a point spread (or more than half of our profit) to get out. To guarantee that we would sell at the Ask, we discounted the stock by $^1/_{16}$ in order to beat our competitors at 74. In addition, S&P futures had made an intraday double top and was heading down, thus shifting much of the momentum in stocks to the downside. Because the spread between the Bid and the Ask is much wider than on high-volume stocks, scalping in this type of wide-spread stocks takes a much higher degree of precision. The risk if you are wrong involves hitting the Bid right away before the Bid leaves, because price levels are very shallow. In addition, exiting the position with momentum versus hitting the Bid after the momentum reverses could mean the difference between a good profit and a small or even no profit. Stocks like these don't move enough for a good scalp very often, so day traders should be very selective when attempting to scalp these stocks. When they do move, precise timing is of utmost importance to take advantage of the price move. Remember that the most important thought in your mind when entering this type of trade is not how much money you will make, but where the Bid is if you have to get out because the momentum shifted suddenly. Knowing how and when to get out if you are wrong will give you more confidence to enter risky trades than just having made money on a few lucky trades.

| NSDQ: PHSYB | | | | | | | |
| BID | | | ASK | | | T&S | |
MM ID	Price	Size	MM ID	Price	Size	Price	Size
ISLD	73 3/8	22	ISLD	73 15/16	10	73 5/8	2
GSCO	73 1/8	10	MWSE	74	2	74	1
REDI	73	5	MONT	74	10	74	1
SBSH	73	10	SHWD	74	10	74	1
SELZ	73	1	MLCO	74	1	74	2
BTAB	72 5/8	1	PWJC	74	2	73 7/8	1
INCA	72 5/8	10	FBCO	74 1/4	1	73 3/4	1

Figure 9-4. PHSYB scalp sequence 4.

Example 2: Novellus (NVLS)

On Friday, February 12, 1999, the market had been selling off but NVLS could not break the 66's on the down side. So when NVLS traded its way up to 67, we looked for a rally once the S&P futures retraced back up near the end of the day, anticipating some short covering (short sellers buying back the stock) before the weekend. Once sellers at $66\frac{3}{4}$ and $\frac{7}{8}$ were cleared and GSCO jumped on the Bid at $66\frac{13}{16}$ (Figure 9-5), we looked for the first print at 67 and sent a SOES market buy order. We opened long 1,000 shares at 67, with risk of selling at $66\frac{13}{16}$ Bid if we were wrong about the oncoming breakout. Eventually, not only did the 67's clear, but ISLD jumped on the Bid at $67\frac{1}{16}$ while the prints showed trades at $67\frac{1}{4}$, despite MSCO still on the Ask at $67\frac{3}{16}$, indicating overrides (Figure 9-6). Because NVLS had not been moving very fast throughout the day, we were not sure whether the $67\frac{1}{4}$ would clear. So we sold half (500 shares) at $67\frac{1}{4}$ and held the rest to 68. We sold the other half at 68, for a profit of $625 altogether. By selling half of the position for a profit when we were uncertain, we mitigated the risk, while allowing the balance to trade out the noise. Even if the other half went against us and we were stopped out for a flat or small loss, we would have made money on the first half, and therefore, not all would be lost.

After touching $68\frac{1}{8}$, NVLS pulled back to $67\frac{1}{2}$, then made its way back to $68\frac{1}{8}$. Once the $68\frac{1}{8}$ cleared and INCA jumped to the Bid at $68\frac{1}{8}$ (Figure 9-7), we bought 1,000 shares at $68\frac{1}{4}$ through ISLD (which we had the order set to in anticipation, so that all we had to do to send the order was hit "enter"). This time, our risk was $\frac{1}{8}$ point if we were wrong, since the spread was only $\frac{1}{8}$. At $68\frac{1}{2}$, ISLD constantly popped in at $68\frac{1}{2}$ after being taken again and again (Figure 9-8). We too sold at 68½ by offering on ISLD, because a shift in momentum could mean losing the Bid at 68¼ and maybe even GSCO at 68³⁄₁₆. The last thing we wanted was to be stuck with a flat trade after having had the opportunity to take a $250 profit.

This example shows how a stock that cannot go down in a weak market is showing strength. We anticipated that a shift in market sentiment at the end of the day would give NVLS a chance to rally. Our timing and precision came from recognizing a good entry point and assessing the risk if we were wrong. You must never anticipate a market move and get into a position without also anticipating how to get out if the market proves you wrong.

NSDQ: NVLS							
BID			ASK			T&S	
MM ID	*Price*	*Size*	*MM ID*	*Price*	*Size*	*Price*	*Size*
GSCO	66 13/16	10	SLKC	67	1	67	1
ISLD	66 13/16	10	COWN	67	1	66 7/8	6
INCA	66 3/4	5	PERT	67	4	66 7/8	5
LEHM	66 5/8	1	NFSC	67	10	66 7/8	2
ADAM	66 1/4	1	TNTO	67	4	66 7/8	5
HMQT	66 1/8	1	HRZG	67	1	66 3/4	7
MONT	66 1/8	10	MONT	67	10	66 3/4	1
MSCO	66	1	NITE	67	1	66 3/4	1
WARR	66	1	WARR	67 1/8	1	66 3/4	10
NITE	66	1	MSCO	67 3/16	10	66 3/4	1

Figure 9-5. NVLS scalp sequence 1.

NSDQ: NVLS							
BID			ASK			T&S	
MM ID	*Price*	*Size*	*MM ID*	*Price*	*Size*	*Price*	*Size*
ISLD	67 1/16	10	MSCO	67 3/16	10	67 1/4	3
REDI	67	10	PRUS	67 1/4	1	67 1/4	1
GSCO	66 13/16	10	ADAM	67 1/4	1	67 1/4	1
BTRD	66 13/16	1	NITE	67 1/4	2	67 3/16	1
INCA	66 3/4	10	SLKC	67 1/4	1	67	1
LEHM	66 5/8	1	TNTO	67 1/4	2	67	1
WARR	66 5/8	1	HRZG	67 1/4	1	67	10
FBCO	66 3/8	2	BTRD	67 1/4	1	67	3
ADAM	66 1/8	1	ISLD	67 1/4	26	67	1
HMQT	66 1/8	1	INCA	67 5/16	17	67	10

Figure 9-6. NVLS scalp sequence 2.

NSDQ: NVLS							
BID			ASK			T&S	
MM ID	*Price*	*Size*	*MM ID*	*Price*	*Size*	*Price*	*Size*
INCA	68 1/8	10	COWN	68 1/4	1	68 1/4	1
ISLD	68 1/8	1	AANA	68 1/4		68 3/16	1
DLJP	67 7/8	10	RSSF	68 1/4	10	68 3/16	2
GSCO	67 3/4	10	SLKC	68 1/4		68 3/16	5
HRZG	67 3/4	1	PERT	68 1/4	2	68 1/8	6
ADAM	67 5/8	3	MASH	68 1/4	29	68 1/8	3
FBCO	67 1/2	1	ISLD	68 1/4	10	68 1/8	1
MONT	67 1/2	1	OLDE	68 5/16	2	68	10
WARR	67 3/8	1	PRUS	68 3/8	1	68	20
MLCO	67 1/4	2	MONT	68 3/8	10	68 1/6	2

Figure 9-7. NVLS scalp sequence 3.

NSDQ: NVLS							
BID			ASK			T&S	
MM ID	*Price*	*Size*	*MM ID*	*Price*	*Size*	*Price*	*Size*
ISLD	68 1/4	10	ISLD	68 1/2	14	68 1/4	1
GSCO	68 3/16	10	ADAM	68 9/16	1	68 1/2	10
FBCO	68	2	SWST	68 5/8	1	68 1/4	10
RSSF	68	1	WARR	68 5/8	10	68 1/2	10
DLJP	67 7/8	12	NITE	68 5/8	5	68 1/4	1
HRZG	67 3/4	3	MWSE	68 5/8	2	68 1/2	10
MLCO	67 5/8	1	BTRD	68 11/16	5	68 1/2	2
HMQT	67 5/8	10	NFSC	68 3/4	4	68 1/2	3
COWN	67 9/16	1	MONT	68 3/4	10	68 1/4	6
MASH	67 1/2	1	SBSH	68 3/4	10	68 1/2	3

Figure 9-8. NVLS scalp sequence 4.

Example 3: Intuit (INTU)

On Friday, February 26, 1999, Intuit (INTU) gapped up at the open to 93 and change due to a favorable earnings report the night before. INTU was expected to report $1.30 per share earnings, but it came in at $1.34 per share. On this day it showed strength at the open, but eventually traded down due to the continuing sell-off in the tech sector. However, INTU never got below the previous day's high of $90\frac{1}{2}$ to 91 level. Again, this stock showed strength in a down market, and we anticipated a rally if the sentiment in the market were to shift to the upside. That opportunity came toward the end of the day as some short-sellers began to cover their shorts going into the weekend.

As INTU slowly traded its way back to the opening price of 93, we looked for a point where a breakout might occur. Prior to reaching 93, we noticed that there were many sellers at $92\frac{3}{4}$ and $\frac{7}{8}$ with GSCO holding the Ask at $92\frac{7}{8}$, even with ISLD Bidding at $92\frac{3}{4}$ (Figure 9-9). Although our risk was only $\frac{1}{8}$ point if we were wrong, we didn't buy the $92\frac{7}{8}$ from GSCO because our reward was also only $\frac{1}{8}$, and we would have to compete with other sellers at 93. Furthermore, we didn't know if GSCO had a big order or size to sell at $92\frac{7}{8}$, because it was holding the Ask at the moment. However, as soon as GSCO left the Ask, we knew that this was the opportunity we were waiting for. The buyers had cleared all the sellers at $92\frac{3}{4}$ to $92\frac{7}{8}$ and the sellers would now try to buy back the shares if a breakout occurred. We waited for one print at 93, then sent a SOES market buy order and a SelectNet Preference order to INCA (Figure 9-10). We were fortunate to have bought 1,000 shares, because the rush of order flow was so great that a split-second hesitation would have caused us to miss the 93's. INTU cleared all the levels up to $94\frac{1}{8}$ in a matter of seconds, as the rush of orders kept the demand strong throughout the rally. We sold our 1,000 shares at 94 for a profit of $1,000 by offering on ISLD on the Ask side at 94, while the momentum was in our favor.

The reason we sold early on the initial breakout was that experience has taught us that the initial breakouts usually attract sellers as the buyers during the consolidation take profits with the breakout. It turns out that others felt the same way we did, because INTU hit $94\frac{1}{8}$ before retracing back

NSDQ: INTU							
BID			ASK			T&S	
MM ID	*Price*	*Size*	*MM ID*	*Price*	*Size*	*Price*	*Size*
ISLD	92 3/4	10	GSCO	92 7/8	10	92 7/8	1
HRZG	92 5/8	1	WARR	93	1	92 7/8	10
INCA	92 9/16	10	PERT	93	1	92 7/8	10
FBCO	92 1/2	1	NFSC	93	2	92 7/8	10
MASH	92 1/4	10	SWST	93	3	92 3/4	1
MLCO	92	1	SLKC	93	1	92 3/4	1
PWJC	92 9/16	1	INCA	93	10	92 5/8	10
BTRD	92 3/8	1	HRZG	93	2	92 5/8	10
GSCO	92 3/8	10	BTRD	93	1	92 5/8	1
MONT	91 1/4	1	MADF	93 1/16	5	92 5/8	1

Figure 9-9. INTU scalp sequence 1.

NSDQ: INTU							
BID			ASK			T&S	
MM ID	*Price*	*Size*	*MM ID*	*Price*	*Size*	*Price*	*Size*
ISLD	92 3/4	10	WARR	93	1	93	3
HRZG	92 5/8	1	INCA	93	10	93	2
INCA	92 9/16	10	BTRD	93	1	93	1
FBCO	92 1/2	1	RSSF	93	1	93	3
MASH	92 1/4	10	SLKC	93	10	93	2
MLCO	92	1	MADF	93 1/16	5	93	1
PWJC	92 9/16	1	SHWD	93 3/16	5	93	1
BTRD	92 3/8	1	MONT	93 1/4	1	92 7/8	1
GSCO	92 3/8	10	MLCO	93 1/4	1	92 7/8	10
MONT	91 1/4	1	FBCO	93 3/8	2	92 7/8	10

Figure 9-10. INTU scalp sequence 2.

NSDQ: INTU							
BID			ASK			T&S	
MM ID	*Price*	*Size*	*MM ID*	*Price*	*Size*	*Price*	*Size*
ISLD	94 1/2	10	INCA	94 3/4	10	95	2
FBCO	94 3/8	1	MSCO	95	10	94 15/16	1
SLKC	94 1/4	1	MONT	95	10	94 15/16	2
INCA	94 1/4	5	SWST	95	2	94 15/16	1
BTRD	94 1/16	1	MADF	95	1	94 15/16	2
JPMS	93 1/2	1	MLCO	95	10	94 7/8	1
NITE	93 3/8	10	AANA	95	1	94 7/8	1
HRZG	93 1/4	1	HRZG	95	1	94 7/8	1
MONT	93	1	SHWD	95 3/16	1	94 7/8	1
GSCO	93	10	WARR	95 3/16	1	94 7/8	5

Figure 9-11. INTU scalp sequence 3.

to 93$\frac{1}{4}$, finding support there. Then, as INTU worked its way back up, we waited patiently for another breakout. Our opportunity came at 95. INTU traded back up to 94$\frac{3}{4}$ with constant jiggles as traders took profits all the way up (and possibly even some short-sellers). When ISLD got on the Bid at 94$\frac{1}{2}$ with INCA on the Ask at 94$\frac{3}{4}$ (Figure 9-11), we noticed a print of 95. This could not have been a late print since INTU never hit 95 this day. So we tried to buy the 94$\frac{3}{4}$ from INCA, but it was too late. INCA was taken before we even sent the order in, and had cleared. Immediately, 95's were printing, and we jumped in with a SOES market buy order and a SelectNet

Preference to INCA at 95 (Figure 9-12). We finally got 1,000 shares at 95 before all the 95's cleared. This time, however, we decided to let the trade ride to the close as long as INTU didn't pull too far back. We had already locked in $1,000 in profit from the previous trade, so we set a mental stop at $94\frac{1}{2}$ (half of our previous profit) and let the position ride. INTU almost triggered our stop as it traded from $95\frac{3}{4}$ down to $94\frac{3}{4}$, but the Bid at $94\frac{3}{4}$ never left so we sat with our hands on the keyboard, ready to hit the sell, but never had to execute our mental stop.

NSDQ: INTU							
BID			ASK			T&S	
MM ID	*Price*	*Size*	*MM ID*	*Price*	*Size*	*Price*	*Size*
ISLD	94 13/16	9	MONT	95	10	95	1
FBCO	94 3/4	1	SWST	95	3	95	6
SLKC	94 3/4	1	MADF	95	1	95	5
INCA	94 3/4	5	MLCO	95	10	95	2
JPMS	94 1/2	1	AANA	95	1	94 15/16	1
NITE	94 3/8	10	INCA	95	10	94 15/16	2
BTRD	94 3/8	10	BTRD	95 1/16	3	94 15/16	1
HRZG	94 1/4	1	SHWD	95 3/16	1	94 15/16	2
MONT	93	1	NITE	95 1/4	10	94 7/8	1
GSCO	93	10	ISLD	95 1/4	10	94 7/8	1

Figure 9-12. INTU scalp sequence 4.

NSDQ: INTU							
BID			ASK			T&S	
MM ID	*Price*	*Size*	*MM ID*	*Price*	*Size*	*Price*	*Size*
ISLD	99 1/2	10	INCA	99 1/2	20	99 1/2	1
FBCO	99 3/8	1	GSCO	100	1	99 1/2	2
SWST	99 3/8	1	WARR	100	1	100	7
MONT	99 1/8	1	MWSE	100	200	100	2
MASH	99 1/8	5	BRUT	100	1	100	1
MLCO	98 1/4	1	SLKC	100	1	100	1
WARR	98	1	SBSH	100	11	99 7/8	5
PWJC	97 15/16	1	MONT	100 1/8	1	99 7/8	5
MADF	97 1/2	2	FBCO	100 3/8	1	99 7/8	5
RSSF	97 1/8	1	BTAB	100 3/8	1	100	1

Figure 9-13. INTU scalp sequence 6.

NSDQ: INTU								
BID			ASK			T&S		
MM ID	*Price*	*Size*	*MM ID*	*Price*	*Size*	*Price*	*Size*	
MONT	99 1/4	10	INCA	99 5/16	10	99 1/4	2	
ISLD	99	15	ISLD	99 5/16	15	99 5/16	2	
FBCO	98 5/8	1	REDI	99 3/8	3	99 1/4	3	
BTRD	98 5/8	1	BTRD	99 3/8	1	99 1/4	7	
MLCO	98 1/2	1	PWJC	99 1/2	1	99 5/16	1	
SWST	98 3/8	1	MASH	99 3/4	1	99 1/4	2	
NFSC	98 1/8	1	DEAN	100	2	99 5/16	6	
MASH	98 1/8	2	SBSH	100	6	99 5/16	1	
AANA	98 1/8	1	SWST	100	1	99 5/16	6	
JPMS	98	1	BRUT	100	2	99 1/4	8	

Figure 9-14. INTU scalp sequence 7.

Eventually, INTU traded all the way up to 100 that day. As the buyers started to take out 100, INCA popped in at 99½ on the Ask, locking the market against ISLD on the Bid at 99½ also. This stopped the rally short (Figure 9-13). Notice that MWSE (Midwest Stock Exchange) was showing 20,000 shares to sell at 100. This was basic evidence, besides the round number, that there were many sellers at 100, ready to take profits before the day ended. INCA was taken out but other sellers jumped in front of 100, as the sellers competed to unload with the momentum. Supply overcame demand and the stock started trading down as momentum began to shift. We missed the ISLD Bid at 99½, and eventually sold at 99¼ to MONT for a profit of $4,250, as supply started building, evidenced by the narrow spread on the Ask by INCA and ISLD at 99⁵/₁₆ (Figure 9-14). INTU traded down to 98⅜ as traders continued to take profits, and INTU closed the day at 98¹⁵/₁₆. By letting the stock trade through the jiggles all the way up, we knew that we would not sell at the absolute high for the day. By being objective, we recognized that the momentum and trend had reversed near the close as profit-takers took the stock down. Our reaction was just a little too slow to hit the 99½ Bid, but quick enough to get out at 99¼, before the stock traded down another ⅞ point before the close.

The initial INTU trade was a quick scalp, but the second was closer to taking a position in a swing trade. If the 95 buy was the first trade, we would have taken a quick profit before the stock traded back down. However, because we had locked in some profits previously, we were willing to risk half of the profits from the earlier trade to see what the second trade could do. By having the comfort of playing with the "house money," we were able to take more risk with the second trade. If the second trade had stopped out at $94\frac{1}{2}$, that would have been the end of that risky venture, and we would not have attempted to take a position again unless we were near a good support level with a logical and tight stop. This would then be considered a swing trade as we held through the noise. For scalping, quick in-and-out trades should be the norm. However, a position that goes in your favor fast can be held longer as long as the momentum and short-term trend are in your favor. Do not mistake this with holding onto trades that go against you. These, as you know, should be exited quickly. In this example, we were able to give the second INTU trade a little more room because the first trade had given us the profit to provide a comfort level for the second trade—a simple practice of risk management. Nevertheless, the second trade had a stop that by no means would exceed the profit amount of the first trade.

Example 4: Cisco Systems (CSCO)

The narrow-spread stocks with high volume are much more difficult to scalp than it appears. Although the risk seems reduced due to the narrow spread, the incredible volume that exchanges hands in these stocks creates too much volatility or noise within a price move. Therefore, the expected profits need to be lower, which is consistent with the narrower spread and high volume. The high volatility requires the scalper to be extremely attentive and much faster with both reflexes and speed of execution. In addition, this type of scalping for quick in-and-out profits leads to a higher number of trades, which results in high commissions that eat into your P&L at the end of the day. Needless to say, traders should learn to filter out the noise when taking a position in these stocks within a trend. However, there will be times when a trend or strong momentum cannot be recognized, especially during consolidation, range trading, and slow periods of the day. These occasions require that a trader learn to take very small profits by scalping, while cutting losses quickly, or exiting trades before they turn into losses when the momentum appears to be shifting. Scalping is a good way for the day trader to pick up those coins while getting out of the bulldozer's way if it gets too close. What triggers the proficient scalper to enter and exit a trade? How do you know that the momentum appears to be shifting? Let us walk you through several CSCO trades, while explaining the methodology and thoughts behind a scalper's decision-making process.

On March 2, 1999, CSCO was having a tough time as it approached 100. Like any stock that approaches a round number, especially 100, there were many sellers in front of the number to take profits (and some getting short). Nevertheless, when the S&P futures started to rally, the $99\frac{7}{8}$ Ask cleared, and ISLD and INCA jumped to the Bid at $99\frac{7}{8}$ with GKMC on the Ask at $99\frac{15}{16}$ (Figure 9-15). Traders who anticipated a breakout were already taking the 100 on the Ask for overrides, as seen in the Time and Sales window. We sent a SOES market buy order and an ISLD buy order at 100. The ISLD buy was filled instantly, while the SOES order was filled at 100 once GKMC left the Ask. GKMC had already filled a previous order and was late in leaving the Ask (see the $99\frac{15}{16}$ print in Figure 9-15). We normally would have bought just 1,000 shares, but the momentum felt strong, and we were willing to risk the $\frac{1}{8}$ point on 2,000 shares for a greater profit if the breakout proved true. In order to reduce the risk of carrying 2,000 shares to test the breakout, we sold 1,000 shares at $100\frac{1}{4}$ on the Ask on the way up by offering on ISLD against the momentum. We were taken instantly, as CSCO pushed through $100\frac{1}{4}$. However, the S&P futures started to sell off from its near-term peak. Realizing that CSCO may retrace back to test the 100 level for support and confirmation of a breakout, we offered out the remaining 1,000 shares at $100\frac{3}{8}$ on ISLD while the momentum was still on our side (Figure 9-16). We sold the 1,000 shares at $100\frac{3}{8}$ within a second, for a profit of $375 on this trade and $250 on the first trade, for a total profit of $625. It turns out that our suspicion that CSCO would retrace back to 100 proved correct. After our sell at $100\frac{3}{8}$, other sellers joined the Ask at $100\frac{3}{8}$, and the momentum soon reversed, as profit takers started hitting the Bid at $100\frac{1}{4}$ and lower to 100.

NSDQ: CSCO							
BID			**ASK**			**T&S**	
MM ID	*Price*	*Size*	*MM ID*	*Price*	*Size*	*Price*	*Size*
ISLD	99 7/8	10	GKMC	99 15/16	10	100	4
INCA	99 7/8	25	LEHM	100	10	100	2
SLKC	99 3/4	10	SBSH	100	9	100	8
SHWD	99 11/16	10	MSCO	100	10	100	10
NITE	99 5/8	9	TNTO	100	2	100	2
GSCO	99 9/16	10	MLCA	100	10	100	6
SELZ	99 1/2	1	MADF	100	1	100	4
DLJP	99 1/2	10	PERT	100	10	99 15/16	10
MASH	99 1/2	10	ISLD	100	23	100	2
HRZG	99 1/2	7	INCA	100	15	100	6

Figure 9-15. CSCO scalp sequence 1.

NSDQ: CSCO							
BID			**ASK**			**T&S**	
MM ID	*Price*	*Size*	*MM ID*	*Price*	*Size*	*Price*	*Size*
REDI	100 1/4	10	GSCO	100 3/8	10	100 3/8	10
TNTO	100 1/4	23	JPMS	100 3/8	10	100 3/8	4
INCA	100 1/4	5	OPCO	100 3/8	9	100 3/8	2
NITE	100 1/4	1	ISLD	100 3/8	14	100	10
ISLD	100 1/4	30	JOSE	100 7/16	1	100 5/16	2
SBSH	100 3/16	10	PWJC	100 7/16	10	100 3/8	3
DLJP	100 1/8	10	TWPT	100 1/2	1	100 3/8	2
SHWD	100 1/16	10	OLDE	100 1/2	1	100 3/8	2
MONT	100 1/16	10	HRZG	100 1/2	2	100 5/16	2
BEST	100 1/16	10	CANT	100 1/2	1	100 5/16	10

Figure 9-16. CSCO scalp sequence 2.

Between focusing on the Market Maker window and the S&P futures, there was very little time to contemplate our decisions to enter and exit. Most novice day traders find difficulty in watching other indicators while keeping an eye on the Market Maker window. Add to that the ability to make split-second decisions, then send out the correct order execution, and scalping can be confusing and even overwhelming. Experience should help you to train your eye to observe more than one area of your computer monitor, while staying objective will help you to react quickly to opposing indicators from your original strategy. Also, especially when you are already in a position, have your orders set to get out of your position as soon as you have reached that conclusion. This should help you to save some time in sending your order by just having to hit the "send" or "enter" key. A day trader attempting to scalp a quick trade should constantly anticipate and be prepared to exit at the first indication that the momentum has stalled and the profit potential has become exhausted. If you miss the price level that you wanted to get out at, do not panic. Simply evaluate the situation and get out of the position at the next price level if the momentum is continuing against you.

Sometimes a scalp will get away from you while your eye wanders for a brief moment. If you had been anticipating the move to get into a position and you have missed it, let it go. Look for another opportunity. If you are in a position and it gets away from you, again, do not panic. Evaluate the situation and get out right away or wait for the first bounce. If the momentum is strong against you because it broke out of a range or support level, bite the bullet and get out. As a scalper, your risk should never be greater than your profit potential. A trade that gets away from you briefly should be contained as quickly as possible in order to avoid a disaster. Instead, get out and look for the next opportunity. Never let a trade that gets away continue to run against you. Not only will it ruin your day, but it also violates the rules of scalping. By anticipating how to get out of a bad situation and setting your order to execute the instant you realize the momentum has shifted, you can eliminate some of the timing errors and keep your losses to a minimum.

On March 4, 1999, CSCO appeared to have found some intermediate base or support at 96 and was starting to trade up, while the S&P futures could not find a direction. So when ISLD jumped to the Bid at $96^{13}/_{64}$ for 1,000 shares with REDI below at $96^1/_8$ for 2,000 shares, we quickly placed a SOES market buy order and a SelectNet Preference order to GSCO (Figure 9-17). We bought 1,000 shares at $96^1/_4$ from GSCO, while canceling the SOES order because it was not getting filled. This suggested that there were other buy orders in front of ours, so the momentum was on our side. Notice the number of prints or trades on the Time and Sales window at $96^1/_4$, which also confirms the momentum. Also, the Bid was $96^{13}/_{64}$ and $96^1/_8$ right below. If the momentum were to shift suddenly, our risk was only $^3/_{64}$ or $^1/_8$ if we missed the ISLD Bid. When the $96^1/_4$ cleared, we immediately offered the stock out at $96^3/_8$ on the Ask through ISLD (Figure 9-18). The S&P futures could not break out to the upside so CSCO and other stocks would have a hard time maintaining the upward momentum. Our offer was taken within a second, but CSCO had a tough time clearing the $96^3/_8$.

A few minutes later, CSCO was trying to clear the $96^5/_8$ when futures selling off stopped the momentum short. ISLD jumped in front of the $96^5/_8$ Ask with a $96^{19}/_{32}$ offer ($^1/_{32}$ below the $^5/_8$) of 2,800 shares, while REDI and INCA were still on the Bid with an uptick at $96^9/_{16}$ (Figure 9-19). We quickly hit the INCA Bid for 1,000 shares with a short-sell SelectNet Preference order to go short at $96^9/_{16}$. Our risk was $^1/_{32}$ or $^1/_{16}$ at worst if we were wrong. Thinking that we had just picked the top of a short-term peak, we thought that this would surely be a winner. When the $96^9/_{16}$ Bid left to become the Ask with $96^1/_2$ printing on the Time and Sales window, we had an order prepared to Bid back the shares at $96^3/_8$ for a $^3/_{16}$ profit (Figure 9-20). When all the $96^9/_{16}$ sellers disappeared rapidly, and ISLD jumped on the Bid at $96^9/_{16}$, we quickly adjusted our ISLD to take out the order for 1,000 shares on the Ask if the Time and Sales window printed once at $96^5/_8$ (Figure 9-21). No sooner was our order set than someone had taken 1,000 shares from ISLD, reducing the share size from 2,000 to 1,000 (Figure 9-22). We immediately hit the "enter" key to send the ISLD order to take the remaining 96⅝ Ask and were filled instantly for a $1/16$ or $62.50 loser. The 96⅝ Ask cleared soon after, and if we had not reacted fast enough by adjusting our ISLD order to take the 96⅝ Ask, we may have missed the 96⅝ Ask and would be facing a $3/16$ loss at 96¾. Our mistake was thinking about where to take our profit, without anticipating how to take the 96⁹/₁₆ Ask for a flat if there was no momentum to clear the 96½ Bid. When the 96⁹/₁₆ Ask left, we knew that we were wrong. Had we been stubborn about taking a profit and refused to take a loss after expecting to make a profit, we would have missed taking a very small loss and would have faced a larger loss.

NSDQ: CSCO							
BID			ASK			T&S	
MM ID	Price	Size	MM ID	Price	Size	Price	Size
ISLD	96 13/64	10	MLCO	96 1/4	10	96 1/4	3
REDI	96 1/8	20	GSCO	96 1/4	10	96 1/4	10
USCT	96 1/16	1	COWN	96 1/4	8	96 1/8	3
BEST	96	10	FBCO	96 1/4	10	96 1/4	10
AGIS	96	10	SBSH	96 1/4	10	96 1/4	9
NITE	96	1	INCA	96 1/4	9	96 1/4	10
INCA	96	10	ISLD	96 1/4	6	96 1/4	2
MASH	96 15/16	5	TNTO	96 5/16	20	96 1/4	1
SELZ	95 7/8	1	RSSF	96 3/8	1	96 1/4	1
DEMP	95 7/8	4	LEHM	96 3/8	1	96 1/4	10

Figure 9-17. CSCO scalp #2 sequence 1.

NSDQ: CSCO							
BID			ASK			T&S	
MM ID	Price	Size	MM ID	Price	Size	Price	Size
TNTO	96 1/4	20	LEHM	96 3/8	1	96 5/16	1
USCT	96 1/4	2	PWJC	96 3/8	10	96 5/16	1
REDI	96 1/4	11	MASH	96 3/8	1	96 5/16	6
ISLD	96 1/4	1	AXCS	96 3/8	10	96 5/16	10
NITE	96 3/16	1	BTRD	96 3/8	10	96 3/8	10
ATTN	96 3/16	7	ISLD	96 3/8	12	96 3/8	10
INCA	96 3/16	14	NEED	96 7/16	10	96 3/8	2
SBSH	96 1/8	10	HRCO	96 7/16	10	96 1/4	5
HRZG	96 1/16	10	AANA	96 1/2	1	96 5/16	7
BEST	96 1/16	10	MSCO	96 1/2	10	96 5/16	2

Figure 9-18. CSCO scalp #2 sequence 2.

NSDQ: CSCO							
BID			**ASK**			**T&S**	
MM ID	*Price*	*Size*	*MM ID*	*Price*	*Size*	*Price*	*Size*
REDI	96 9/16	1	ISLD	96 19/32	28	96 9/16	4
INCA	96 9/16	16	PWJC	96 5/8	8	96 19/32	2
AXCS	96 1/2	10	REDI	96 5/8	20	96 5/8	2
BTRD	96 1/2	20	INCA	96 5/8	18	96 5/8	2
ISLD	96 1/2	1	LEHM	96 3/4	1	96 5/8	1
MSCO	96 3/8	10	SBSH	96 3/4	10	96 5/8	2
SLKC	96 3/8	10	JOSE	96 13/16	1	96 5/8	8
SELZ	96 3/8	1	NITE	96 13/16	1	96 5/8	5
MASH	96 3/8	10	DLJP	96 7/8	10	96 5/8	2
MLCO	96 1/4	10	BRUT	96 7/8	4	96 5/8	1

Figure 9-19. CSCO scalp #2 sequence 3.

NSDQ: CSCO							
BID			**ASK**			**T&S**	
MM ID	*Price*	*Size*	*MM ID*	*Price*	*Size*	*Price*	*Size*
AXCS	96 1/2	10	TNTO	96 9/16	9	96 1/2	1
BTRD	96 1/2	10	INCA	96 9/16	8	96 1/2	1
ISLD	96 1/2	7	ISLD	96 9/16	3	96 9/16	1
REDI	96 7/16	1	PWJC	96 5/8	8	96 1/2	1
MSCO	96 3/8	10	REDI	96 5/8	20	96 9/16	2
SLKC	96 3/8	10	LEHM	96 3/4	1	96 9/16	2
SELZ	96 3/8	1	SBSH	96 3/4	10	96 5/8	1
MASH	96 3/8	10	JOSE	96 13/16	1	96 5/8	5
PERT	96 3/8	6	NITE	96 13/16	1	96 5/8	2
INCA	96 3/8	20	DLJP	96 7/8	10	96 5/8	1

Figure 9-20. CSCO scalp #2 sequence 4.

NSDQ: CSCO							
BID			**ASK**			**T&S**	
MM ID	*Price*	*Size*	*MM ID*	*Price*	*Size*	*Price*	*Size*
ISLD	96 9/16	10	PWJC	96 5/8	10	96 9/16	1
BTRD	96 1/2	8	INCA	96 5/8	13	96 9/16	1
AXCS	96 1/2	10	ISLD	96 5/8	20	96 9/16	1
REDI	96 7/16	1	LEHM	96 3/4	1	96 9/16	2
MSCO	96 3/8	10	SBSH	96 3/4	10	96 9/16	1
SLKC	96 3/8	10	REDI	96 3/4	30	96 9/16	1
SELZ	96 3/8	1	JOSE	96 13/16	1	96 1/2	1
PERT	96 3/8	5	NITE	96 13/16	1	96 1/2	1
MASH	96 3/8	10	DLJP	96 7/8	10	96 9/16	1
INCA	96 3/8	25	GSCO	96 7/8	10	96 1/2	1

Figure 9-21. CSCO scalp #2 sequence 5.

NSDQ: CSCO							
BID			**ASK**			**T&S**	
MM ID	*Price*	*Size*	*MM ID*	*Price*	*Size*	*Price*	*Size*
ISLD	96 9/16	10	PWJC	96 5/8	10	96 5/8	10
BTRD	96 1/2	8	INCA	96 5/8	13	96 9/16	1
AXCS	96 1/2	10	ISLD	96 5/8	10	96 9/16	1
REDI	96 7/16	1	LEHM	96 3/4	1	96 9/16	1
MSCO	96 3/8	10	SBSH	96 3/4	10	96 9/16	2
SLKC	96 3/8	10	REDI	96 3/4	30	96 9/16	1
SELZ	96 3/8	1	JOSE	96 13/16	1	96 9/16	1
PERT	96 3/8	5	NITE	96 13/16	1	96 1/2	1
MASH	96 3/8	10	DLJP	96 7/8	10	96 1/2	1
INCA	96 3/8	25	GSCO	96 7/8	10	96 9/16	1

Figure 9-22. CSCO scalp #2 sequence 6.

In scalping or any type of trading, you must always remember that you will never have all winning trades. Even the most proficient trader will have losing trades or sometimes even a bad day, when your timing is completely off and everything you do is wrong. You can never eliminate losing trades or losing days. However, by remaining objective, you can exercise discipline and reduce the losses on bad trades or bad days, while maximizing your profits when your timing is good. Do not confuse objectivity with having no knowledge of the market and, therefore, no bias. You must learn to digest and interpret the information, then reach your own conclusions and observe the market's reaction to the same information. Is the news late in reaching the market? Probably not. Is the information old and has it already been factored in? More likely. Whatever the reason may be, if the market is reacting differently, then you must learn to react and adapt to the current market condition that will best benefit your P&L. There is a saying: "It's not what you think that matters, it's what the market thinks that matters." To understand what the market is thinking, you must first understand what it is that the market is thinking about. Through experience, you will develop an intuition for market psychology. This intuition will help you to see the supply and demand for a stock that leads to price action and momentum and, ultimately, to your ability to time your entry and exit points.

10
Swing Trade Examples

What we call swing trades are any trades that last longer than scalps, up to what is commonly known as "intermediate term" to day traders—a few days. This is quite different from scalping not only because of the length of time, but also because these types of trades hold through price fluctuations and noise. The stops, mostly mental stops, are normally wider, and these types of trades rely heavily upon technicals and market sentiment. Charting comes very much into play, and while daily charts are indeed very helpful, most of our swing trades arise from observing patterns and trends in intraday charts that span several trading days, usually set to 15- or 30-minute intervals. In the search for potential swing trades, being attuned to the current and recent market sentiment is the first important factor. For example, if we anticipate the market will begin or continue a bullish trend, we search for strong stocks that are potentials for breakouts beyond any recent or perhaps even historical resistance points. We also look for retracement levels, breaks beyond popular averages, and popular patterns such as double or saucer bottoms, pennants (very tricky), head and shoulders, or triple-top forms. We consider any untraded gap that may have been left from recent days. The search for swing trade candidates is no easy task, because we can literally flip through hundreds of charts only to find a select few that possess the most ideal risk-to-reward possibility of pattern follow-through. Our software settings are linkable and thus allow us to look at more than one type of chart simultaneously as we enter the symbol, so it is easy to immediately view the stock from different perspectives. Aside from looking for patterns in the intraday charts, the daily charts are considered for the same patterns that may be forming. A good *intraday* chart pattern verified by a favorable *daily* chart pattern as well as matching market sentiment is the ideal situation we look for. The longer the length of time on your chart scales, the more significant the signal is. This cross-referencing of different evidence is the ideal way to formulate a swing trade. The technical patterns themselves are not complicated, because these are mostly based on simple trend, support, and resistance concepts, as well as other rudimentary and popular patterns. However, it is the careful mix of all facts, including order execution and consideration of wide spreads (if applicable), that makes swing trading no easy task. Add to this some nerve-rattling volatility (especially in the NASDAQ), and not only do you have a challenge in planning, but also the psychological challenge of doubt in weathering price fluctuations. In swing trading, while you will often find yourself just waiting (in fact, you may even get bored), when the volatility comes, whether it is in your favor or not, we can assure you of a real and sometimes hair-raising trading challenge.

Quite appropriately introduced, perhaps the most indispensable factor to include in all swing trades is the presence of the protective stop-loss. The fact that no trader can win on every trade should be very clear to you. The only protection you have against incorrectly anticipating the market is a well-selected stop-loss. This is more often a mental stop-loss for us, because we have the advantage of keeping vigil over all our positions.

Swing Trade Example 1: Merrill Lynch (MER)

In selecting the first example for swing trading, we chose a trade that befits the topic of our book. In late February 1999, a widely anticipated announcement was made. The great brokerage house Merrill Lynch, a pillar in the traditional ways of the stock market, finally bought into the new world. Merrill bought D.E. Shaw, a developer of online trading systems and an online day trading firm. The previous year, MER had hit highs of 109 before tanking to below 40 on bad Asian exposure, the difficulties of the entire financial sector in the summer of 1998, discounting lesser profits on trading, and loss of customers due to high commission costs. Besides the excitement of witnessing the old world blend with the new, the magic number 80 immediately came into mind. For some reason, a technician's mind is always filled with apparently meaningless inventory of numbers. We were very familiar with the price territory and in fact had often participated in good core and swing trades on Merrill (MER) before. This, however, was significant. The buyout news was that fundamental push that this stock needed to break that technical resistance point: 80. In fact that was the very same exit target we had had on a long core trade in 1998. MER really had a tough time at this price (Figure 10-1). The significance of the news, especially in light of the market's fascination with Internet stocks and the online day trading frenzy, seemed to be the very factor that would create a solid technical follow-through for the breakout. This was one of those times when fundamentals lead the technicals. Our plan for this stock was to open an initial position for a swing trade exactly at the breakout point and, subsequently, open a core trade later for another attempt at 100, as long as the support at 80 held and the trend of the financial sector or the general market did not reverse to head south. While Merrill was still in the 70's upon the announcement, we did not buy into it either for swing or core because the short-term market conditions were unfavorable. The market had just come off its highs, and in the last several sessions was experiencing a tough correction. To add to this, inflation was in the news, and in fact a great majority of our other targets were on the short side. So we set the trade aside and waited for the right time, which came along on March 4th. Merrill had just introduced online day trading to a select group of its customers and, at the same time, favorable economic news and a pact between Dell and IBM created some excitement in the markets that morning. This was just what the market needed for a boost to the upper range of the recent correction, and in fact might even cause the Dow to test highs. Among a number of other stocks to target that day, Merrill was ripe for a key price move. In fact, the Specialists had MER gapped open right at the previous day's high, but under 80. The opportunity came early in the trading day when MER began to trade at 80 and with solid momentum. We had been watching since $79\frac{1}{2}$ and while it was tempting to get in, we waited for some confirmation from the market, which we got, and just before 80 we sent a market buy order to the Specialist. Shortly after, the confirmation came in: 1,000 long at the magic number. MER never turned back— until 82. This was the next obstacle, which throughout the day was frustrating. While the general market seemed firm, Merrill would just break 82 and then retrace, and in fact repeated this three times. The third time we almost exited the trade, but we anticipated a strong close. The market seemed to be firm and was hovering on the upper half of the trading range all day, looking like it had enough legs to push higher into the close. During the last hour, Merrill staged a breakout to new intraday highs; this was enough reason to double down at $82\frac{7}{8}$, in expectation of testing 84. While the momentum continued to beyond 85, a sell-off before the close caused us to exit out of half the position at $84\frac{9}{16}$ and to keep the remainder for a gap-up. We were gaining over 4 points into the close and our profits here, along with those we had booked, would protect us from any bad gap-downs. On this overnight position, the coast seemed to be clear against any gap-down with the exception of an announcement of the employment situation in the morning. Because of the large gain, the

Figure 10-1. Daily chart for Merrill Lynch (MER).

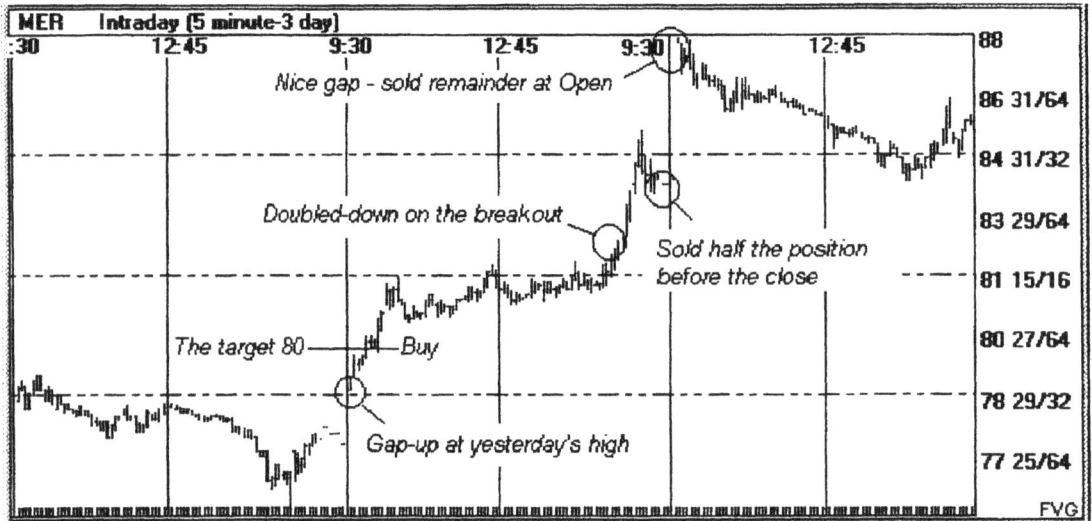

Figure 10-2. Merrill Lynch intraday chart.

bullish sentiment, and the technical significance of the breakout, we kept the overnight position. The following morning, we could not have asked for any better results (Figure 10-2). The employment announcement came in favorably enough to dispel any inflation fears the market had discounted. The bullishness was coupled by a short-cover rally in the bond market. Even better yet, Merrill was gapped open 4 points higher. Following the usual technique, we sold the remainder of our position during the first few minutes of trading to book the ideal swing trade.

Swing Trade Example 2: Infoseek (SEEK)

There wasn't anything big in the news on February 11th. However, led by the technology sector, stocks had been selling off for three days in a row on the usual fears of overvaluation and the overheating economy, which leads to the stock market's biggest fear: inflation. The bearish analysts had also been coming out of hibernation and were all over the news with the usual, nevertheless valid, gloom and doom outlooks. However, there really was nothing in actual news that would support the sell-off. The market over the last few days had used this opportunity to discount its uncertainty after a strong bull run late in 1998 and in January 1999. The prevailing sentiment seemed to be too bearish on no real news and better yet, we had sold off in a very hard way over the last three days. Overbearishness without validity led us to anticipate the opposite: The market was due for a bounce to the upside. In fact, the lack of significant headlines indicated more concentration on technical activity. The market gapped open on a deal between Marketwatch and AOL, and it was a perfect time for the oversold tech stocks to retrace. There was a lot of bargain hunting due today. One of our targets was Infoseek, which on the previous day had bounced off the round support number at 50. We correctly anticipated that the strength of large-gap NASDAQ stocks would be sold immediately. This is a common symptom during corrective market phases, when participants use the strength of every rally and gap-up to sell positions they are caught in. Today, however, we were looking to buy, but not at the open. We gave the stock a little time to fill that gap and our first entry point target would be yesterday's high. The stock had gapped open above this point; however, the bargain-hunting sentiment, preceded by gap selling, would probably merit support at yesterday's high. The sentiment seemed to be bullish enough today that it should find some sort of support there. The futures, the Tick, and the NDX also appeared to be stabilizing. First, we confirmed the bounce off yesterday's high. This was our ticket to open the first position: a small, 300-share lot long at $56\frac{1}{4}$ stop below yesterday's high with momentum, $55\frac{1}{4}$—an original risk of $300, and conveniently one point below our entry. When trading Internet stocks, we keep a close tab on share exposure because of their volatility. Within minutes, the stock rallied to $57\frac{1}{2}$ before retracing right back. We were looking to hold for the whole day so long as the trend remained intact—that is, if there was going to be one. We got in and held very early, not only on account of SEEK bouncing off support, but because of an intraday breakout on the NASDAQ composite as well (Figure 10-3). As Infoseek followed through to the upside and we were in profit territory, we moved our stop to a one-point trailing stop. If SEEK retraced more than one point with strong momentum, we were looking to sell the position to lock profits. About an hour and a half into the trading day, Infoseek broke out again. Here we doubled the position at $59\frac{1}{16}$ (Figure 10-4). While having to watch it hover around that area for a few minutes, raising the question of a false breakout, our other positions, also long, indicated that everything seemed to be intact and holding

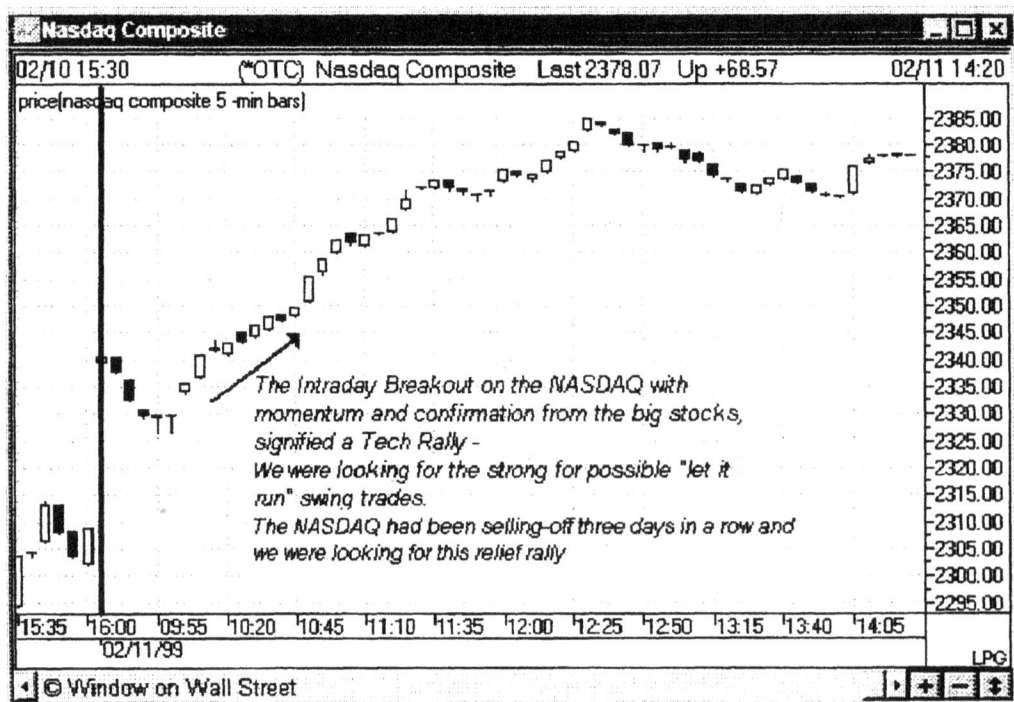

Figure 10-3. NASDAQ composite intraday.

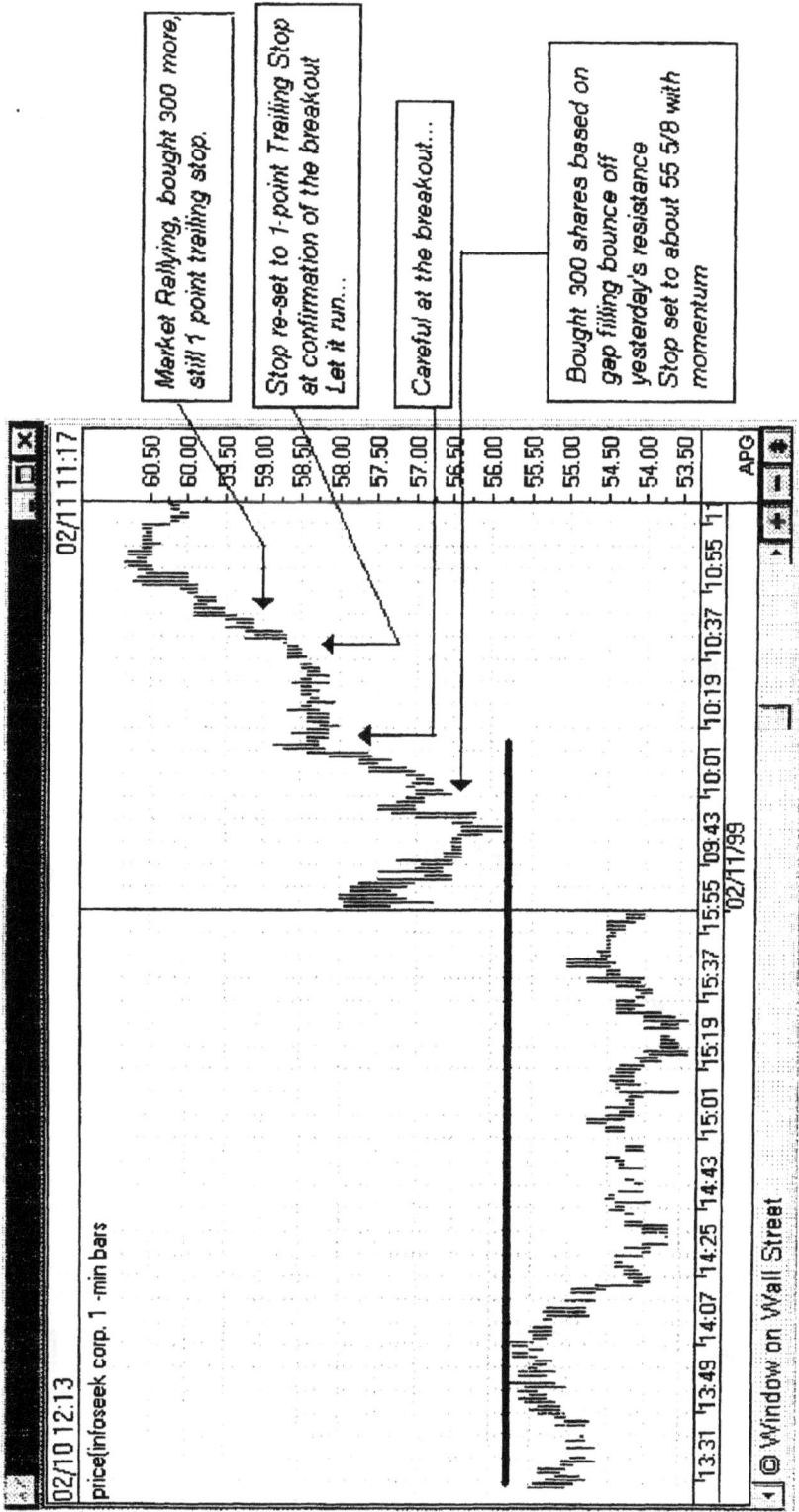

Figure 10-4. SEEK intraday one-minute chart.

163

well. The NASDAQ composite and the futures were consolidating as well. Nevertheless, it was questionable for SEEK because it had already moved 3 points from its low. SEEK's break to 60 and beyond was very fast, as is usual for Internet stocks; however, the new round number looked tough. Had it not been for our other open positions, as well as the NASDAQ composite and the futures, we would have looked to exit here. Instead we chose to hold, perhaps just as a gamble because we had some room. The market was demonstrating the evidence we needed to convince us that it had the strength to push higher: shallow pullbacks on our other open long positions, the NASDAQ composite, and the S&P futures. Between bargain hunting and short covering, the market had a lot of legs. We soon confirmed our expectations on SEEK, as it tested 60 once, was successful, and ripped up to 62 in minutes. We were still maintaining the one-point trailing stop, but at this level we were 6 points in the money, and it was getting choppy. It was time to book the profit with an ISLD Offer that was hit

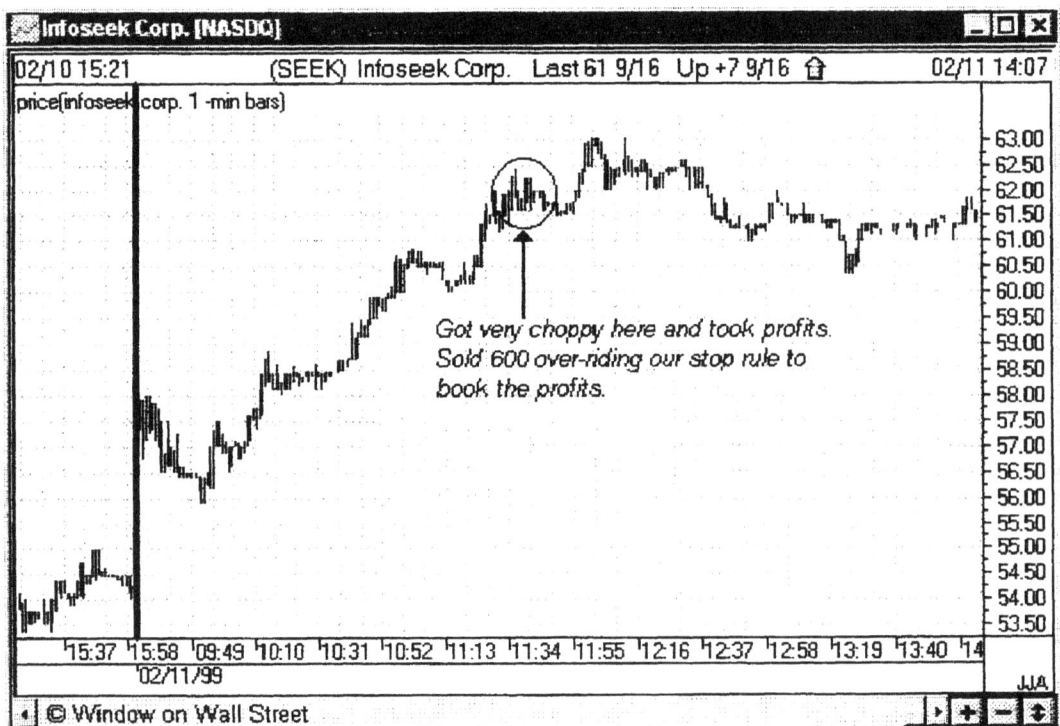

Figure 10-5. Infoseek intraday 1-minute chart.

instantly on momentum at exactly 62 (Figure 10-5). While we had to watch the stock go higher to 63 a short while later (and in fact the next day it went to 66), we were happy enough with a 6-point profit on the first 300 and about 3 points on the second lot, which totaled roughly $2,700 profit. While the profits would have been a lot higher had we placed more share size, looking back at the original risk of $300 reminded us that the trade had been well worth it.

Swing Trade Example 3: Cisco Systems (CSCO)

Among our favorite patterns for swing trades is the simple Fibonacci retracement derived from a multi-intraday chart. Sometimes it is even tempting to trade purely on the technical pattern without the help or distraction of any fundamental input. However, our habits of combining both is too well-established to break. As with most evidence of technical follow-through, the announcement of fundamental news typically gives a stock the needed push to follow-through on the pattern. It may also break it, however.

In this example, our technical clue that CSCO was probably going down today appeared to be supported by news that came on the morning of March 2nd. Alcatel, the French telecom giant, was buying Xylan, a data networking company long rumored, along with Fore Systems, to be a takeover candidate. What did this have to do with Cisco today? Everything, for today at least. In the fierce race to find the networking company with the biggest muscle, the entire sector had been consolidating, as evidenced by big mergers and buyouts such as the recent Northern Telecom-Bay Networks and Lucent-Ascend deals. With Alcatel buying Xylan and room for other cross-Atlantic players such as Siemens and Ericsson to do the same, Cisco's reputation of being the 800-pound gorilla of networking was threatened. Well, for at least *today* it was. Or was it? Don't takeovers or mergers often rally the entire sector? Isn't that a good thing? At the time, and as with most situations, we didn't know whether the market for Cisco would interpret the news to be bullish or bearish or nothing at all. However, being day traders in search of a good swing trade, we need to interpret all big fundamental news in "today" terms, and reserve the rest of the complicated analysis or fundamental mumbo-jumbo for other people or perhaps for future use. Just like everyone who day trades, what we needed to know was whether Cisco was going up or down *today*. This is a situation in which technicals came into play. In looking at Cisco's chart, we were in luck. On the morning of March 2nd, one of our

favorite patterns was staring right back at us: a simple 50 percent retracement (Figure 10-6). Charts with these patterns often remind us of a ball
bouncing half way up off the floor and pausing, just before gravity pulls it
back down. Unfortunately, trading is not this perfect. In looking at this
chart, adding the high point on February 24th to the low point two days
later on the 26th and dividing it by two results in, quite conveniently, the
price area of 100—50 percent up and very near where Cisco had left its last
trail. The difficulty was in trying to decide whether to short at 99, 100, or
101. While Cisco did look like it was going to tank down to around 98
(some support there), or perhaps even retest the low of the 26th (just under
96), it would all depend on where Cisco opened to determine an exact
entry point for our short position.

Prior to the market open, Cisco showed normal price activity on Instinet.
The prices being traded were near yesterday's close. In fact, by the open
Cisco was barely unchanged, at just under 100. This made it all the more
difficult. So we waited for some sort of confirmation to open a swing trade,
and in the meantime scalped it in anticipation of clearing 100. During the

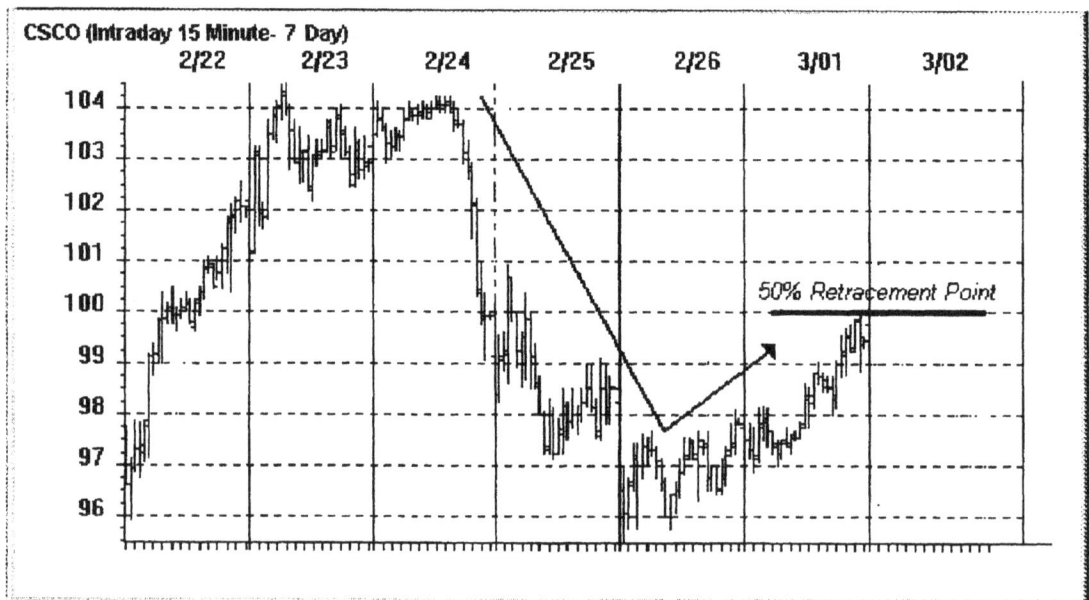

© CyberCorp 1999

Figure 10-6. Cisco 7-day intraday chart, 50% retracement.

first half hour, CSCO bounced off a low of 99. We scalped the breakout to the upside to anticipate clearing 100, which turned out to be a good trade. We were very uncertain here and decided that if we were going to swing short it, it was going to be at the break of the intraday low established early in the morning at 99. Two hours into the market, Cisco showed weakness and broke that low. We opened a short exactly at 99 by an ISLD short Offer of 500 to pick off an uptick Bid, and a stop-loss at $99^5/_8$ resistance with market momentum. While the intraday low had already broken, CSCO's volatile nature came out to hand us a loss. We stopped-out as planned at $99^5/_8$ (Figure 10-7), on its way back up to 100.

As in all other swing trades, sometimes you have to try more than once, as long as the pattern is still intact. Cisco had not yet broken the intraday high. Later on in the day another opportunity came, and this time on the account of the lower high established at midday, and the apparent weakness of the futures, we shorted again another 500 at $99^5/_8$ and stop at $100^1/_4$—the most recent high. If Cisco was going to do what we wanted it to do, this would be a good time. It took its time, fluctuating at around that

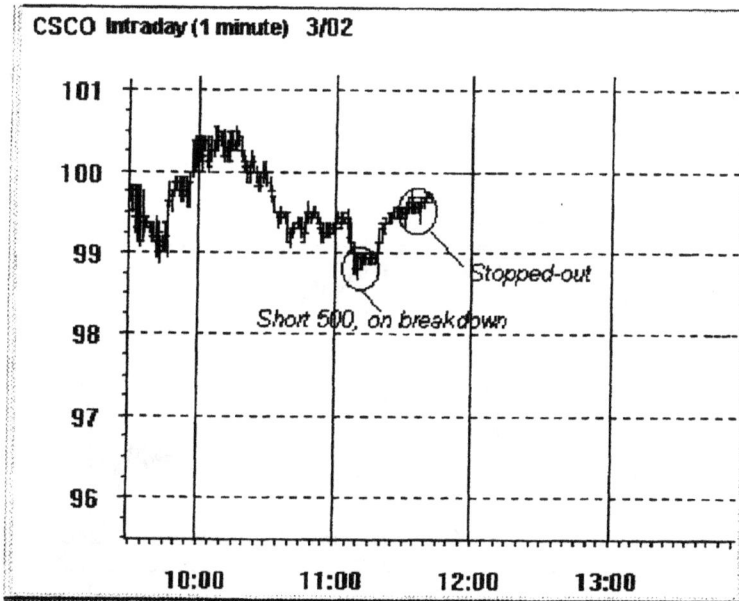

© CyberCorp 1999

Figure 10-7. Cisco 1-minute intraday chart on 3/02.

price without much activity. With a little patience, we watched as CSCO drifted down toward 99 and at 1:30 broke down hard to $97^3/_4$. It bounced here, but the bounce was very weak, and there was a lot of selling by Market Makers and INCA right into the short covering, so we got another chance to short 500 more at just under 98 with a tight stop. If CSCO was going to break the high of that bounce, we would cover everything. The market still did not appear to stabilize, and there was enough weakness to confirm that we indeed were headed to retest the low of 96 from a few days before. Again CSCO broke down hard, and our patience paid off as we watched CSCO trade right into the low 96's, and in the process decided to book our profit by bidding right into that momentum. We exited out of the entire position at $96^7/_{16}$ and $96^3/_8$ (Figure 10-8) before the stock bounced off this significant price area. The simple Fibonacci retracement pattern had been completed on the intraday level (Figure 10-9).

The lesson on this swing trade is important. While you may be faced with a technical pattern that is very strong, the randomness of the market may hand you a loss. Also, in stock trading, sometimes it may take more than one try to benefit from a good pattern.

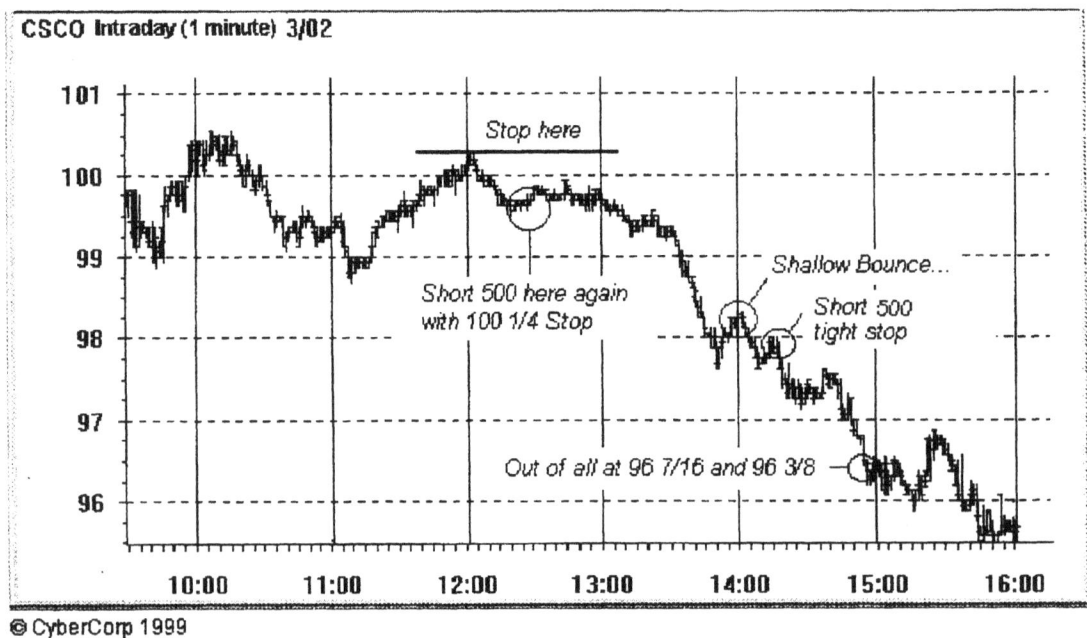

Figure 10-8. Cisco intraday 1-minute chart on 3/02, whole day.

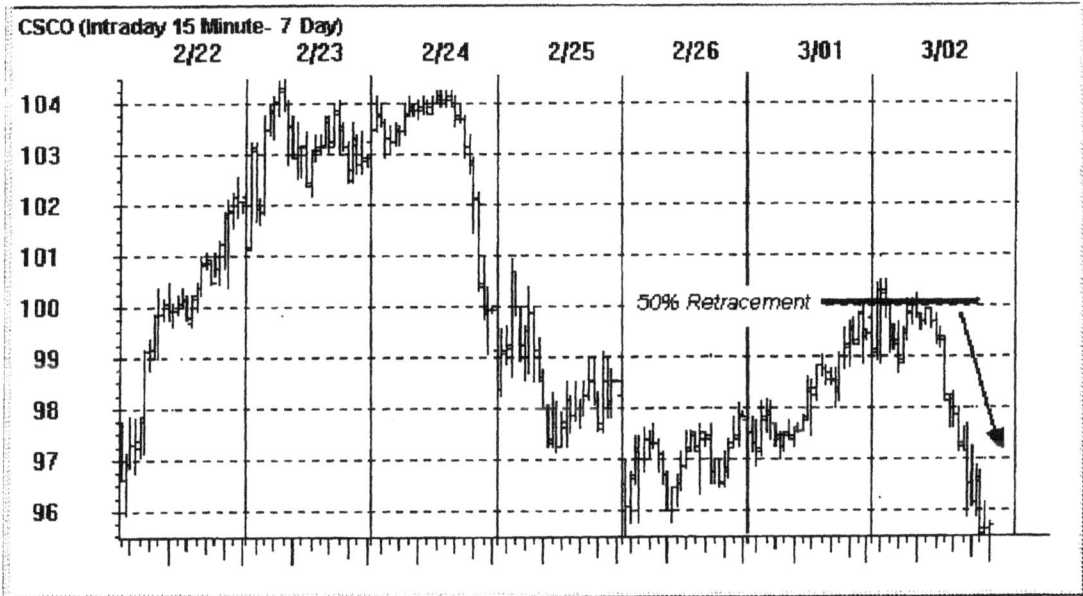

Figure 10-9. CSCO intraday 15-minute, 7-day chart

11
Core Trade Examples

A little quiet time in the evening at home is the time for picking and planning our core trades. There is a special reason for this. As discussed in Chapter 8, the psychology in core trades is very different from that of the intraday swing and scalp plays. Because we spend a lot of time during market hours tackling the twists and turns of the intraday world, it is detrimental to commingle our mind-set during the day with the more relaxed and less panicked approach needed to effectively capitalize on opportunities in the longer-term market. Core trades take advantage of large and impending price moves that may take longer time to develop. The target list always begins with an attempt to take the longside on the technology market's cream of the crop. Also included here is the cream of the crop from whatever sector is in fashion. While this may be the start of our list, it is followed by the rest, just like our list for scalp and swing trades, which are components of the S&P 100, the NASDAQ 100, and a number of other stocks we add to keep our list updated. During the market hours we take note of stocks that we think show good potential for core trades, and later on in the evening after the market closes, we take a little time to analyze—in peace and quiet—the longer-term perspectives on these stocks. If the stocks on the target list demonstrate through a little technical and fundamental research (thanks to the Internet) that they are worthy of buying or shorting, we will find a good day to take a position and open the risk exposure. While we do maintain a separate account for core trades (as discussed in Chapter 8) that enables us to place orders overnight, we never place them until the following day to ensure ourselves of a good execution that is not subject to the overnight risk of gaps or bad news. The key to finding and maintaining a good core account that will beat the market by the end of the year is combining solid fundamentals with solid technicals. We consider the stock's internal fundamental aspects as well as the fundamental environment of its proper sector and of the general market itself. In technical analysis we give strong consideration to the stock's relative strength against its peers within the same sector, and we also measure the sector in comparison to the general market. The technical research, in addition to all the basic technical analysis, also entails a never-ending attempt to forecast the direction of the general market.

If the evidence is pointing to a weaker general market, we begin to dispose, usually by scale, our long positions. Our approach is quite simple: We are not afraid to eliminate a good long core position if we feel that the market is going to decline strongly, because odds are, we will be able to reestablish it if the market demonstrates that our forecast was wrong. We will take full advantage of the speed, lower costs, and other benefits that come with trading the market full-time.

It is no surprise that we have consistently found the technology sector to be the strongest and, in fact, the leader of our markets. Thus, our best plays have always come from technology-related issues.

Example 1: EMC Corp (NYSE: EMC)

Perhaps one day it might not be true anymore, but at this writing, EMC has been a reliable source of many good core trades. Throughout 1998, it was one of these stocks that kept giving and giving, and in fact reminded us of our old-time favorites, DELL and, further back, MSFT, while not quite as volatile. Our consistent success in it, be it scalps, swings, or core, puts us in quite a good mood. As traders, this is also a terrifying thought. We are very well aware of the danger of letting our guard down, even for our favorites. This is what many years of trading teaches you: You are friends with a stock only when it makes money for you, and you are quick to cut the ties when it doesn't.

After the October 1998 lows of the market, it seemed possible that the entire stock market was set up for a massive double-bottom pattern that would launch it to the 10,000 Dow level. The debacle of the world financial markets as well as the crash landing of the highly profiled Long Term Capital group set quite a negative tone for the market, and the October 8th lows were frightening. They were more frightening because of their broadness than the meltdown in 1997, especially now that Russia's troubles suggested possible contagion in Europe. However, if the market needed to wash out the weak hands, the activities during and after October 8th seemed to point to just that: a washout. And how was EMC performing during these terrifying times? It was always the last to sell off. What we had for ourselves was a stock that was on our primary target list, and was behaving like a champion warrior among the kings. It held up better than some other Wall Street favorites, and stayed away from its 200-day moving average (MA), unlike most other stocks that had cut through the key MA like butter. The success of our core trades in EMC earlier in the year and the technicals pointing higher suggested that the bearish market in the summer and early of fall of 1998 was the only thing that was keeping EMC down. Its fundamentals were very solid and the market for its software and storage solutions was high, thanks to the unending growth of networks and the Internet. In November the market was appearing to show some life, and EMC was technically demonstrating a readiness for breakout. We were ready as well to reopen our exposure to EMC. We had missed EMC's move from its lows because of our wariness to open any core trades at all. However, we chose a new high as a first entry point, expecting EMC to make an attempt to rally to 100 over a few months, if the market, and of course its internals, allowed it. The technology sector had been going up virtually every day, while the general market had been chugging along behind it. On October 29th, a particularly bullish market day, we bought EMC's breakout, and the Specialist returned our first package: 300 long at $64^3/_{16}$. Our initial stop was set to below 60 with bad market news. It is not very common to find a core trade that immediately makes money. In this case, however, the most heat we took was a one-point pullback a few days later. After that, EMC blasted off along with the entire stock market. We were very pleased to watch the market rally and be fully exposed. Our other trades in SUNW, AOL, INTC, YHOO, MSFT, and ATHM, among several other positions, were also flying (we use a couple of these as examples in the following sections). The only one of the tech favorites that had performed poorly was DELL, which we took notice of and eliminated from the portfolio (unfortunately just before it went up as well). We added more to our exposure on EMC on November 24th: 500 at $72^1/_8$. The market proceeded over the next few weeks in one of the most incredible bull runs we had seen. In the first week of the year, the market had shot up with even more force, as the exuberance and money flow of the new year came in. It was here we began to take some profits off the table from our other holdings, but remained fully exposed to EMC. On January 13th, bad news, which we were beginning to miss, hit the market. Brazil's Central Bank president had announced his resignation. This dreaded news from Brazil, which had been looming for months, finally hit the market, and with big force. The market reacted with a large and terrifying gap-down; however, the market's immediate reaction to that gap was again exhilarating—it rallied immediately, in spite of the uncertainty. This was our cue to get out of some of our exposure to EMC, in case the situation got worse. We were very deep in the money on almost all our positions and this was our mark-

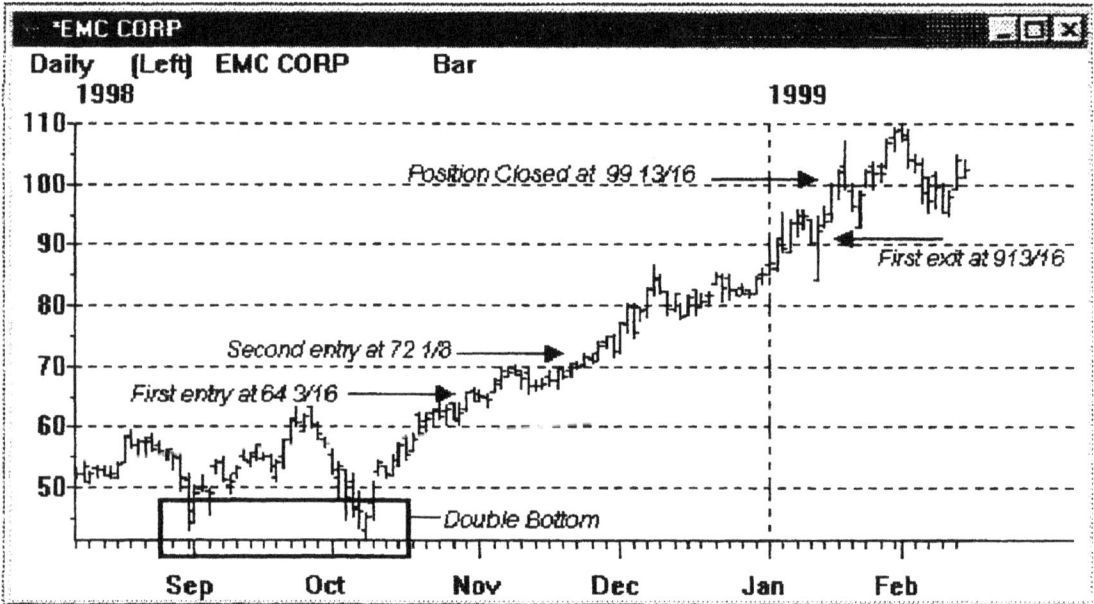

Figure 11-1. Core trade: EMC.

er to begin reducing our exposure. Thus, we sold 500 shares of EMC at $91^3/_{16}$, and held on to 300 with the intention of selling into the next rally. This came three days later at $99^{13}/_{16}$, just before our target price of 100. We were out of EMC. (Figure 11-1). Although we had to watch EMC go a bit higher, we were nevertheless happy that we achieved our objective and that we were able to mark another winner from EMC. Given that the market had such an unexpectedly strong and steep bull run, we were very wary of jumping back in, and opted to stay on the sidelines for a while as far as core trades were concerned.

Example 2: Intel Corp. (NASDAQ: INTC)

After establishing its all-time high at exactly 102 points in August 1997, INTC spent the next year in the doghouse of a widely followed semiconductor analyst from Merrill Lynch. Although the stockholders of semiconductor companies were not pleased with his gloomy prediction, the analyst had nevertheless correctly forecasted a slowdown in the semiconductor industry. This kept the entire sector at bay while the rest of the market rallied. Despite being the best, INTC was not spared. INTC had visited the 70's a number of times and in fact in June of 1998 visited the mid-60's. We were not very interested in INTC until it showed some life; after all, it had established an up-and-down pattern that we were not very impressed with. It seemed a little too vulnerable against bad news, and we felt that there were better opportunities than being exposed to yet another gap-down on INTC. We wanted to see some long-awaited strength before getting in, and INTC was demonstrating nothing but weakness. On the two occasions during the year that it broke above 90, it failed miserably. What we wanted to see was solid and consistent trading in that area. During the lows of October 8th, we took note of INTC's good performance. Its chart suggested that if the market sold off the way it did, INTC would revisit the sub-70 area. However, INTC maintained above 70, and in fact was even trading closer to 80 during these bad market days. We were not yet convinced, because we interpreted this as buyers cutting the probable bounce-off of the 70 area (Figure 11-2). As the general market was entering rally mode, led by the techs (the NASDAQ was unbelievably showing green arrows almost every day), INTC was giving us what we wanted: solid trading in the 90 area. Our first commitment was small: On

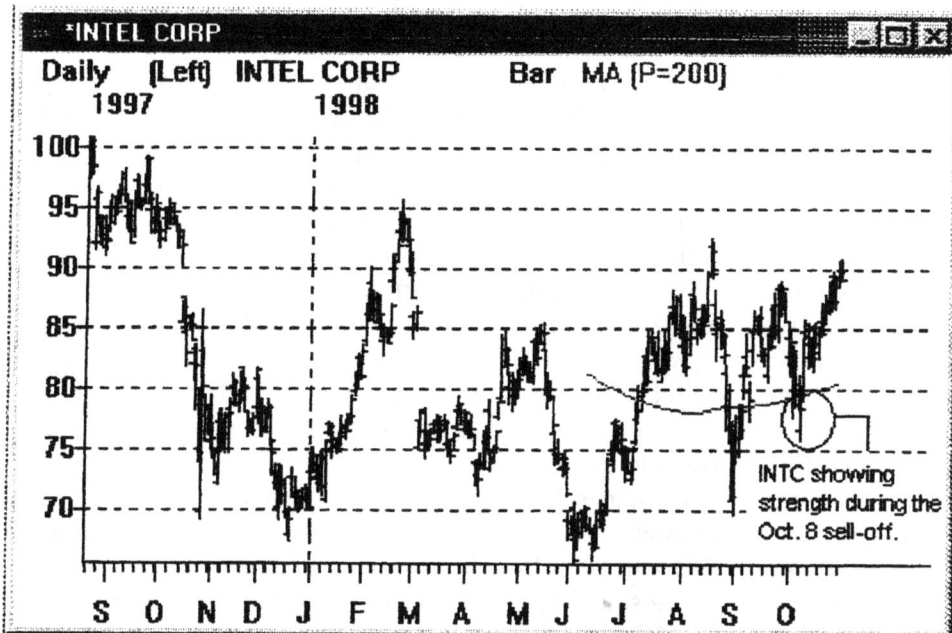

Figure 11-2. INTC Corp.

November 5th, we bought 300 shares at $94\frac{1}{8}$. A few days later, right into the NASDAQ rally, we committed another small lot of 200 shares at $97\frac{11}{16}$. If INTC was going to new highs, we were expecting a move to at least 120 to 125 within a few weeks (if the market conditions were suitable). This would mean that INTC would double from its 65 lows in the summer. Our stop-loss on the entire position was below 90, and like our other core trades, with bad market news. The bad news never came, and in fact, the next day we were rewarded with a gap-up and good news from INTC. INTC opened at just under its previous all-time high. This meant one of two things for us: breakaway gap or exhaustion gap. The market conditions favored breakaway and because we were showing some profits on other positions, we took the risk and bought 300 more exactly at 102 and set an initial stop to unload half the position below the previous close of $97\frac{9}{16}$. Now we had 800 shares at the average price of 98. Within a few days, the pattern was establishing well. As each day passed, we were wary of the gap-up, wondering if it would get filled; however, we watched in amazement (along with the rest of our positions) as INTC moved to 115 with relative ease. Our trailing stop was set to 10 percent pullback—if INTC retraced more than 10 percent, we would eliminate the position on the next rally, and if there wasn't going to be one, we would eliminate the position anyway, for fear of INTC closing its gap back on November 11th. We set a stop that was a little wider than usual for two reasons. First, we had room to risk, considering that we were in the money on a lot of positions. Second, we expected that INTC would experience a rotation in ownership or distribution because now that it was hitting new highs, the owners of INTC who had been in the doldrums for over a year would use this rally to put an end to their misery. On December 14th, INTC did just what we expected—it retraced exactly 10 percent. This triggered our signal to sell half into the next rally, and if INTC traded more than $\frac{3}{16}$ below 110 (spread overshoot), we would exit the entire position. The next day INTC snapped back to the 115 area, where we sold 400 shares. This turned out to be a mistake, as we watched INTC move to 126 over the next week. However, this was the reason we kept half, and this is an example of the benefits of scaling. Nevertheless we held on to the remaining 400 shares with the same 10 percent stop-loss and watched INTC greet the new year, along with the rest of the market, with new highs—to our astonishment, at 140. A few days later, on January 13th, came the Brazil gap-down, and along with some of our other positions, we sold into the morning rally at $135\frac{3}{8}$ (Figure 11-3). While we watched INTC and many of our other positions eventually trade higher, we were quite pleased that we had reduced our exposure to a market that was now uncertain. Better to enjoy the fortunes of good risk management and an incredible bull run.

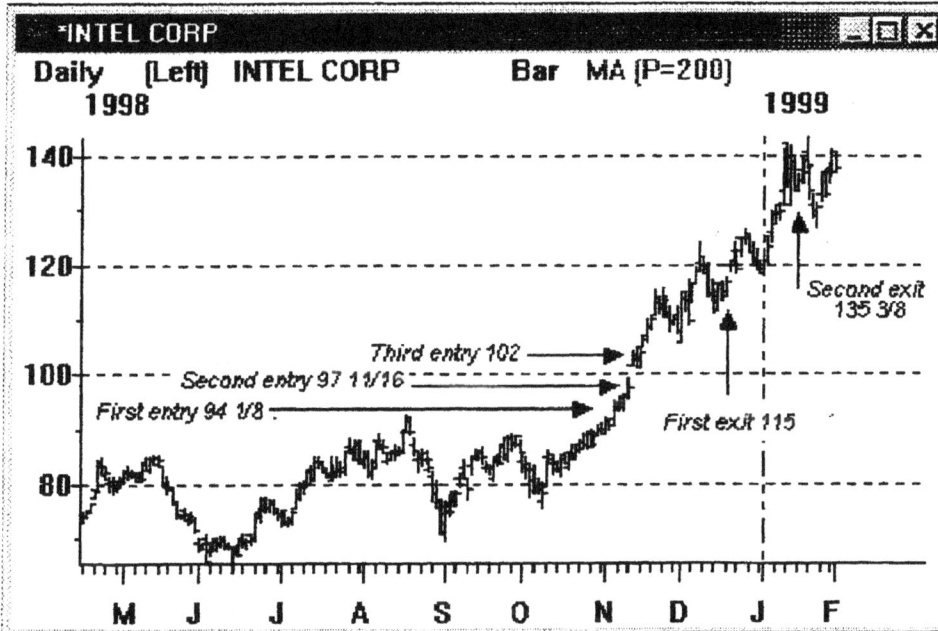

Figure 11-3. INTC Corp. (2).

Example 3: Yahoo! Inc. (NASDAQ: YHOO)

The name of this stock suits this core trade. Since its IPO, we had been successfully in and out of YHOO frequently. It was our favorite Internet stock for a simple reason: They were number one. We had never dared to short this or any other Internet stock; the mere thought of it was too painful. If we had profited so much from this stock on the long side before, imagine if we had shorted it because we didn't like it. As we have previously discussed, we are firm believers in the idea that the majority of the money to be made is on the correct side of a trend, and not against it. We would watch in horror as people, some of them our own friends, would take their shots at shorting what was then the hottest stock on the planet and end up with a disintegrated trading account.

While our exit strategy was never perfect on this stock (or any other stock), and as a result we would miss a lot of good moves, we liked YHOO for one thing when it searched for a new price territory. YHOO had established a simple pattern to us that we had successfully utilized a number of times before: Whenever it broke new highs, it acted like a rocket blasting off into outer space. However, our experience always told us that anything too easy will end sooner or later, and we were not about to take any chances. In late October of 1998, the market had been rallying off its October 8th bottom and, while we had begun to take other core positions, we were stalking for the new high on YHOO. YHOO had performed well during the sell-off, but we are so careful with this or any other Internet stock that we wanted to see some strength. On November 2nd we got what we wanted and bought YHOO in a fast market at 142. A small, 100-share lot was enough. Since this is a stock that was very volatile, our stop-loss was set to 10 points, and our objective was to take around 50—that is, if YHOO was going to behave as it did before. This was the last time we saw YHOO trade at that price, and it was indeed acting very strong. A few days later, we bought 200 more at 156. Our average price for 300 shares was around 151; our stop-loss on all was below 150. The market, was gathering a lot of momentum, and we were piling up for a strong move off the summer double-bottom. At one point, we had close to 30 open core positions— the most we had ever had. YHOO hit a high of 227 on November 24th, and during the next week pulled back very strongly. But we wanted to give it a lot of room. We were expecting YHOO to find support at its previous high of 185 on November 10th. As we discussed in Chapter 8, when you are dealing with a volatile and wide-spread stock and you are looking at support or resistance, always add a few points around the price area for over- or undershooting and give special consideration to spread mechanics. In this case, we were ready to stop out if YHOO closed below 180. As we had done previously, because YHOO was like a wild horse that needed a little room, we gave it that. This explains why we started with small share sizes. What if we had entered for the first time at that 227 high with a heavier share size? The pullback would have been painful, even with just a hundred shares. Because we were in the money on this and the others, we had the luxury of a wide spread. What we were concerned with, however, was that the stock was getting too expensive and if we had to add more, we wouldn't have enough equity to buy. On December 4th, YHOO had retraced to exactly our stop point at 180, and then proceeded over the next few days to bounce off that level. It was here that we bought an additional 200 shares at just above 204, because we felt that with the market's momentum, YHOO would probably be ready to test the 227 high. Our 500-share average was now 172. We were careful to keep an eye out for YHOO trading below 200 while the market rallied. This would mean that YHOO probably was out of steam and we should get out with whatever profit we still had. We set an ultimate stop at exactly 175—below YHOO's support area. On December 21st, YHOO broke the 227 high, and we added a couple of hundred shares more to round off our total exposure to 700 shares at an average of 189. We watched YHOO, as a Christmas present, hit 286.

During the period between Christmas and New Year's Day, the volume was very light, as expected. Because YHOO had made a large move on that low volume, we sold 300 shares at 269. In hindsight, this was yet another demonstration of our less-than-perfect exit strategy (although we will probably never change it). Over the next few days, we watched in disbelief as YHOO blasted off yet again, this time for an incredible nonstop 200-point rally. This happened only about ten days after we sold those 300 shares. What we had here was an awesome display of short covering and panic buying as everyone could feel the split announcement coming soon. On January 11th, YHOO had gapped-up yet again, and we sold the remaining 400 shares at the open at 370. It was simply too much—370 points! In great pain, we were now spectators to watching YHOO rally another 75 points higher only *a few hours later* to 445. (Figure 11-4).The thought of having sold at almost the dead low for that day made us feel terrible. We had gotten spoiled and we wrote it off as yet another proof that the market will never cease to amaze us. A few days later we watched YHOO retrace over one hundred points. Only a week or so later, YHOO tanked 200 points from its 445 high, on massive profit-taking aggravated by the Brazil news.

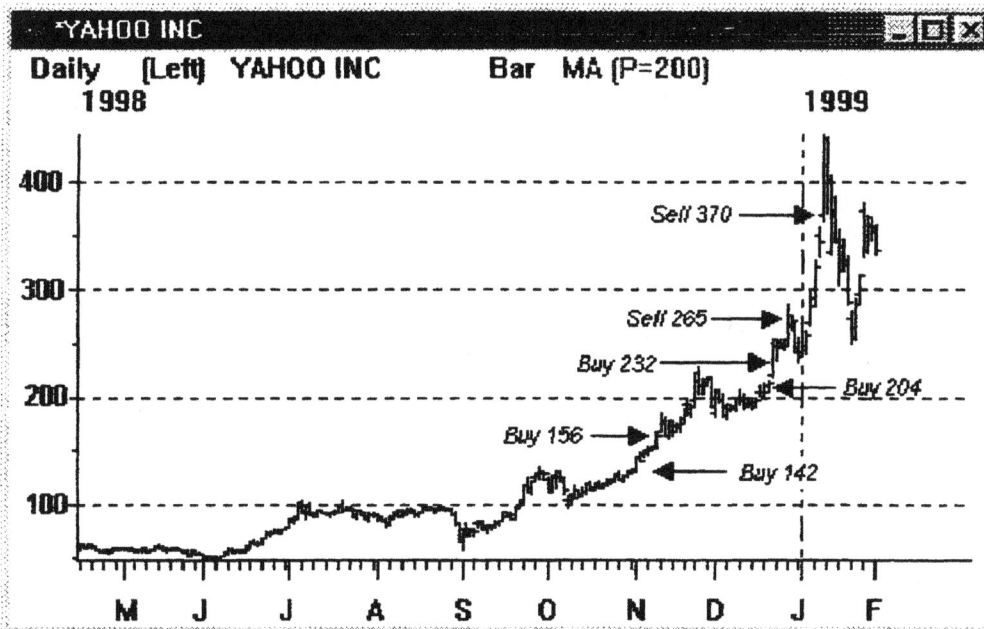

Figure 11-4. Yahoo! Inc. daily chart.

Both the rally and the sell-off on YHOO were incredible displays of frenzy. We were happy to have participated in it correctly and, considering the risk-to-reward ratio, it was one of our very best trades. We look at it as a gift from the stock market for practicing good risk management and respecting its ways.

12
Trading Notes

Account Maintenance

The amount of information needed to learn how to manage risks in day trading is overwhelming to many. The market's unpredictability and the focus required for active participation in the markets often distracts the trader from a highly important factor that may seem ordinary to many: the proper maintenance of an active trading account. While technology has facilitated our ability to keep track of our many transactions, the occasional errors in our technology (in addition to the potential for human error) may add large risks to our capital. If you are trading actively in the markets, keep in mind that every transaction you make involves an instantaneous exchange of equity that runs in the tens, and for some, even hundreds of thousands of dollars. A missing trade, a computer glitch, human error, or sometimes even fraud can cause large damage to your equity. In other words, maintaining your account is a key part of risk management. Because we focus on the market's price fluctuations so heavily and tend to trust our computers to take care of our transactions, the fact that the smallest error in your account can cause significant damage is an aspect of risk management that is too important for a day trader to ignore. You must maintain and check your account on a constant basis, the same way a pilot checks to make sure that everything is working on the plane while flying. Here are some tips for proper account maintenance:

- **Create a daily trading journal.** Ideally, this journal should be separate from the computerized records of your brokerage firm, online account, or even your own PC. As you make a transaction, record it by hand. Create a binder that historically records all your transactions, entry and exit prices, times, order size, and profit or loss. It is surprising to us that many traders track the common checking account closer than the trading account. While there is only a small possibility of error in your account, all it takes is one small error to cause large damage. Make the effort to eliminate that possibility.

There are other advantages to having a daily trading record. Aside from having the security of your own list of transactions that you can use to reconcile your account with the record provided by your brokerage house, you can use this journal to write down important notes for planning or for future reference. It is highly useful for novices to write down your learning process, the rules that you find important, your restrictions, and your plans or goals for today, as an overall guide and a reminder while tackling the many challenges of the trading day.

- **Reconcile your account every day.** Do not let the challenges and excitement of the market or other matters distract you from closing out your day by making sure that your account is in order. Go through every transaction and make sure, in detail, that it reconciles with your brokerage firm's records. Make a habit of doing this so as to avoid getting behind, especially if you have more than a few transactions in one day.

- **The sooner you find an error and report it, the better.** If you find an anomaly, report it immediately to your broker; do not waste time. Making this a priority increases your odds of getting the problem fixed without any more fuss. It is far easier for your brokerage house to look through recent records than to sift through historical records.

- **Avoid trading unless the anomaly has been reconciled.** Piling on more transactions on top of an erroneous one may create a snowball effect of more problems. These can include an erroneous margin call, an interest charge, a commission rate, the creation of an unwanted position, the elimination of a good position, or worse, a combination of any of these.

- **Keep all your records.** While you may accumulate months or years of manual records, do not discard them. Maintaining a long history of records adds more legitimacy to your journal. Needless to say, you never know when you will need them.

Risks of Commissions and Other Trading Expenses

Ten-or twenty-dollar commissions sure look attractive, especially when your former broker charged you hundreds of dollars for the same thing. To many, the risks of low commissions and other trading expenses such as SEC, exchange, ECN, or data fees may seem negligible. However, we can assure you that the more actively you participate in the market, particularly if you are using a low-equity account, the more significant these expenses become. Consider them not merely as operating expenses, but as real and significant risks to your capital. It is common to find that the majority of trading losses is made up of commissions and fees that are seemingly cheap, but in the end are a deciding factor. For active traders, these can run in the tens of thousands of dollars. Keep a close tab on your commission costs and fees. If they are taking chunks out of your capital that is not growing, perhaps you need to lessen the frequency of your trades, whether they seem low-risk to you or not. You may need more time to allow yourself to mature as an experienced trader who can clear commissions and other costs easily because of hard-earned trading skills.

Trading IPOs and High Volatility

Watching extremely high volatility is truly exciting. The key word here is *watching*. Many novices in the market are tempted not only to watch these situations, but to participate. Sometimes the most attractive aspects of the market present the most dangerous situations for the inexperienced. Even the most skilled traders are often humbled to the sidelines by the ferocious price swings on some stocks. Sometimes we remove them from our view to avoid being drawn in by the excitement or even buying or selling them by mistake—this does happen! Wouldn't it be a good idea for the inexperienced to follow suit? Sure, you can make a lot of money in these stocks, and witness others make tremendous profit. However, make it a habit to always confront the potential downside.

Data Accuracy

The highest priority in efficient order execution is the accuracy of the data you are receiving. In other words, all bets are off if your data is distorted. If you are experiencing this problem while you are about to execute an order, this is equivalent to being blindfolded before crossing a freeway.

Internal brokerage and computer quote problems aside, the market as a whole commonly suffers from bad quotes when volume is heavy and when the market is moving at a very fast pace. It can happen to an entire market or it may be limited to a specific stock. This typically happens during:

- the opening and closing periods;
- big market, heavy-volume days; and
- days when an individual stock is experiencing abnormal volume and volatility.

With heavy volume, our networks typically suffer from bottlenecks, which result in delayed quotes. Some order execution systems built into the market may even be down and totally nonfunctional. Keep in mind that when quotes are running late, your screen may be reflecting the trading reports on a stock at 61, for example, when the real market could already be trading 2 or more points away in either direction. Make it a habit to know, at all times, if your quotes are delayed. You can usually confirm correctness by seeing that the Time and Sales report corresponds with the Bid and Ask prices. Some stocks trade so heavily on big days that the if the Time and Sales were reported immediately as they were coming in, they would be going by so fast it would be merely a blur of running numbers. Time and Sales must go by in a manner that is readable, and if the market is moving at a very fast pace, your reports may be inaccurate. As much as possible, avoid trading in these situations. Not only do you run the risk of not knowing where the price of the stock is really trading, but you will also be competing directly against Market Makers and Specialists, who have a tremendous advantage over others during this time. Market Makers and Specialists have a greater ability to measure order flow as it is coming in; if you have bad quotes, you will suffer the consequence of not knowing what is going on while other players do.

In high-volatility situations, such as with IPOs (particularly tech or Internet-related NASDAQ issues), the problem is different. The Bid, Ask, and Time and Sales can be so frantic that it is often difficult to tell the exact value of the stock. IPOs literally trade in uncharted territory. The stock is seeking equilibrium and speculation may be very high. In these situations, ferocious price swings can occur in minutes or seconds. As much as possible, avoid these situations until the price has stabilized to some degree. There are innumerable other stocks to trade. If you must open a position on an untamed IPO or highly volatile stock, use limit orders, not market orders. Your market order can be filled at a price that may be too hot to handle—especially in the NASDAQ.

Profiting via Faulty Methods

From our experience, we have found that perhaps the most frightening thing to see in day trading is an inexperienced trader making large amounts of money. This is because he is about to be taught a lesson. This was particularly prevalent during the bull runs of the Internet stocks whose price movements went literally by the hundreds of points in a very short period of time. However, these stocks also reversed direction with equal magnitude. We witnessed, despite constant and stern warnings, an incredible phenomenon of greed, gold-rush fever, and self-destruction that for many, ended in large losses of capital. Regardless of whether it is participation in volatile stocks or simply participating in a market that is staging an incredible rally, the fact that the inexperienced can make a large amount of money very easily in this market creates a false impression that they are blessed with natural trading skills. All ships rise with the tide.

If the market is rallying and we are buying every pullback or breakout and make tremendous amounts of money from it, then the next logical step would be to do it again tomorrow. In fact, our greed will drive us to a more dangerous conclusion: that if we do it again tomorrow, *but with larger share exposure,* we can make even more money tomorrow than we did today. Every time any individual books a large winning trade, the temptation is to think: "If I only had ten, five, or even just one thousand shares of that..." Dreaming is okay, so long as you keep it in your imagination. In many years of observing traders of all levels, including ourselves, we have seen that acting upon greed without acknowledging dumb luck seems to always end in the loss of some or all previous winnings, or even more. As an active participant in the markets, you must know the how's and why's of your profitable trades. You must be able to define exactly why you made money. This is far easier to do in hindsight. Did you make money because of your skills, or dumb luck, or perhaps a combination? While luck is always a factor, your position should have been opened based on an educated decision, rather than on a heads-or-tails choice. Many inexperienced traders make money during a market rally because of the natural inclination for an investor to go long and hold on pullbacks. If you are inexperienced and have profited from doing this, do not think you have now acquired the skills to trade. Anyone can make money when the position happens to go in your favor; but the true test of a trader's skill is how you react when the position is going against you. A professional's true skills are reflected in the ability to come out unscathed in the face of adverse conditions. While you may be better at some conditions than others, you can identify when a trade is suited to your style and when not. An inexperienced trader will apply one single method (for example, buy and hold) to different conditions; that can be detrimental to his bottom line, because of the market's natural tendency to fluctuate. The market or a single stock does not always go up, but rather moves in stages on the way. If the test for a certain price level fails and you do not realize this, you may be facing a large loss. Quite ironically, as we pointed out in Chapter 6, it is when the pain of loss is largest and when the fear is greatest that a trader is convinced to exit a trade that often eventually turns around to the upside, right after you exit. A climactic sell-off that precedes a rally is signified by the surrender of the firmest of bulls. If you are making money on your trade, that is always good. However, the idea in professional trading is to educate yourself enough to distinguish whether you made money through your own skills at anticipating mass psychology, or whether you profited from a situation that was merely circumstantial.

Finally, you must also acknowledge that in a roaring bull market, the profits on a trade can extend to much larger amounts than originally intended. The market often presents us with these opportunities; however, it can just as often trade in a narrow range where profits need to be taken quickly because of poor trends. Again, you must focus not on a specific technique, but on the most applicable technique for the current conditions.

Trading Myths: Spread Trading

The ability to participate directly alongside professionals, to Bid and Offer like Market Makers, to display and cancel at high speed, and to see detailed price activity are fascinating to many. It is disappointing, however, to see so many suffer from the myth of spread trading, because of the illusion that powerful trading tools are the answer to trading success. Nothing could be further from the truth. Spread trading, by our definition, is getting an order executed to buy at the current Bid price and then subsequently turning around to sell it at the Ask price—the profits of which amount to the spread, just like a Market Maker's or Specialist's take. While it sounds rather simple, too many traders are attracted to this concept only to discover that in practice, it leads to unending losses more often than not. Why? Because when a trader's displayed Bid gets hit, there is usually good reason for it: A seller was willing to meet that price. Odds are, there are more sellers that will follow suit to do just the same. Why? Because they couldn't get executed over at the Ask side. Once the inexperienced trader's Bid gets hit, your attempts to sell it over at the Ask side will only increase the number of displayed sellers. This is the beginning of a common problem. As we discussed in Chapter 7, doing this simply aggravates the bad situation the trader may have already gotten into. When the Bids are getting hit, the sellers are coming in; if the trader is long while this is happening, the downward momentum will lead you to sell for a loss. Inexperienced traders often find themselves in these situations, and in their panic, make bad decisions. Combined with other common novice errors in order execution, poor timing, lack of discipline (What if you decide to hold it overnight?), and with destruction of the ego, fighting back with doubling down, and facing fear and greed, the uneducated trader is faced with a real psychological challenge that is relived over and over again until he ends up with significant losses. In the stock market, what may appear to be simple and profitable is probably too good to be true. Unfortunately, the words *simple* and *profitable* rarely go hand in hand in the stock market—or anywhere else for that matter. Think like a trader by trusting your basic instincts and keeping a constant eye out for "the catch." In most cases, you will probably be right.

Trading Myths: Instinet and After Hours

Another trading myth that attracts many newcomers is the ability to trade on Instinet and after hours. The idea of being able to load up or dispose of a position in the after hours while everyone is away is, again, a fascinating concept. Unfortunately, it usually ends there: It is just a concept. It is still a competitive arena, just like the open market. Note that in the after-hours many rules that apply to protect the investor during market hours do not apply. To some degree, there is use for after-hours trading; however, the myth is that prices are more attractive during these times, or that prices slowly graduate to certain levels. When news is announced, prices in the after hours can jump faster than they do in the open market. This is equivalent to a parking lot deal while the mall is closed: Anything can happen.

After-hours trading carries a much higher liquidity risk, reducing a trader's level of safety. Aside from the absence of other participants, Market Makers are not required to take any sides during this time, as they are during market hours. If you need to dispose of a position, there may literally be nobody there to take the other side.

In addition to liquidity risk, you also assume the overnight risk in after-hours trading. It is difficult to judge momentum and actual value, or whether the stock will open the next day at a price that is anywhere near the after-hours trades. How many times have we seen a stock trade up to $178 on after-hours Instinet, for example, only to see it open at 172 and tank to 165? If you bought 1,000 shares of that stock because it announced better than expected earnings, there is a real risk that the stock will not see that price again for a while. What if the stock has already risen over the past few weeks by 40 points in anticipation of these earnings? Did you consider this before buying on Instinet after hours? Leave Instinet alone until you gather more experience.

As we write this book, several changes are coming into the market, among them online brokerages that are beginning to offer customers the ability to trade after hours. It has already been proposed to the NASDAQ and the NYSE to increase trading hours. However, until there is any significant liquidity during after hours, our position remains the same on this subject: Placing trades in the after hours should be kept to a minimum, and avoided unless absolutely necessary. You are a trader, and one of your best friends is liquidity.

Enduring the Stresses of Trading

It is a known fact that trading is a high-stress profession. However, a factor often overlooked by rookies in the business is the effect of stress on decision making. The pressures on any day trader in this enormous market are constant and end only at the closing bell. In fact, if you have open positions, then the challenges continue overnight and right into the next day. The opening period in itself—the first couple of hours of the trading day—takes a toll on any trader, and even more so on the newcomer. The lack of being able to withstand mental tension and to maintain focus all the way into the market close often has a negative effect on the decision-making process and, thus, on the bottom line. Because the potential of mental stress to affect your bottom line is very real indeed, making a conscious effort to keep yourself in tip-top mental shape is part of the practice of good risk management. If you are a rookie, you must learn how to take care of your mental state in order to maintain focus. It may take many weeks or months to learn how to endure the trading day, or a succession of trading days. Take as much time as you need within the day or even take days off to come back relaxed but prepared and focused. Newcomers are often excited about facing the market and overlook the toll it may be taking, both mentally and physically.

Don't accept the mistaken notion that the market will run out of opportunities and perhaps may not have as much tomorrow. Rookies often try to shoot for as much fortune as they can today without paying attention to the effect this may have on their decision-making process. Don't believe that today is the terrific trading day and perhaps the opportunity will not come again. The market is always active with innumerable opportunities. Odds are, you will see an even better day soon—perhaps as soon as tomorrow. You must go at your own pace. The idea in trading is to take hold of this market, not the other way around. Be patient, relax, take many breaks—as many as you want—and have fun. Wasn't this one of the reasons you chose this endeavor? Make use of the privilege.

Cutting-Edge Technology

Possessing cutting-edge tools does not necessarily mean that your trading will improve. These tools may help improve order execution, and may in fact be indispensable in many ways, but they will have little effect on your ability to anticipate price movement without proper use. Take the time to know the ins and outs of your trading software as a *tool*, while learning the markets as a *skill*. These are two separate things. The power of your software will work for you, but you have to know that it can work just as well against you. While the merits of efficient order execution are substantial, we would undoubtedly prefer to have good overall trading with less-than-perfect executions, to the other way around.

Trading with a Simulator

Simulated trading has its advantages and disadvantages. There are excellent simulator packages out there to help you "paper trade" electronically on the same software you will be using for actual trades. The advantage of using a simulator is to familiarize yourself with the software. It is important to know where the correct buy and sell keys are, how to track your positions and track price movements, how to adjust views and create charts, because you do not want to be fumbling around while you are trading.

The disadvantages in simulated trading are twofold: psychology and order execution. In simulated trading, there is no psychological reaction to profits and losses. Cutting a loss that does not affect your account is easy. In fact, if you are showing losses, it is simple to restart the software and start from zero. On the other hand, a simulator is also unable to test your reaction to making real money, which may lead to overexuberance. Either way, the simulator will never be able to test your psychology and discipline, which are deciding factors in your profitability or lack thereof. If you want to test those, test them in the real market with real risk exposure, and compensate by limiting the share size of your trades.

The next disadvantage is false order execution. A teenie here and a quarter there in inaccurate order execution add up to tens of thousands of dollars. Trading on a simulator (or paper trading) will test your ability to pick correct direction. Order execution skills, like discipline and psychology, will be tested in the open market, not on the simulator. Use the simulator to familiarize yourself with the software, reading the tape and picking direction. Use this time to explain, in retrospect, how and why you would have made and lost money. If you have "made" money on the simulator, do not let it lull you into thinking the same will happen in the real market. This will cause you to enter the market with your guard down, and it may happen that you cannot believe how different the real thing is and how much money it cost to come to that conclusion.

Goal Setting

No undertaking is well started without a statement of goals. This is just as true in trading as in any other endeavor. Setting goals for your trading will help you meet many of its challenges. You must first be educated enough to understand the large risks in trading, many of which we have discussed in this book. You must also gather information from other sources by communicating with people who are a few steps ahead of you and by reading as much as you can about the subject.

In trading, your inner self is revealed. Listen to your inner self and be conscious of how you react when your natural greed or fear try to take over. Most people have an inclination to want profits *now* that is stronger than the tendency to protect capital. A written set of goals and a trading plan will remind you to control the imbalance of emotions. In the beginning, your expectations should be conservative and focused on *defense*. The initial approach to day trading is capital preservation and maximum learning. Your goals and trading plan must be geared toward this. Practice it on a daily basis until your defensive technique becomes an instinct. Your offense will come naturally as you learn to identify what can hurt you and to distinguish a good from a bad probability trade.

Conclusion

The stock market, once safeguarded as an institution for the wealthy and privileged, has opened up to you. While once the individual investor was only allowed to participate in the market as an isolated customer through secondary sources, the favorable action by regulators has opened the playing field to individual traders. With more efficient order entry systems, competitive commissions, and technological advancements in data transfer and networking, individual traders now have at their fingertips the power to face the challenges of the market on an equal footing with professionals on Wall Street. The open playing field provides many opportunities for victory and equivalent risks of failure. For you as for the professionals, there are no shortcuts to success in this market. We have outlined in this text the psychology and strategies for trading that we feel are important and that have worked for us. However, it is up to you, the individual trader, to take the reigns in acquiring the skills necessary to tame the market and profit from it. As much as we would like to deliver an all-in-one book that will contain all the answers to your trading questions, no one can accomplish that task because of the nature of the market. If you don't have the ability to manage your risks and exercise discipline, the market can be severe, as well as apathetic to your needs or prayers. If you don't have confidence and the ability to remain objective, the market will taunt and tempt you when you are most vulnerable. However, never attempt to take revenge on the market. It is not the market that is your adversary; it is your lack of the priceless traits of risk management and discipline that makes you susceptible to large risks. The qualities common to most successful traders can be cultivated, with practice and a strong commitment to protect your capital.

The deciding factors that we are unable to quantify in this book are your determination and passion for trading. Practice, experience, the willingness to educate yourself, an immeasurable amount of patience, and perseverance in the pursuit of your goals will allow you to realize your dreams and build equity.

Finally, we would like to convey to you the privileges that come with trading. Have fun! Do not let your passion for trading keep you from enjoying its freedoms or allow you to lose focus on what is important to you: your family, your friends, and your life. We wish you the best of luck!

Appendices

Appendix A: NASDAQ 100 Stock List

To get the most recent listings visit: **www.nasdaq100.com**

Company Name	Symbol	Company Name	Symbol
3Com Corporation	COMS	Centocor, Inc.	CNTO
Adaptec, Inc.	ADPT	Chancellor Media Corporation	AMFM
ADC Telecommunications, Inc.	ADCT	Chiron Corporation	CHIR
Adobe Systems Incorporated	ADBE	Cintas Corporation	CTAS
Altera Corporation	ALTR	Cisco Systems, Inc.	CSCO
Amazon.com, Inc.	AMZN	Citrix Systems, Inc.	CTXS
American Power Conversion Corp.	APCC	CMGI Inc.	CMGI
Amgen Inc.	AMGN	Comair Holdings, Inc.	COMR
Andrew Corporation	ANDW	Comcast Corporation	CMCSK
Apollo Group, Inc.	APOL	Compuware Corporation	CPWR
Apple Computer, Inc.	AAPL	Comverse Technology, Inc.	CMVT
Applied Materials, Inc.	AMAT	Concord EFS, Inc.	CEFT
Ascend Communications, Inc.	ASND	Corporate Express, Inc.	CEXP
At Home Corporation	ATHM	Costco Companies, Inc.	COST
Atmel Corporation	ATML	Dell Computer Corporation	DELL
Autodesk, Inc.	ADSK	Dollar Tree Stores, Inc.	DLTR
Bed, Bath & Beyond Inc.	BBBY	Electronic Arts Inc.	ERTS
Biogen, Inc.	BGEN	Electronics for Imaging, Inc	EFII
Biomet, Inc.	BMET	Fastenal Company	FAST
BMC Software, Inc.	BMCS	First Health Group Corp.	FHCC
Cambridge Technology Partners, Inc.	CATP	Fiserv, Inc.	FISV
CBRL Group Inc.	CBRL	Food Lion, Inc.	FDLNB

FORE Systems, Inc.	FORE	PacifiCare Health Systems, Inc.	PHSYB
Genzyme General	GENZ	PanAmSat Corporation	SPOT
Herman Miller, Inc.	MLHR	Parametric Technology Corp.	PMTC
Immunex Corporation	IMNX	Paychex, Inc.	PAYX
Intel Corporation	INTC	PeopleSoft, Inc.	PSFT
Intuit Inc.	INTU	QUALCOMM Incorporated	QCOM
Jacor Communications, Inc.	JCOR	Quantum Corporation	QNTM
KLA-Tencor Corporation	KLAC	Quintiles Transnational Corp.	QTRN
Level 3 Communications, Inc.	LVLT	Qwest Communications Int.	QWST
Lincare Holdings Inc.	LNCR	Reuters Group PLC	RTRSY
Linear Technology Corporation	LLTC	Rexall Sundown, Inc.	RXSD
LM Ericsson Telephone Co.	ERICY	Ross Stores, Inc.	ROST
Maxim Integrated Products, Inc.	MXIM	Sanmina Corporation	SANM
McCormick & Company, Inc.	MCCRK	Sigma-Aldrich Corporation	SIAL
MCI WorldCom Inc.	WCOM	Smurfit Stone Container Corp.	SSCC
McLeodUSA Incorporated	MCLD	Staples, Inc.	SPLS
Microchip Technology Inc.	MCHP	Starbucks Corporation	SBUX
Micron Electronics, Inc.	MUEI	Stewart Enterprises, Inc.	STEI
Microsoft Corporation	MSFT	Sun Microsystems, Inc.	SUNW
Molex Incorporated	MOLX	Synopsys, Inc.	SNPS
Network Associates, Inc.	NETA	Tech Data Corporation	TECD
Nextel Communications, Inc.	NXTL	Tellabs, Inc.	TLAB
Nordstrom, Inc.	NOBE	USA Networks, Inc.	USAI
Northwest Airlines Corporation	NWAC	VERITAS Software Corporation	VRTS
Novell, Inc.	NOVL	Vitesse Semiconductor Corp.	VTSS
NTL Incorporated	NTLI	Worthington Industries, Inc.	WTHG
Oracle Corporation	ORCL	Xilinx, Inc.	XLNX
PACCAR Inc	PCAR	Yahoo! Inc.	YHOO

Appendix B:
Standard & Poor's
100 Stock List

To get the most recent listings visit: **www.standardandpoors.com**

Company Name	Symbol	Company Name	Symbol
AT&T Corp.	T	Brunswick Corp.	BC
Alcoa Inc.	AA	Burlington Northern Sta Fe Corp.	BNI
Allegheny Teledyne Inc	ALT	CBS Corp.	CBS
American Electric Power	AEP	CIGNA Corp.	CI
American Express	AXP	Campbell Soup	CPB
American General	AGC	Ceridian Corp.	CEN
American Int'l. Group	AIG	Champion International	CHA
Ameritech	AIT	Cisco Systems	CSCO
Atlantic Richfield	ARC	Citigroup Inc.	C
Avon Products	AVP	Coastal Corp.	CGP
Baker Hughes	BHI	Coca Cola Co.	KO
Bank One Corp.	ONE	Colgate-Palmolive	CL
BankAmerica Corp. (New)	BAC	Columbia/HCA Healthcare Corp.	COL
Baxter International Inc.	BAX	Computer Sciences Corp.	CSC
Bell Atlantic	BEL	Delta Air Lines	DAL
Bethlehem Steel	BS	Dow Chemical	DOW
Black & Decker Corp.	BDK	Du Pont (E.I.)	DD
Boeing Company	BA	Eastman Kodak	EK
Boise Cascade	BCC	Entergy Corp.	ETR
Bristol-Myers Squibb	BMY	Exxon Corp.	XON

FDX Holding Corp.	FDX	Monsanto Company	MTC
Fluor Corp.	FLR	National Semiconductor	NSM
Ford Motor	F	Norfolk Southern Corp.	NSC
General Dynamics	GD	Northern Telecom	NT
General Electric	GE	Occidental Petroleum	OXY
General Motors	GM	Oracle Corp.	ORCL
Halliburton Co.	HAL	PepsiCo Inc.	PEP
Harrah's Entertainment	HET	Pharmacia & Upjohn, Inc.	PNU
Harris Corp.	HRS	Polaroid Corp.	PRD
Hartford Financial Svc. Gp.	HIG	Procter & Gamble	PG
Heinz (H.J.)	HNZ	Ralston-Ralston Purina Gp	RAL
Hewlett-Packard	HWP	Raytheon Co.	RTN.B
Homestake Mining	HM	Rockwell International	ROK
Honeywell	HON	Schlumberger Ltd.	SLB
Intel Corp.	INTC	Sears, Roebuck & Co.	S
International Bus. Machines	IBM	Southern Co.	SO
International Flav/Frag	IFF	Tandy Corp.	TAN
International Paper	IP	Tektronix Inc.	TEK
Johnson & Johnson	JNJ	Texas Instruments	TXN
K Mart	KM	Toys R Us Hldg. Cos.	TOY
Limited, The	LTD	U.S. Bancorp	USB
Lucent Technologies	LU	Unicom Corp.	UCM
Mallinckrodt Inc.	MKG	Unisys Corp.	UIS
May Dept. Stores	MAY	United Technologies	UTX
McDonald's Corp.	MCD	Wal-Mart Stores	WMT
Merck & Co.	MRK	Walt Disney Co.	DIS
Merrill Lynch	MER	Wells Fargo & Co. (New)	WFC
Microsoft Corp.	MSFT	Weyerhaeuser Corp.	WY
Minn. Mining & Mfg.	MMM	Williams Cos.	WMB
Mobil Corp.	MOB	Xerox Corp.	XRX

Appendix C: Glossary of Day Trader Terms

10Q—*See* Quarterly Report.

ADR (American Depositary Receipt)—Evidence of ownership of a foreign security and tradable on U.S. Exchanges.

AMEX—American Stock Exchange.

Analyst—A person with supposed expertise in investment analysis.

AON (All or None)—An order to execute the entire trade in one transaction.

Ask (or Offer)—The price and order size at which a seller is offering to sell stock.

Bear or Bearish—Bias to lower prices.

Best Ask (or Best Offer)—The best current selling price. *See also* Inside Ask.

Best Bid—The best current buying price. *See also* Inside Bid.

Beta—A measure of a stock's volatility in comparison to the overall market.

Bid—The price and order size at which a buyer is willing to buy stock.

Block or Block Trade—A transaction of 10,000 shares or more.

Bull or Bullish—Bias to higher prices.

Ceiling—*See* Resistance.

Circuit Breakers—When the market hits extreme levels of selling, trading in all stocks is halted to prevent further panic. Circuit Breakers depend on the percentage of change in key indices and are periodically updated to reflect current market values.

Close—*See* Previous Close.

Closing Period—Commonly referred to the last one or two hours of trading, when volume is heavy and trading activity is high.

Crossed Market—When the Inside Bid is greater than the Inside Ask.

Date of Record—The registered date of ownership of stock.

Deleted or Delisted—A security that has been removed from public trading.

Downtick (NASDAQ)—Created when a lower Inside Bid is exposed after a higher Bid was removed (by a transaction or cancellation).

Downtick (NYSE)—Created when a transaction is lower than the previous reported trade.

ECN—Electronic Communication Networks utilized by day traders and institutions to post Bid and Offer prices on the NASDAQ.

Fill or Kill (FOK)—A command to immediately execute the order in its entirety or cancel.

Fundamental Analysis—Analysis of valuation based on the study of a company's financial statements, earnings power, products, market, etc. May also include the study of the economy in measuring the health of the stock market.

GTC Order (Good-till-Cancelled)—An order that is open to execution until cancelled.

Halted—*See* Trading Halt.

Hit the Bid—Urgent sell to the current Bid price.

Hit the Offer—Urgent buy from the current Ask price.

Inside Bid—The best current buying price and order size.

Inside Ask—The best current selling price and order size.

Inside Market—The highest Bid and the Lowest offer prices among all competing Market Makers or ECNs in a NASDAQ security.

Instinet System (INCA)—An ECN now widely used, but originally designed to allow institutional investors to display anonymous Bids and Offers to other institutional investors.

Intraday Activity—Trading activity between the opening and closing periods.

IPO—Initial Public Offering. A new security available for public trading.

Last Sale—Most recent transaction on a stock. Must be reported within 90 seconds on NASDAQ.

Liquidity—Refers to volume of available buyers and sellers.

Limit Order—An order to buy or sell a stock at a trader- or customer-specified price.

Listed Stocks—Stocks traded on an exchange (not NASDAQ). Listed stocks are represented by a one-, two-, or three-character symbol.

Locked Limit Down—Implemented on the futures during a rapid selloff to prevent panic or any further downside transactions. Only trading at higher prices is allowed during this period. *See also* Circuit Breaker.

Locked Market—When the Inside Bid is equal to the Inside Offer.

Long Position—Stock ownership. A trader with a long position is seeking an upside price move in order to sell the stock at a higher price.

MA—Moving Average.

Mark to Market—The value of a position as of the most recent closing price.

Market Capitalization (MCAP)—The total market value of all shares (Price × Outstanding Shares).

Market Makers—NASD member firms who represent the stock to the public. They must make a reasonable market at all times (post a buying and selling price). They trade to fill internal customer orders and also trade internal accounts for profit.

Market Maker Spread—The difference between the price of the Market Maker who is closest to the Inside Bid and the price of the Market Maker who is closest to the Inside Ask. Market Maker spread does not consider the presence of ECNs.

Market Order—An order to buy or sell a stock at the market's best available price.

Market Value—The most recent price traded on a stock.

Market Value Weighted Index—An index that is influenced in proportion to each security's market value. Larger stocks affect the index more than smaller stocks.

Most Active—Stocks with the highest trading volume for the day.

Midday Period—Loosely refers to the hours between 11:30 a.m. and 1:30 p.m. EST of any trading day. Also known as the Lunchtime Period. This is the period when the volume of trading usually subsides to its lowest levels of the day. *See also* Opening Period and Closing Period.

NASD—National Association of Securities Dealers. A self-regulatory organization responsible for overseeing and regulating the NASDAQ stock market.

NASDAQ—National Association of Securities Dealers Automated Quotation System. The electronic network on which trading of NASDAQ listed stocks is conducted. Stocks traded on the NASDAQ are represented by a four- or five-character symbol.

NASDAQ 100 Index—A market value weighted index that measures NASDAQ's top 100 stocks.

NASDAQ Composite Index—A market value weighted index that measures the activity of all NASDAQ listed stocks.

NASDAQ National Market—NASDAQ's Large-Cap Stocks (3,000-plus listings).

NASDAQ SmallCap Market—NASDAQ's Small-Cap Stocks (1,400-plus listings).

NYSE—New York Stock Exchange.

NYSE Composite Index—A market value weighted index that measures the performance of all NYSE listed stocks.

Odd Lots—An order that has less than 100-share multiples; for example, 82 shares, or 543 shares.

Offer Price—*See* Ask.

Open—A market's first price traded for the day.

Open Order—An order that is open to execution.

Opening Period—Commonly refers to the first hour to two hours of the trading day, when volume is heavy and trading activity is high.

P/E Ratio (Price to Earnings Ratio or Multiple)—A measure of a stock's market valuation versus actual earnings. Higher P/E ratios reflect high performance expectations, risk, and expensiveness.

Partial Fill—An executed order that did not fullfill the requested share size.

Previous Close—The previous trading day's last reported price.

Prints—Real-time report of actual trades with price and size. Also known as Time and Sales report. Usually found at the right-hand portion of the NASDAQ Level 2 or SuperDOT window.

Quarterly Report—A report that publicly traded companies are required to submit to the SEC on a quarterly basis reflecting performance and financial health. Also referred to as 10Q.

Range—The difference between the highest and lowest prices traded during a given period of time.

Real-Time Trade Reporting—A requirement imposed to immediately report all transactions to the market.

Refresh—When a Market Maker or ECN posts more size to buy or sell after filling an order at the same price.

Resistance—A price at which a stock has historically found sellers that prevented any further increase in price. Also known as Ceiling.

Retained Earnings—Net profits left to accumulate in a business after dividends are paid.

S&P 500—A broad and value-weighted index that represents the top 500 stocks selected by Standard & Poor's.

SEC (Securities and Exchange Commission)—The federal agency commissioned to protect the investing public against fraudulent or manipulative practices in the securities market.

Short Interest—The total number of shorted shares of a specific stock.

Short Sell—The sale of shares that are not owned by the trader in anticipation of buying back later at a lower price.

Slippage—The difference in price from the trading level at the time a market order is placed, to the actual execution price.

SOES—The Small Order Execution System.

SOES Order Entry Firm—An NASD member firm that is registered as an Order Entry Firm for purposes of participation in the Small Order Execution System (SEOS).

Spread—The difference between the Inside Bid and the Inside Ask.

Stock Dividend—Payment of a corporate dividend in the form of stock rather than cash.

Stop Loss—A level that a trader selects as a point to exit a trade in order to limit any further losses.

SuperDOT (Super Designated Order Turnaround)—An electronic system for a day trader to communicate orders directly to the specialist for a stock that is traded on the NYSE.

Support—A price area at which a declining stock historically found buyers to prevent any further decline in price.

Surprise—Difference between the actual and expected earnings.

Symbol (NASDAQ Stocks)—A four- or five-letter symbol assigned to a NASDAQ security. Four-letter symbols are assigned to common stock. Five-letter symbols are assigned to issues that are represented as follows:

A—Class A

B—Class B

C—Issuer qualifications exceptions

D—New

E—Delinquent in required filings with the SEC

F—Foreign

G—First convertible bond

H—Second convertible bond, same company

I—Third convertible bond, same company

J—Voting

K—Nonvoting

L—Miscellaneous

M—Fourth preferred, same company

N—Third preferred, same company

O—Second preferred, same company

P—First preferred, same company

Q—Bankruptcy proceedings

R—Rights

S—Shares of beneficial interest

T—With warrants or with rights

U—Units

V—When-issued and when-distributed

W—Warrants

Y—ADR (American Depositary Receipt)

Z—Miscellaneous.

Symbol (NASDAQ Market Makers or ECN)—A unique four-character symbol that identifies a Market Maker or ECN.

Symbol (NYSE Stocks)—A unique one-, two-, or three-letter symbol that represents a security traded on the New York Stock Exchange.

Technical Analysis—The study of price and volume based mostly on chart pattern formation and with no concern for fundamental information such as financial statistics or statements.

Teenie—1/16 of a point.

Time & Sales—*See* Prints.

Today's High—The intraday high trading price.

Today's Low—The intraday low trading price.

Trading Halt—A temporary suspension of trading on a specific stock due to pending news that may significantly affect the stock price, an imbalance in order flow, or regulatory reasons.

Two-Sided Market—The obligation imposed by the NASD that NASDAQ Market Makers make both firm bids and firm asks for each security for which they make a market.

Underwriter—An investment firm that brings a company to public trading.

Uptick (NASDAQ)—A Bid that is posted higher than the previous Bid. *See also* Downtick (NASDAQ).

Uptick (NYSE)—A trade that is higher than any previous reported trade. Also known as Zero Plus-Tick. *See also* Downtick (NYSE).

Volatility—The degree of price fluctuation of a security.

Volume—Total number of shares traded on a specific stock or in the entire market within a given time period.

INDEX

www.ingramcontent.com/pod-product-compliance
Lightning Source LLC
Chambersburg PA
CBHW061415210326
41598CB00035B/6222